The Timing of Events

Bepin Behari

MOTILAL BANARSIDASS PUBLISHERS
PRIVATE LIMITED • DELHI

First Edition: Delhi, 2002
Reprint: Delhi, 2005

ISBN: 81-208-1887-3 (Cloth)
ISBN: 81-208-1888-1 (Paper)

MOTILAL BANARSIDASS
41 U.A. Bungalow Road, Jawahar Nagar, Delhi 110 007
8 Mahalaxmi Chamber, 22 Bhulabhai Desai Road, Mumbai 400 026
120 Royapettah High Road, Mylapore, Chennai 600 004
236, 9th Main III Block, Jayanagar, Bangalore 560 011
Sanas Plaza, 1302 Baji Rao Road, Pune 411 002
8 Camac Street, Kolkata 700 017
Ashok Rajpath, Patna 800 004
Chowk, Varanasi 221 001

Printed in India
BY JAINENDRA PRAKASH JAIN AT SHRI JAINENDRA PRESS,
A-45 NARAINA, PHASE-I, NEW DELHI 110 028
AND PUBLISHED BY NARENDRA PRAKASH JAIN FOR
MOTILAL BANARSIDASS PUBLISHERS PRIVATE LIMITED,
BUNGALOW ROAD, DELHI 110 007

THE TIMING OF EVENTS

Contents

Preface

The Timing of Events fulfils an important gap in classical astrological literature. The ancient seers with yogic *siddhis* did not need rules for predicting future events. They clairvoyantly saw the future course of events. The astrological principles are given for those who are not so evolved. The astrological principles aim at helping those who are interested to live a life according to the evolutionary course of their everyday life. Each individual unfolds his life events according to his own unique future. On the basis of astrological indications it is expected that the different individuals could have a an understanding of their goal of life and mould their life style in order to attain this goal. Only on the basis of such an understanding of the life process, could an individual have a meaningful and full quota of his happiness and equipoise. The general astrological principles should be modified according to his individual uniqueness. This applied even in the case of the principles relating to the timing of events. The esoteric principles relating to the constitution of man as revealed by the septenary nature of man and the special ray on which the individual is evolving must be taken into account prior to applying the general principles of astrology including those of the timing of events. Another important principle that should be well considered in ascertaining the timing of events is the course of egoic evolution. These are difficult conditions but for an effective astrological prognostication which could be helpful to the individual they must be taken into account. The ancient astrological savants gave different principles relating to the timing of event which they thought could be helpful for different categories of individuals; they did not intend to provide any exhaustive and well integrated treatise on this special subject. In this way we find different texts giving different principles highlighting certain special features of the subject. Presently there are many books on the subject but a consolidated documentation of theses principles is difficult to obtain at one place. Even among the present astrological writers there has been a tendency to deal with certain special categories of the rules. The present study attempts to fulfil this need to some extent in a very modest manner. The present study does not try to present any new theory on the subject but its primary aim to compile together, giving at one place the most popular principles on the subject.

Three aspects of Vedic astrology ought to be understood carefully for astrological prognostications. The general influence of planetary configurations forms the foundation of all astrological considerations. The location of planets and their interrelationships indicated the broad pattern of events that would take place in the life of an individual. Secondly, the astrologers have to find out the specific time when these influences could fructify. All the planetary influences are not able to produce their result for ever. Only under special conditions they make their impacts felt. There are many combinations such as *Gaja Kesari Yoga,* and *Kala Sarpa Yoga* which are mere conditions of general welfare. Such combinations produce their impact throughout the life of the individual concerned. Their influence on specific occasions should be very carefully delineated. On the other hand there are combinations for Raja Yogas or the occurrences of special auspicious celebrations such as birth of a child or the construction of a house or acquisitions of royal vehicle. Such events have to be timed on the basis of the principles of the timing of events. The third aspect of astrology with which very few astrologers are interested in recent times is related with the rationale of the occurrence of an event in the life of an individual. This is very difficult subject which cannot be approached by a novice unless he is deeply learned in esoteric aspects of astrology. Every event in the life of a person has some purpose for his egoic unfoldment. This goal is related with the unfoldment of the individual's various latent faculties. The Lunar Mansions and the Zodiacal Signs have in built influences that constantly and gradually lead the individuals towards their ultimate destiny. Unless an event in significant in regard to the fructification or drawing the individual near his ultimate goal the specific event even if that is possible on the basis of usual astrological principles will not occur. Every individual has a unique way to unfold his real self. Every important event in the life of a person stands at the crossroad of his life. It is only under such situations that the same can be importantly prognosticated under astrological configurations. Every event in the life of a person results of the past planetary impulses which are generated under the impact of the Law of Karma. But it is not only the past that certain events are arranged in the life of a person at a particular time during the course of his egoic unfoldment. In this way every event in one's everyday life resulted from the actions of omission and commission of the individual which constituted his karma as well of his egoic mission which is hidden in the veil of future. The practicing astrologer has terefore to take a well-integrated view of the life of an individual while attempting to predict the likely events that might take place in the life of the consultee. The prognostications regarding the future of an individual should not therefore be made in isolation of other factors impinging on the person. A successful and helpful astrologer has to have adequate knowledge of all the three aspects of Vedic astrology but to be effective and helpful to the individuals consulting him he should have exposure to scientific theories regarding the evolutionary process and the scriptural injunctions for an ethical life. On a sensible base of scientific knowledge with various researches in different aspects of life process and proper grounding in spiritual subjects with an open mind could an astrologer hope to be helpful in proper guidance to the persons approaching him for advice. In this context it is also important to emphasize that the astrologer should completely purge his own psycho-mental propensities and prejudices as well as close-mindedness before undertaing serious astrological prognostications.

Every event is a double faced feature. It results from the past impulses generated by the individual. This is regulated under the law of Karma. It is for this reason that this law is given much importance in astrology. The astrologers studying the timing of events seriously must have a thorough grounding in this doctrine of action and reaction much emphasized in religious scriptures of all countries. This doctrine is related with the law of reincarnation without which astrology is incomplete. Every event in the life of a person pushes him towards his future goal which is accomplished through the process of reincarnation. These requirements devolved great responsibility on the practicing astrologer. He needs proper studies of many sujects related with the life process. He cannot remain isolated from the great wind of intellectual openness blowing presently in different fields. This exposure requires that the astrologer to be properly effective must have an open mind, a pure heart and an eager intellect and completely objectivity about his own personality.

An important consideration in predictive astrology is to assess the interregnum between the astrological configurations which related any specific event with the fructification of its results. In some cases, as in the case of Sun and Mars, the result is often immediate. But if the planets are suggesting that the impact would be on the psycho-mental frame of the individual, then a time gap is usually expected This is an important consideration which the astrologer would do well to recognize. The ancient seers who gave us several treatises on predictive astrology were very reticent in giving details of timing of events. It was so because they were aware of several intricacies of the subject which could not be easily described in everyday common astrological texts. The experience and understanding of the basic and long-term implications of the general principles of astrology are necessary for a sound astrological comprehension of the timing of events and for any light on the evolutionary course of the individual's behaviour.

The present work therefore should be considerd within these various limitations and the wider perspective of the subject suggested above. In this sense with all its limitations this work should be considered an important link wider perspective of Vedic astrology.

C-505, Yojana Vihar, BEPIN BEHARI
Delhi-110092

Introduction

The ancient seers gave us the knowledge of impending events. They gave it so that we could understand our destiny and live accordingly. The question of destiny according to ancient Vedic seers was very different from what it is? They used the word *dharma* to connote the purpose and process of manifestation. While describing the cosmic manifestation, they began with non-existence and affirmed the incomprehensible nature of the same. "The non-existent was not then, nor was the existent i.e. the Earth, nor the firmament, not that which was beyond. When there was nothing then what could cover what, Where and under whose care? Did the waters and the bottomless deep then exist?"[1] On this background of skepticism they postulated the *Puruṣa,* the cosmic creative principle that is all-pervasive. "Puruṣa is perceptible everywhere, as if he has thousands of heads, thousands of eyes, thousands of feet....The Puruṣa alone is this alone, that what was and will be. And he is the Lord of immortality, and that which grows with food, is mortal".[2] This cosmic man and his relationship with every terrestrial form of existence is the basic foundation on which the Vedic astrology was based.

The timing of events as described in astrological texts aimed at identifying the stage at which the individual and the cosmic man tended to work together. Everything that happened to the individual was an expression of the Will of the Supreme and this relationship was described as the *karma* of the individual. The manner in which the individual was expected to react to them was considered as his *dharma.* Within this basic framework of *karma* and *dharma* the subject of timing of events described in Vedic astrology has to be studied.

The aspect of astrology, which is often found to be overlooked, whether in Eastern or Western, is the paradigm of astrological science.

1. The Rig Veda. Quoted from Glimpses of the Vedas by Satyavrata Siddhantalankar, Milin Publications, Delhi (1980).
2. Ibid.

Absence of proper appreciation of the basic framework in which this revelation was made often raised controversy. The occult sciences are neither experiential nor are they the results of innumerable examples of observed occurrences. The occult knowledge is essentially intuitive, revelationary and imparted in a mystic manner. Hence the understanding of occult truths demands that the student raise his or her consciousness to the level of consciousness of the seers who have codified them for the benefit of humanity.This approach requires that the occult subjects are studied in their proper perspective and within the framework of general philosophy and such other teachings related to them. This is especially so when we study the deeper aspects of Vedic astrology, which postulates that every event in the life of an individual is an expression of the Supreme.

The main difficulty with regard to Vedic astrology arises from the fact that it was conceived as a part of the ancient Indian teachings contained in the *Vedas.* It was acknowledged as a limb of the *Vedas.* It was therefore called *Vedāṅga.* Before a disciple was introduced to the mystic teachings, he was expected to be proficient in several subjects including astrology. There was no contradiction between astrology and the metaphysical teachings of the *Vedas.* They supplemented each other. But none of these philosophical or religious subjects was revealed just for the curiosity of the so called intellectuals. This knowledge was intended for those who wanted to comprehend the deeper aspects of manifestation and adapt themselves to the requirements postulated under the scheme. The ancient world religions, which were esoteric in character, were practical guidelines. The religious philosophy, rituals and performances of one's everyday duty were all different aspects of a comprehensive and well-integrated system.

There was a great danger that the selfish and unwary individuals could misappropriate the knowledge, which was imparted after ages of contemplation, purification and initiation in secret mysteries. The emergence of Black Magic is a glaring example of this kind of misuse. It was for such reasons that knowledge was contained in a language, not easily decipherable, unless some one had the necessary keys to them and had the requisite astro–mental preparations to comprehend the teachings in the right manner. The use of mystic and symbolic language in the description of such subjects therefore became the general rule. The recent researches and studies in myths and symbols of scriptures reveal that they contain very profound truths though we have not yet succeeded in deciphering the full meaning of them.

One of the methods for comprehending the ancient wisdom is to approach them through astrological revelations and test their efficacy in revealing the truth and falsehood in one's own life. The general description of astrological principles in relation with the natal horoscope describes one's life in general terms but the identification of specific incidents in one's life can indicate the invisible thread that binds the individual with the all pervading cosmic creator, the Cosmic man.

It is unfortunate that there has been a big interregnum between the ancient Indian civilization and our contemporary society. It has happened due to the fact that the ancient Indian society was oriented towards living the life of righteousness and not getting entangled in mere theoretical discussions. To the ancient Indians any knowledge was useful only if it could be lived and adapted to one's life. The wisdom was a part of the life and it was not codified in a comprehensive treatise for someone to read. Whatever is found about it presently are mostly in fragments aimed at guiding the individuals in their everyday life towards righteousness.

The ancient philosophy describing the nature of the all-pervasive natural powers as anthropomorphized gods or supernatural powers in absurd physical forms and incredible deeds and powers was an acknowledgement of the various degrees of natural powers with whom the individuals interacted and functioned in their everyday life. The austerities and *yajñas* were expressions of this cooperation. The astronimical details given in *Purāṇas* and different epics indicated their awareness of planetary deities actively participating in the affairs of men.

In spite of such elaborate knowledge and celestial awareness, the seers did not document or codify the rules of planetary impulses. These were included in the general scheme of understanding, which included knowledge of occult sides of things, the method of cooperation with these powers, and the rules guiding these planetary impulses. The Brāhmaṇas devoted their whole life in studying them. They used the knowledge thus obtained for guiding the people. That was the relationship between a priest and devotees, between the hierophants and the neophytes. The Brāhmaṇas and the temples were the chief fulcrum around which the ancient Indian society revolved.

The temples were also located at the spots where the stellar forces poured in a special way. The knowledge of this downpour was available to the priests who were experts even in *Vaṣtu* principles[1] as well. With the advent of foreign invaders when the aggressors rensacked the country and the temples were desecrated, the temple-based society got destroyed. The priests went into oblivion and the mysterious knowledge of the East went into concealment.The spiritual custodians of the mystic knowledge however saw that the outer husk of this knowledge remained with the common masses.The available treatises on astrological knowledge which are presently being discovered at various places on palm leaves and such other parchments are remnants of this concealed knowledge available for mass consumption. The esoteric principles operating behind these astrological impulses were not included in them. These could open to the casual and prying readers, unprepared to absorb them, immense power and could even ruin their life by arousing their animal passions and desires. This has been the main cause for the concealment of esoteric astrological knowledge during the last 2,000 years or so. The available treatises indicate how to calculate and apprehend the coming events and the likely future of the individual but they do not reveal the inner guiding principles.

During the last 1500 years or so the Indian astrologers have been primarily concerned with maintaining and preserving the predictive astrology. The astrological paradigm that sustains this occult science has its metaphysical base in spiritual philosophy. It is very abstruse and full of occult hints and suggestions. It reveals so much that it can not be left in the hands of the unscrupulous and unprepared prying individuals. It is therefore, preserved in the sacred custody of the initiated seers. But the predictive aspect of astrology, which makes the individuals interested in this subject and makes them aware of their mission in life, can be disseminated among the people.The predictive astrology is very attractive and many people are attracted towards it. This dissemination is helpful even to preserve astrology because by its attraction it has the potential of enlivening the interest of some serious students sometimes to explore the metaphysical aspect of the subject. The esoteric base of the subject is still preserved in the secret mysteries but the outer husk, which contains the predictive portion of it, has been disseminated widely for more than thousand

1. *Vastu* is the science of astrological principles, which guided architecture so as to derive the best results of the stellar forces for the specific purpose for which the building was constructed.

years. The itinerant religious preachers went from village to village and aroused the interests of the masses in predictive astrology by predicting daily events likely to happen towards them. On the international level many international visitors can be seen to be taking interests in the subject who are trying to get the available knowledge translated and sent to their mother country. It is in this way that Al Beruni and many others came to India and managed to learn Indian astrology. During this period, many Indian scholars were also invited to Arabian and Middle East countries. Their services were mobilized for translating the Indian [esoteric] texts in local languages. One often comes across these translations in the libraries of ancient countries in different regions.These are some of the indications, which are for the historians to investigate.But the fact remains that the metaphysical aspect of astrology has been kept secret and the esoteric astrology has widely been disseminated. Even in India the astrological texts available presently pertain to this period.In order to go deeper into the basic principles of Vedic astrology it is necessary to transcend the esoteric astrology and delve deeper to comprehend the essential features of astrology and the divine forces which it describes. Only this kind of knowledge can satisfy the modern mind and help them in orientation of their lives based on these occult forces and cooperate with the planetary hierarchy to achieve one's fullness of life.

During recent years some attempts have been made to explore the esoteric dimensions of astrology and come to an understanding of its relationship with metaphysical teachings of world religions. In this regard the works of H.P. Blavatsky stands supreme. She made bold attempts to revive the ancient occult sciences but was very hesitant in revealing them to the common man. She however made the people interested in the subject and lifted a little of the veil over the subject[1]. She emphasized that the physical planets were external expressions of the inner planetary spirits that ensouled them and were carrying out the will of the Absolute All through the stellar impulses in the world of causes or the world of physical manifestation. Blavatsky laid great stress on the evolutionary aspect of these stellar impulses.The zodiacal signs, constellations and the planetary hierarchy were all collectively arranged in such a way that they revealed the stages,

1. See *Isis Unveiled* and *The Secret Doctrine*, which gave many details of the world religions, occult teachings and esoteric astrology.

through which the divinity in man was exposed and externalized. They also indicated the process by which the human ego, the society in which he lived and the terrestrial globe he dwelt were finally transformed. The transformation took place according to the archetype, which existed, for the humanity in the mind of the Supreme. Blavatsky also revealed the esoteric nature of various teachings available in sacred scriptures. She declared that the religious myths and symbols could lay bare vast potential of nature provided the secret was unlocked with proper keys. According to her there were seven keys for unlocking these secrets. These keys were given to the aspirants only towards the end in different levels of initiations, which were given in various mystery schools. She revealed much about the nature of astrological principles but she clothed her teachings in mystic language.Very few modern astrologers are interested in her brand of astrology, but some of those who delved in them have reaped precious harvests. She had insisted that one has to step beyond the visible world of matter and enter into the domain of transcendental spirit in order to comprehend the true nature of astrology.Rudolf Steiner, Alice Bailey, and Dane Rudhyar and others took the lead given by Blavatsky. All of them have tried to weave a pattern in astrological predictions, which exposes a little of the divine pattern existing in every event in everybody's life.

The relationship between the planets and the human individuals still remains a deeply mystical subject. One of the most outstanding Vedāntists of the 19th century who was held in great esteem even by H.P. Blavatsky was T.Subba Rao. He was very reluctant to discuss esoteric teachings to unprepared students. In some of his writings he has however given some hints and suggestions which are very valuable for astrological students. Therein he has indicated some of the basic principles of stellar operation as well as the mechanism through which these influences affect the individuals and the human society.[1] He mentioned that the zodiacal cycle revealed the pattern of evolutionary courses. It indicated the various cosmic processes through which the individuals as well as the terrestrial existence were manifested. He mentioned that the various religious monuments and the places of worship were not expressions of crafty priests to exploit superstitious worshippers. These monuments served the purpose towards harnessing of stellar forces. They were intended to flow to the earth,

1. *Collected Writings of T. Subba Rao.*

move through the various channels and pervade throughout the globe as streams of divine consciousness. It was expected that these forces gradually and appropriately spiritualized the humanity at large. He also indicated that the planets were related with various force centers known as *cakras* in yogic literature.

A well-known German mystic Johann Georg Gichtel, a pupil of Jakob Boehme in his book *Theosophia Practica* (1696) indicated some correspondence between the different planets and the various portions of the human anatomy. This information was rather a camouflaged version of the relationship existing between the planets and the *cakras*. It nonetheless revealed that the Middle Age mystics of Europe were also acquainted with the relationship existing between the planets, and the yogic force centres related with *kuṇḍalinī śakti*[1]. They studied this subject in their religious books but did not reveal them to the masses. This view is strengthened even by recent psychological studies of Carl G. Jung. He made intensive research in alchemy of the Middle Ages and came to discern the surprising relationships assumed by these mystic philosophers. These provided valuable clues to the understanding of psychology, astrology and spiritual development.[2] An important aspect of these mystic teachings has been the emergence of a pattern in all mental conflicts and psycho physical conditions of a human being. The emerging pattern in these studies is the intimate relation with planetary impulses. These studies show that the religious myths and symbols are related with deeper teachings concerning human evolution. They have been given a language not easy to understand unless one possesses the necessary keys for unlocking them.

The scope of astrology is very extensive. It includes almost everything that exists in the universe. Its laws apply to every created thing that comes into existence, grows and is ultimately dissolved. Every movement is goal–oriented and it leads the object towards the fulfilment of its destiny. This movement can be observed in sentient as well as insentient objects. Astrological keys decipher the sequence of this movement. If it is carried further in depth it can reveal the goal towards which the movement is taking the object. Whatever exists in the universe is subject to the movement of origin, change, unfoldment and dissolution. All objects have their own special features but the

1. In modern yogic and mystic language it is known by the name *Serpent Fire*.
2. See Carl G. Jung. *Alchemy and Psychology*.

seeming differences in their mode of unfoldment are very superficial. All of them are essentially different aspects of the cosmic man, *Puruṣa* and they are modified in the course of their unfoldment by his basic impulse. The cosmic man includes everything that lives and breathes in him. The variety in the manifestation has led to enormous possibilities for every item. The path through which they grow and attain their destiny is however controlled by some universally applicable cosmic law, the central impulse of the cosmic man. The esoteric principle of astrology studies this universal impulse of causation.

The various astrological laws are generally studied under four heads. These are (i) mundane, which includes within its scope the application of stellar impulses to meteorology, seismology, husbandry and so on, (ii) *state* or *civic* which studies the fate of nations, kings and rulers. The ancient rulers of all nations were much concerned with this branch of astrology. This branch of astrology is currently much in popular demand. (iii) *Aorary* which examines the possobilities of answering a query or doubt arising spontaneously in the mind of a questioner. The exact moment of a spontaneous question seems mysteriously linked with the result of the question or the doubt that may take place in future.The metaphysical aspect of this branch of astrology takes us to the very core of the timing of events (iv) Jātaka or the personal horoscopy is that branch on the basis of which the fate of individuals from the moment of their birth to their death is prognosticated. Apart from these four main categories of astrological prognostication, an astrologer deals with *muhūrta.* It is concerned with finding out the most auspicious time for beginning of an enterprise such as starting of educational activities, undertaking of a journey, performance of marriage, laying down of the foundation of a new construction, commencement of any *yajña* or religious celebrations and such other activities. The matching of horoscopes for the marital relationship is presently also an important astrological task. *Upāya* or the prescriptions of remedial measures so as to ward off difficulties encountered by an individual is also studied under astrology. Very few astrologers are concerned with the rationale of these astrological functions but all of them essentially relate to the study of stellar forces as they impinge upon the affairs of men and women. At the back of all these prognostication–studies the main objective is either toward off the likelihood of any unwanted consequences or to adapt oneself to the most preferred situation.

The goal of all astrological studies is to study the nature and operation of stellar forces. This is done on the expressed or assumed belief that there is a relationship between the stars and life on earth. The urge for prognostications comes from the desire to adapt oneself to the most fulfilling course of life. The timing of events is a study to answer these questions.

The primary assumption of Vedic astrology is the identity between the individual and the cosmic creative principle. In astrological textbooks this aspect of the subject is not discussed generally. In religious scriptures the relationship has been described in terms of absurd and ridiculous myths and symbols. The metaphysical doctrines suggest the identity between the two in highly abstruse language. The Vedas describe it as *"Tat Tvam Asi"* meaning "that art thou". This philosophical statement is not reconciled with astrological rules. Hence any effort to discern the significance of one's everyday occurrences seems fruitless. The *Vedāntic* doctrine of cosmic ideation is however firmly established in the very structure of astrological system of the East. If the basic features of this doctrine and the way they are embedded in astrological paradigm are properly understood, one could easily assess the significance of various major and minor events occurring in one's everyday life.

We have already mentioned that the Vedic concept of the cosmic ideation and the nature of the Supreme are very different from what is considered in the so-called pantheistic society. The motion as perpetual state of existence is the only eternal and uncreated Deity. The universal perpetual motion never ceases never slackens nor increases in speed not even during the interludes between the 'nights of Brahma' but goes on like a mill set in motion, whether it has anything to grind or not. This peculiar faculty of the involunatary power of the infinite mind is eternally evolving subjective matter into objective atoms or comic matter to the later developed into form. The *Purāṇic* stories describe the process of objectification at various stages of externalization, differentiation, and concretization through several myths. One of these mythologies relate to Brahmā, the cosmic creator, dividing himself into *Brahmā -Virāj* and *Vāc -Virāj,* the male and the female and inducing them to marry and beget thousands of children of different categories. At the stage of human creation, the process of manifestation discusses the emergence of human being into his subjective aspect comprising *ātma-buddhi-manas* represented as 'individuality' of the person. His objective part described as his 'personality' comprised the physical form, as we perceive. The scriptures have laid down the process in different manner depending upon the system of philosophy one followed to study the composition of man. Essentially, it consisted of the creation of *Pañca Tattvas,* which comprised the five basic elements viz.earth, water, air, fire and ether or *ākāśa.* These were later transformed as *Mahābhūtas,* which provided the five primary faculties for experiences. Later on there were the five *Indriyas* for action and five for acquiring knowledge. Then emerged ahaṁkāra, the egotism. The physical body is described as the *sthūla śarīra,* the physical body which is energized by *Prāṇa Vāyu, the Vital Airs.* The human body constituted on the background of incessant motion becomes subject to birth, growth, decay and dissolution. But the perpetual scheme of motion or movement continues on its never ending course. The ultimate dissolution of manifested beings leads to their final nerging in the perpetual motion which never ceases, never slackens whether there is anything to grind or not. It is on this background that the various doctrines of karma and reincarnation along with the goal of final redemption or Nirvāṇa have to be understood.

The astrological prognostications of events based on the natal chart or according to any other system apparently do not seem to take into consideration this vast cosmic perspective. The various methods of prognostications that would be discussed shortly indicates that the zodiacs and chain of asterisms which provide the basic structure on which the planetary configurations existing either at the birth time or an occurrence are intimately related with the evolutionary impulse of the cosmic man. The zodiacs and the Lunar mansions are stellar descriptions of the stellar forces which ever engaged in implementing the scheme of cosmic ideation. The externalization of such subjective core into objective forms is carried out in nasture by certain subjective and objective powers of which these stars and the planets are important constituents. When an event is predicted as likely to occur at any time, it implies that these cosmic forces are actively concerned with guiding the individual to move under the divine impulse towards his final destiny. The actualization of the event, the form and psychological significance affecting different levels of personality of the individual are outer expressions of the inner forces inducing him since eternity. They expect that the individual would gradually fall in line with the ultimate destiny as inherent in the initial germ, which began concretizing and giving him the present form. This metaphysical plank of Vedic astrology providing the esoteric foundation of Vedic astrological prognostications is vital for deciphering the significance of different events occurring to the individual.

The timing of events is calculated on the basis of one 's natal chart.The different planets in their relationship with the signs of the zodiac and lunar mansions show their linkages with magnetic points in the sky, which are ever radiating specialized cosmic energy for the manifestation of certain results. The response is based on his constitution of the personality which is greatly restricted by his different sheaths. These sheaths covering the inner man are described variously in different scriptures. Various planetary impulses affect these sheaths and gradually enable them to absorb the planetary impulses. The Egyptian, theosophical and Vedāntic literature have described the same in different ways. The various planetary impulses affect these sheaths and gradually enable them to abort finer planetary impulses and their power of absorption of these impulses. The study of a natal chart could be made to examine the quality of individual's different sheaths, which greatly restrict him to react in any specific manner under the given situation. The natal chart essentially shows the latent potential of the individual. Whether these faculties are destined to be actualized or not should be examined and determined. The third aspect of predictive astrology is to find out whether these latent possibilities will find their expressions and expose the individual for reaction to those events.

Luminaries at the Centre-Stage

The third aspect of Vedic astrology deals with timing of events which discusses in detail as to the period when the latent possibilities bestowed by the natal planets could find expression in actual life. These depends upon three sets of considerations. The first is related with planetary rulership. The highly magnetic points, which are sensitized by the planets at the birth time, become a kind of guardian angel for the individual. They are important for him intoning valuable planetary impulses, which always affect him. As a result of planetary configuration at the time of birth, the planetary magnetic field is arranged in such a way that the different planets align themselves in a manner appropriate to let them have their sway over the individual in a specific order. This order is studied under various Daśā Systems. Many systems of this kind have been specified in astrological texts, which are applicable to different types of individuals born under different planetary configurations. All the systems, however, have the common feature of basing their planetary position of the Moon in an asterism.The most important common feature is the significance attached to the Moon and the asterism; the planets begin to operate only when the Moon depending upon its position at the birth epoch commands them to operate.

The third plank of astrology consists, as we have said earlier, of the planetary rulership, the planetary transits and progressed horoscopes. The planetary transits also hinge around the position of the Moon in the sign or the asterism at the time of birth. They are important deciding the timing of events but the rules guiding them are difficult to master. At the root of these planetary transits lie the resulting forces of transformations due to the angular relationship between the transiting planets and their relationships with the natal planets. All these relationship are considered around the central position of the Moon in the horoscope. So far astrological texts, the ancient myths and symbols have to some extent indicated the nature and disposition of the planets, zodiacal signs and the *nakṣatras,* but the chemical changes that take place as a result of their mutual interblending have remained mysterious. One has to accept what the texts have indicated about them and attempt to explore their inner dimensions on the basis of one's own experiences. These relationships are codified under the *aṣtakavarga,* which has to be carefully calculated for each planet, and on the basis of this aṣtakavarga calculation the influence of transiting planets is inferred. One countervailing factor in this regard is the presence of certain obstructing forces, which do not enable the planetary transits or have their full impact. These are usually known as Vedhas meaning obstructions. But the vedhas *do not* operate for Sun and Saturn, as well as between Moon and Mercury. But the real esoteric reason for this still remains to be explored.

Progressed horoscope relates the existing planetary configuration which re-magnetises the field of radiation at the time of birth. In planetary rulerships, the Moon is the central figure around which all the results are determined. The progressed horoscope assumes that the natal Sun releases very powerful stellar impulse, which remains an ever-radiating influence. Whenever the Sun passes over this highly energized point on the ecliptic, there is revival of the natal impulse. As the Sun as well as other planets at the moment of solar ingress on the natal point is different from what they were at the time of birth, their total impact is accordingly different. Progressed horoscope attempts to study the possible interaction of these two sets of planetary configurations with a view to assessing their possible results during the ensuing sojourn of the Sun on its zodiacal path. The annual horoscopes thus prepared also attempt to examine the strength of different planets. They also have identified certain important points resulting from the combined position of different planets in the different houses. Presently about hundred *Sahama* points are identified. They are based on relationships between the angular distances of certain planets or the Lords of different houses established in relationship with the ascendant or the Sun. These points need very careful examination in the context of annual horoscopes.

Conclusion

Vedic astrology forms a part of the *Vedas and it is said that the former is an essential step for understanding the deeper wisdom contained in the latter. The Vedas have emphasized that the Sun is the soul of the universe and the Moon is the mother of every living being on the globe.*[1]

In the natal chart the importance of the Sun is well recognized. It is also well recognized that the strength of any horoscope depends upon the strength and quality of these luminaries. Varāhamihira has already suggested that the Sun is the cause of the Moon, Mars stands for the will or strength and is related very intimately with the Sun and the latter is the supreme will in the pathway of those who are after eternal bliss, happiness or the fulfillment of their destiny. Mercury is related to self-knowledge and Jupiter with philosophy, righteousness, and religious aspirations which are very different aspects of the Sun. Venus is the embodiment of happiness, an aspect of the Supreme.[2] Saturn stands for the cause of destruction but then ultimate dissolution is also an aspect of the solar deity for its withdrawal of vital energy from the individual leads to dissolution or death. Varāhamihira also implied the Sun to be the cause of the past, the present and the future existence. Presently we have noted that the strength and quality of a natal chart flows from the power of the Sun.

1. *Sūryaḥ Jagatah Ātmā meaning the Sun is the soul of the universe and Moon, or Candramaḥ Janaṇī meaning the Moon is the generator of the universe which stands for Truth, Awareness and Bliss.*
2. Sachchidānanda.

The planetary rulership, which determines the periodicity of the rulership of a planet over the life events of an individual at different periods, is determined on the basis of the Moon's position in an asterism at the time of birth. The planetary transits give their results according to their relationship with the natal Moon. The progressed horoscopes are worked out on the basis of the natal position of the Sun and the return to that very point every year. The Moon reflects the rays of the Sun and directs the same to go back to the earth so as to nurture the living beings on it. The Moon is thus merely an agent of the Sun and so are different planets.Vedic astrology in this way by relating every agent in the life of a person with the Sun, which is considered as the very soul of the universe, relates every individual with a caring and disciplinarian father in heaven. Whatever happens to the individual, he is always under the watchful eyes of his guardian angel that is carefully guiding him towards his ultimate destiny.

CHAPTER#1

Planetary Periodicity

There are three routes, which can be followed in predicting the future course of life. These three channels enable the astrologer to understand the sequence of events and the problems likely to confront the individual These are known as (i) *Mahā -Daśā, Antardaśā* and . *Sūkṣma Daśā* System also known as Planetary Periodicity, (ii) Planetary Transits, and (iii) Annual Progression of natal planets. The last one involves the preparation of annual horoscopes based on the solar ingress to its natal position. It is also known as the Progressed Horoscope. An integrated approach of these three systems of predicting the likelihood of any impending events may give a fairly accurate view of the future course of occurrences.

I. Daśā and Antardaśā System

The Daśā System describes the period of good and adverse experiences. They result from past karmic forces. But it should be recognized that the planets do not cause any event. They are merely channels through which the past karmic forces fructify. These forces are not deterministic. They produce certain conditions of life but they do not compel the individual to react to them in any specific manner. They provide opportunities for self-evolution provided they are taken in the right manner. The psychological reactions to these conditions depend upon the individual's personality. The astrological concept of personality is however very different from what is commonly understood by the term. The scriptures have already described that various sheaths that account for the astro-mental as well as physical well being of the person cover the inner man or the essential core of the individual. His capacity to absorb the finer forces impinging upon the inner man and to react to them depends upon the nature and composition of these sheaths[1]. The

1. See *The Seven Veils Over Consciousness* by C. Jinarajadasa, and *Viveka Cūḍāmaṇi* by Śaṅkarācārya.

planetary forces always affect these sheaths and induce the individual to evolve and to unveil his latent faculties. These forces are ever harmonized with the past karmic forces already generated by him. The planetary deities have arranged them in a specific order in order to help him to evolve in a particular direction. If these forces could be intelligently understood, the individual could utilize them to accelerate his inner development. The planetary periodicity is in this way purposive. They are arranged in a particular sequence in order to help the person. The experiences gained during the different planetary influences can lead him to move securely on his path of evolution. Knowledge of this sequence and the comprehension of one's archetypal goal gives the person strength and foresight to proceed confidently and to bear cheerfully the difficulties of the path.

Ancient astrologers revealed the sequence of planetary prominence for the benefit of the mankind. There are various methods for calculating the sequence and the duration of control by the planets. Presently, we have no information on the rationale of the sequence or of the period of planetary control. Nonetheless even our superficial knowledge of these systems has confirmed their efficacy. Parāśara whose life history and the time of his birth are not well-known, is probably the earliest astrological seer who codified the basic tenets of astrological science and gave some systematic information on the working of the Daśā System. He mentions ten Daśā systems as very important. They are known as (1) Viṁśottarī, (2) Aṣṭottarī, (3) Ṣoḍaśottarī, (4) Dvādaśottarī, (5) Pañcśottarī, (6) Śatāṁśa, (7) Caturaśityabda, (8) Dvisaptatisama, (9) Śaṣṭyabda, and (10) Ṣaṭtriṁśadvatsara. He mentions certain other systems such as *Kāla Daśā, Cakra Daśā* and *Kāla Cakra Daśā* that were also used by some astrologers. He refers to several other systems but considers them less reliable. In this category he included *Cara Daśā, Sthira Daśā, Kendra Daśā, Kārakagrahodaya Daśā, Brahmagraha Daśā, Maṇḍūka Daśā, Śūla Daśā, Yogārdha Daśā, Dṛga Daśā, Trikoṇa Daśā, Rāśi Daśā, Pañcasvara Daśā, Yoginī Daśā, Piṇḍa Daśā, Aṁśaja Daśā, Aṣṭakavarga Daśā, Sandhyā Daśā, Pācaka Daśā, Tārā Daśā,* and others.

The applicability of any Daśā in an individual case depends upon birth time, place of birth and special planetary configurations present in the horoscope. Among the various Daśā systems, Viṁśottarī Daśā system is the most extensively used method in the periodicity of planetary lordship. Some of the important methods of Daśā calculations are given below :

1. Viṁśottarī

This system of periodicity is worked out on the basis of the position of Moon at the time of birth in a Nakṣatra. A planet rules every asterism. When the Moon occupies a Nakṣatra, the planet ruling over it gets the initial control over the individual. So when the Moon's position in a Nakṣatra is found out, one knows the specific planet that controls the newly born child. But no planet controls the life of a person forever. There is a sequence of rulership that decides the order in which different planets influence him or her. Various planets have different periods of their control. The sequence of planetary control over the person follows a particular order. It corresponds the order in which the planet rule over the chain of Nakṣatras. This order is as follows : Sun, Moon, Mars, Rāhu, Jupiter, Saturn, Mercury, Ketu and Venus. The initial planetary chain begins with Sun ruling over Kṛttikā, the third asterism counted from Aśvinī. Once the initial ruling planet or the Moon's position in an asterism at birth is found out, the complete chain of planetary sequence would fall in line with this order. The beginning of any planetary rulership would depend upon the position of Moon in a Nakṣatra but once this planetary rulership is decided, the following period of planetary rulership would adhere to this sequence. If the initial rulership starts with, say, Saturn, then the next Daśā period would be that of Mercury followed by Ketu and so on. If the initial period of a planet begins say, with Mars, then the following period would be that of Rāhu followed by Jupiter and so on.

Table 1
Viṁśottarī Planetary Rulership

Asterisms	*Planets*	*Years*
Kṛttikā, Uttarā Phālgunī and Uttarā Āṣāḍhā	Sun	6 Years
Rohiṇī, Hasta and Śravaṇa	Moon	10 Years
Mṛgaśīrṣa, Citrā and Dhaniṣṭhā	Mars	7 Years
Ārdrā, Svāti, and Śatabhiṣag	Rāhu	18 Years
Punarvasu, Viśākhā and Pūrvā Bhādrapadā	Jupiter	16 Years
Puṣya, Anurādhā and Uttarā Bhādrapadā	Saturn	19 Years
Aṣleṣā, Jyeṣṭhā and Revatī	Mercury	17 Years
Maghā, Mūla and Aśvinī	Ketu	7 Years
Pūrvā Phālgunī, Pūrvā Āṣāḍhā, and Bharaṇī	Venus	20 Years

The sequence of planetary rulership over the life of an individual can be observed from the above table. The total period of this planetary sway over the life of an individual is 120 years. But every planet does not enjoy the same duration of control. The total 120 years of Viṁśottarī Mahā Daśā is distributed over different planets as follows: Sun 6 years, Moon 10 years, Mars 7 years, Rāhu 18 years, Jupiter 16 years, Saturn 19 years, Mercury 17 years, Ketu 7 years and Venus 20 years. The initial period of a planetary rulership, as indicated above, starts with the planet ruling over the Nakṣatra occupied by Moon at birth. Moon very often does not occupy an asterism at its very beginning. It is likely that this luminary has already traversed some distance in the asterism. Consequently, the period of its control is proportionately reduced. The period already elapsed at birth is proportional to the longitude of Moon already traversed in the asterism. If Moon has traveled half of 13° 20' of a Nakṣatra , the planet will have only half the duration of its normal control. The following planets however will have their full Daśā or the period of rulership. The earlier half of the period which the initial planet did not exercise at the beginning of the individual's life will be available to him towards his end provided he lived for 120 years.

All the nine planets have their secondary levels of influence during the main *Daśā* of every planet. The period of secondary rulership is usually known as the *Antardaśā* or the sub -period of planetary rulership. *Antardaśā* of different planets follows the same planetary sequence as in *Daśā* but the initial rulership under the Antardaśā of the initial planetary rulership at birth begins with the rulership of the planet after taking into account the portion already traversed by Moon in the asterism. It implies that the part of the antardaśā or of the sub -rulership of the planet will belong to that planet which would have occupied due to moon's occupancy of that longitude. If Moon has already traversed half or 6° 40' of Aśvinī which is ruled by Ketu, then the main period of rulership would be that of Ketu but the antardaśā would be that of Rāhu. This would not be at its beginning but after the portion already elapsed during its sub -period because of Moon's longitude in this asterism. In this case, Rāhu will have only 5 months 18 days of balance at birth. The antar of the following planets would have their full duration and the sequence would be the same as in Daśā period. Assume Moon in another case of birth has crossed one-fourth of Bharaṇī, that is at 16° 40' of Aries, Venus rules over Bharaṇī which qualifies it to have its main daśā at birth but it will have only 15 years of balance to influence the life of the new born as the first one-fourth or 5 years period of Venus' rulership has already elapsed.

The strength and position of the main Daśā Lord and those of secondary planetary lords affects the interpretation of the Daśā system. All planets whether benefic or malefic, influence different aspects of the individual's life. Their influence harmonizes with their natural disposition. These changes depend upon the basic nature of the planets but the Constitution of the individual as evident from his personality features also intervenes. The final result is the outcome of the basic nature of the planets, their strength in the chart and the general personality aspect of the individual. If the planets are strong and placed in cardinal houses namely, the 1st, 4th, 7th and 10th houses, their influence on the individual is helpful and significant. They affect the individual's life, its pattern and direction in an important manner. The results may or may not be happy from the worldly standpoint. But they aim at individual's evolution. For example, Sun in the 4th house, may make the emotion and temperament of the individual impersonal and universal. He may seem barren and heartless. Many individuals may consider him even inhuman and cruel. The individual however, will have universality of vision. He will be much concerned with life in its universal aspect. Rāhu in this position will draw from the past karmic reservoirs certain material results such as landed property, relationship with foreigners or deeper occult knowledge that may produce in the individual a deep sense of disappointment. In this process he will develop dispassion, an essential requirement for any spiritual development. The outer achievements whatsoever they may be would turn into dust in his mouth under the influence of Rāhu. The basic idea is that a planet in strength placed in a cardinal house during its main Daśā precipitates long-term evolutionary impulses. Their effects may be disquieting if the planets are not in strength or if they are adversely aspected. The planets in all case would be concerned in producing results, which are in accordance with their own inherent qualities.

In trine houses namely, the 5th and 9th houses, the planets make the individual very creative during their main Daśā. The individual is engaged in intense creative activities. He gets several opportunities for participating in social, philanthropic and spiritual work. If the planets are related with the 5th house, the individual is engaged in intellectual and mental pursuits. Even if the impact of these planets is produced on the physical level, which generally leads to birth of offspring, then also their main contribution is in furthering the evolutionary expansion in the consciousness of the individual. Even malefic planets such as Sun, Mars, Saturn, Rāhu and Ketu acquire beneficial attributes in this way provided they are in trine houses. The benefic results are not necessarily from material or mundane considerations. They are related with deeper aspects of the houses in which they are located. The activation and generation of the results may not be apparently pleasant from superficial considerations. But they will awaken creativity at the level where the individual is operating. In the 9th house the planets will involve the individual with creativity at the subjective level. Malefic planets such as Rāhu, Saturn, Mars and Sun if they are not strong and favorably disposed towards the individual will provoke him against traditional mode of thinking and behaviour.

In 2nd, 6th, 8th and 12th houses, which externalize hidden karmic forces coming from the depth of universal reservoir, one prognosticates their results with great caution. In these houses, the planets, good and adverse, that is, benefic as well as malefic, become very powerful. They are so whether they are in strength or in weakness. Their Daśās invariably produce psychological mutation. These are difficult periods and individual has to be very cautious during this period. The astrologer has to be very careful in assessing the Daśā results of such planets.

2. Aṣṭottarī

This method of planetary periodicity is different in certain important ways from the Viṁśottari system. The latter, however, is extensively used and is much in vogue. Aṣṭottarī is used only for special type of natal charts. It is applied when Rāhu enjoys special relationship with the ascendant Lord in the natal chart. If Rāhu is not associated with the ascendant Lord and occupies a quadrant or a trine house, this method of planetary rulership produces effective results.

Under this system of planetary periodicity, Sun's period of rulership begins with Ārdrā, the 6th asterism, instead of Kṛttikā as in Viṁśottarī Daśā system. When Moon occupies Ārdrā in a natal chart, which is susceptible to this system of Daśā calculation, the initial planetary lordship prevails. In fact, if Moon at birth occupies Ārdrā or any of the four asterisms beginning with Ārdrā, that is, Punarvasu, Pushya and Aśleṣā, besides Ārdrā, Sun commences its planetary rulership over the individual under Aṣṭottarī system. Sun's rulership lasts for 6 years. If Moon occupies the following three asterisms namely Maghā, Pūrvā Phālgunī and Uttarā Phālgunī, it has its planetary rulership lasting for 15 years. In case, Moon at birth occupies the following four asterisms namely, Hasta, Citrā, Svāti and Viśākhā, Mars will qualify to have planetary rulership at birth over the newly born and its total period of rulership would be 8 years. Mercury's rulership at birth commences in case Moon at birth occupies any of the following three asterisms namely Anurādhā, Jyeṣṭhā and Mūla and it has the total duration of its rulership as 17 years. In case, Moon occupies at birth any of the following four asterisms that is any of Pūrvā Āṣāḍhā, Uttarā Āṣāḍhā, Abhijit and Śravaṇa, Saturn gets the planetary rulership with a total period of 10 years. It may be noted in this system that Abhijit figures among the asterisms, which are taken into consideration for assigning planetary rulership to different planets (Saturn is the planet, which gets its rulership under its occupancy). Another significant feature of this system is that special magnitude is assigned to various asterisms, which qualify Saturn to get the initial planetary rulership. Pūrvā Āṣāḍhā is permitted to have full extension of 13° 20' consisting 3° 20' as its each Pada or quarter. But the following asterism namely Uttarā Āṣāḍhā is permitted only 10° 00' and Śatabhiṣag only 6° 40' and Abhijit is given 10° 00' which has been taken from these two asterisms. Thus this bloc of asterisms comprises Pūrvā Āṣāḍhā containing 13° 20' starting from 0° or the very commencement of Sagittarius sign of the zodiac, Uttarā Āṣāḍhā beginning from 26°40' in Sagittarius to 6° 40" Capricorn, and Abhijit from 6°40' in Capricorn to 16° 40' in it. After these Śravaṇa would start to end up at 23° 20' of the sign. The following three asterisms namely Dhaniṣṭhā, Śatabhiṣag and Pūrvā Bhādrapadā qualify for the planetary rulership of Jupiter which takes sway for 19 years. Rāhu follows if Moon at birth occupies any of the four asterisms namely Uttarā Bhādrapadā, Revatī, Aśvinī and Bharaṇī. Rāhu is assigned a full period of 12 years. Venus that rules the individual at birth in case Moon occupies Kṛttikā, Rohiṇī or Mṛgaśīrṣa follows Rāhu. Its rulership period lasts for 21 years. Under Aṣṭottarī system of planetary rulership there is no place for Ketu.

Under Aṣṭottarī the planetary rulership is assigned to a bloc of asterism. The portion traversed by Moon over this expanse determines the duration of the planet still to follow. In case, a planet say Mars qualifies for rulership by the virtue of Moon Hasta-Citrā-Svāti-Viśākhā and if Moon is at the end of Svāti and the whole of Viśākhā lies yet to be traversed by Moon, then in that case Mars' three -fourth period of rulership is over. It will therefore have sway over the life of the individual only for two years. After the expiry of these two years, Mercury will assume control on 17 years and the cycle will begin its operation in its full course. In case, Moon has traversed half of, say, Śatabhiṣag in the bloc of three asterisms with Dhaniṣṭhā-Śatabhiṣag-Pūrvā Bhādrapadā which qualified Jupiter to have sway over the child at birth, then half of the period of Jupiter's rulership is over and the next half of 19 years that is, 9 years 6 months of the same will be there for the individual to be under this planet. After the end of this duration, Rāhu will take over its planetary rulership over him with its full 12 years of rulership. After this planet, the cyclic order will operate with each of the following planets having the full course of their periods of rulership. The portion of the initial rulership of Rāhu invariably produces psychological mutation. These are difficult periods and the individual has to be very cautious during this period. The astrologer has to be very careful in assessing the Daśā results of such planets.

Table 2

Blocs of Asterisms Which Qualify Different Planets for Initial Rulership Under Aṣṭottarī System

Planetary Rulership	*Bloc of Asterisms in Which Moon Qualifies a Planet to have the Initial Rulership*	*No. of Aster-isms*	*Years of Rul-ership*
Sun	Ārdrā, Punarvasu, Puṣya, Aśleṣā	Four	6
Moon	Maghā, Pūrvā Phālgunī, Uttarā Phālgunī	Three	15
Mars	Hasta-Citrā, Svāti, Viśākhā	Four	8
Mercury	Anurādhā, Jyeṣṭhā, Mūla	Three	17
Saturn	Pūrvā Āṣāḍhā, Uttarā Āṣāḍhā, Abhijit, Śravaṇa	Four	10
Jupiter	Dhaniṣṭha, Śatabhiṣag, Pūrvā Bhādrapadā	Three	19
Rāhu	Uttarā Bhādrapadā, Revatī, Aśvinī, Bharaṇī	Four	12
Venus	Kṛttikā, Rohiṇī, Mṛgaśīrṣa	Three	21

3. Ṣoḍaśottarī

The total period of planetary rulership under Ṣoḍaṣottarī system extends over 116 years. The system applies to those individuals who are born during the waning phase of Moon. The periodicity of different planets are as follows:

1=Sun (11 years), 2=Mars (12 years), 3=Jupiter (13 years), 4= Saturn (14 years), 5=Ketu (15 years), 6=Moon (16 years), 7= Mercury (17 years) and 0, or 8=Venus (18 years).

The duration of the initial Daśā of the planet depends upon the proportion of the asterism already traversed by Moon, the distance already elapsed represented the rulership period that is already over. Whatever period of that planet still remains to pass would be the balance of its rulership at birth. The rulership of other planets would be in the same sequence as indicated above and they would enjoy their full periods of rulership. Whatever remains of the initial planetary rulership could be available to the person if he or she lives upto 116 years, the full cycle of this planetary rulership.

4. Dvādaśottarī

Dvādaśottarī system of Daśā calculation is very much similar to the earlier one but the similarity ends only in the method of approach. The applicability of this system is different. So is the method of determining the initial planetary rulership. This system is applicable in those cases where the individual is born in the Navāṁśa of Venus. In this system, one counts the number of asterisms from the one in which Moon is located at birth upto Revatī, the last asterism counting the Nakṣatras from Aśvinī. The number thus obtained is divided by 8. The remainder represents the planet ruling at birth. In case the remainder is 0, it is assumed as 8 which represents Moon. In case the remainder is 1, Sun occupies the initial planetary rulership, 2 represents the control of Jupiter, 3 stands for Ketu, 4 for Mercury, 5 for Rāhu, 6 for Mars and 7 Saturn. The years of their control are as follows: Sun 7 years, Jupiter 9 years, Ketu 11 years, Mercury 13 years, Rāhu 15 years, Mars 17 years, Saturn 19 years and Moon 21 years. The total period for all the planets amounts to 112 years. There is no planetary rulership for Venus. The exact duration of planetary rulership at birth depends upon the area already traversed by Moon in the asterism, which is to be subtracted from the total years of rulership assigned to the planet proportionately.

5. Pañcottarī

Pañcottarī system of planetary rulership applies to births, which have Cancer ascendant while the longitude of the ascendant lies in Cancer *Dvādaśāṁśa*. Only the seven planets excluding the shadowy Rāhu and Ketu are taken into consideration under this system. The initial period of planetary rulership is decided by counting the birth Nakṣatra from Anurādhā, which is the 17th asterism. The number thus obtained is divided by 7, the remainder is taken to represent the planetary rulership at birth. In this system, number 1 stands for Sun, which is assigned 12 years of planetary rulership. Number 2 stands for Mercury with 13 years of rulership. Saturn qualifies for this position if the remainder is 3, it has the rulership for 14 years. With number 4 Mars occupies the initial planetary rulership, it has the duration for 15 years. Number 5 gives the initial rulership to Venus for a period of 16 years. Number 6 enables Moon to occupy the beginning rulership. When the remainder is 0 or 7, the rulership at the beginning of the birth belongs to Jupiter with 18 years of control over the individual. All the seven planets complete their course of rulership over the individual in 105 years. The duration not available to the individual at the beginning, will be available to him at the end of the total duration. He will enjoy that rulership period towards the end of the cycle.

6. Śatābdika

Śatābdika system of Daśā calculation applies only to those individuals who are born under a *Vargottama Navāṁśa.* Only 100 years are assigned to the planets for rulership under this system. For determining the initial rulership of a planet, one counts the birth Nakṣatra from Revatī and divides the number thus obtained by 7. The remainder represents the planet that will obtain the initial rulership. Sun's period starts if the remainder is 1 and it gets 5 years of rulership. With 2, Moon has the rulership at the beginning and it also enjoys the rulership of five years. The duration of 10 years is assigned to Venus that assumes the rulership at birth with 3 as the remainder. When there is 4 as the remainder, Mercury becomes the initial planetary ruler and its duration is for 10 years. The duration is doubled if the remainder is 5 and Jupiter assumes the initial rulership of 20 years period. Mars that gets the position with 6 as the remainder enjoys the same duration, that is, 20 years of control. When the remainder is 7,

Saturn becomes the initial planetary ruler and it enjoys the rulership period of 30 years.

Under this system the Nodes namely, Rāhu and Ketu do not get any rulership. The total duration of rulership under this system is 100 years. The initial period is calculated on the basis of the position of Moon within an asterism. The period of rulership is proportionately reduced according to the distance traversed in the asterism and this period is available only towards the end of the total period of 100 years.

7. Caturaśītyabda

This system applies to those persons who have the tenth house Lord occupying the tenth house itself. It takes into account only seven planets, it does not take into account the nodes of the Moon. Under this system, each planet has its rulership period of 12 years and the total period of all the planets taken together amounts to only 84 years.The initial planet to assume rulership over the newly born is decided by counting the birth asterism from Revatī, the last Nakṣatra and dividing the number thus obtained by 7. The remainder represents the planet ruling at birth. The sequence of planetary rulership as well as the planet represented by the remainder is as follows:

Number 1 represents Sun, which has as is the case with every other planet, the rulership period of 12 years. Number 2 represents Moon, Number 3 Mars, 4 Mercury, 5 Jupiter, 6 Venus and 7th represents Saturn. The sequence of planetary rulership under this system follows the same sequence as the weekdays.

8. Dvisaptatisamās

This system applies to those births, which have the ascendant Lord placed in 7th house, or the Lord of the 7th house is placed in the ascendant. It provides rulership to only 8 planets. The descending Node of Moon namely Ketu does not get any rulership under this system. Only Rāhu among the Nodes is included. Each of the 8 planets included under this system obtains rulership period of 9 years and the total duration of one cycle of Daśā period amounts to 72 years.

This Daśā system begins with the planet which is found out by counting the birth asterism, that is, the asterism in which Moon is placed at birth from Moolam which is the 19th asterism and dividing the number thus obtained by 8. The remainder represents the planet, which obtains the planetary rulership at birth.

The remainders represent the planet as follows : Number 1 represents Sun, 2 represents Moon, 3 Mars, 4 Mercury, 5 Jupiter, 6 Venus, 7 Saturn and 8 represents Rāhu.

9. Ṣaṣṭyabda

This system is applicable in those cases in which the Sun at birth occupies the ascendant itself. The planetary rulership at birth as in the Aṣṭottarī system is assigned to a bloc of asterisms rather than to an individual one. The number of asterisms in this system is 28, which includes Abhijit. These asterisms are divided into eight groups. The first three asterisms beginning with Aśvinī are grouped in the first bloc and the second bloc contains four asterisms. The third bloc contains three asterisms followed by four asterisms in the fourth bloc. Thus various blocs alternate between three and four asterisms in one bloc. The first three blocs are assigned to Jupiter, Sun and Mars respectively. Each of these planets qualifies for the rulership period of 10 years. The period of initial rulership is decided by taking into account the Moon's position in the bloc as a whole as in the case of Aṣṭottarī system. The last five blocs are related with Moon, Mercury, Venus, Saturn and Rāhu respectively. Each of these planets qualifies for the rulership period of 6 years. Under this system Abhijit, as indicated earlier, is included. It has the planetary rulership of Saturn and occupies the very beginning of the bloc of asterisms containing Abhijit, Śravaṇa and Dhaniṣṭhā. The inclusion of Abhijit produces some confusion. In order to adjust the discrepancy created by it the previous bloc containing Jyeṣṭha, Mūla, Pūrvā Āṣāḍhā and Uttarā Āṣāḍha is assigned only an extension of 51°00', Uttarā Āṣāḍhā is allowed only 10°00'. The bloc which included Abhijit is assigned to Saturn and it has the total extension of 30°00'. It provides 10°00' for Abhijit, 6°40' for Śravaṇa and 13°20' for Dhaniṣṭhā. The details of working out the planetary rulers under the system are analogous to the Aṣṭottarī system.

10. Ṣaṭtriṁśadvātsara

Under Ṣaṭtriṁśadvātsara system of Daśā calculation only those persons are considered who have their birth in daytime with Sun Hora. If the birth is in night Moon Hora has to be taken into account. The initial planetary rulership is determined by counting the birth asterism from Śravaṇa. The number thus obtained is divided by 8. The remainder represents the planet ruling at birth. Number 1 represents Sun that enjoys rulership period for only one year. Number 2 gives the rulership to Moon with 2 years of rulership. Number 3 gives the control to Jupiter that enjoys the rulership for 3 years. Mars gets the rulership if the remainder is 4 and it enjoys the rulership for 4 years. Number 5 goes to Mercury with 5 years of rulership. Saturn gets the rulership when the remainder is 6 and its duration is also 6 years. Venus has the control over the individual at birth if the remainder is 7 and its duration is 7 years. Where there is no remainder, it amounts to saying that the remainder is equal to 8. In that case, the rulership at birth goes to Rāhu, which enjoys control at birth for 8 years. It may be noted that the rulership under this system is represented by the remainder after the dividing the number of the birth asterism counted from Śravaṇa and the number of years of their rulership is same as the remainder thus obtained. There is no rulership to Ketu under this system.

The Secondary Daśā System

Planets at the secondary level also influence the main Daśā. We have seen before that the initial planetary rulership of the main planet determines the life-long sequence of planetary conditions in a general way. The course of everyday life requires very detailed information on ever-changing events. Detailed information on such events can be had by secondary impulses generated by different planets. The main *Daśā* of every planet has secondary *Daśās* of all other planets. The effective prognostication of the timing of events and the relative significance of those events can be gauged effectively by examining these secondary influences in relationship with the main Daśā influences. These secondary impulses are studied under *Antardaśā system.*

A basic assumption of Vedic astrology is the integrated nature of the planets. They always interact with one another and also at different levels. The central impulse permanently intoned by the Sun reaches the individual at his normal life after crossing the different veils produced by different planets. Each planet affects the primary solar ray. But each of these veils has veils within veils, which obscures the direction towards which the central core of the individual is directing him. This complication makes the understanding of the results of secondary impulses very difficult. The first step in order to resolve this problem is to identify the secondary planets working at any period and also the duration of their influence at that level. This is the main task for the secondary Daśā system. Antardaśā show how various planets operate within the general influence of a planet and generate their own impulses in order to lead the individuals gradually so as to strengthen his faculties in the desired manner effectively and in a consolidated manner.

The task of ascertaining planetary rulerships and sequence of their periodicity as revealed through the main and secondary rulerships depends upon the position of Moon in relationship with various asterisms. These asterisms in their turn represent the areas of special influence. Each of them represents certain impulses necessary for the egoic unfolding of the individual. The Moon carries through it the basic generative energy imparted by the Sun. It implants those faculties in the individual with the help of the asterism in which it is placed. The various planetary implants depend upon the relationship between the Sun and Moon on the one hand and between the Moon and the asterism on the other. Those who wish to pursue the study of astrological occultism need to examine the planetary rulership under its main and various secondary rulerships very carefully.

The initial planetary rulership decides all subsequent stages of Main, Antar and Sūkṣma Daśās. Once the initial rulership is decided, others follow as a matter of course. This cyclic course hinges round the natal position of Moon. Being the reflection of the solar radiance, the primary function of Moon during its various operations and its association of different asterisms is to precipitate the impact flowing through the solar rays. The delineation of planetary periodicity approached in this manner relates the individual with the center of one's cosmic existence. The individual has ultimately to acquire all virtues prior to his attaining his final goal. So every secondary planet contributes during its sub period the special qualities generated by it. Every event, sorrowful or pleasant, reflects the working of different planets in support of this Cosmic Will. No event is an isolated event. Every situation whether temporary or of enduring significance aims at unravelling the necessary latent qualities in the person. The timing of events as shown by different secondary and tertiary planetary impulses is important because these qualities being developed at this time is necessary to meet the different impending challenges to the individual.

The prognostication of the future is an exercise in unravelling the course of individual's efforts in actualizing his or her latent qualities. It is an effort in speculating the ultimate destiny of the individual and the special path chartered for him or her. The impact of secondary and tertiary planets can be studied effectively by relating their specific long and short-term results in relation to the person's ultimate goal. The specific results as indicated for different planets during the course of their secondary and tertiary chain of rulership periods are meaningful only when pursued in this manner.

The route through which sub-periods and sub-sub periods of planetary periodicity affect the individuals is determined is more or less the same. The methods are similar to that which is followed in the calculation of the main Daśā system. It may however be emphasized here once more that the most important step in this regard is the determination of the initial planetary rulership and the duration of it already elapsed on account of the progress made by Moon in the specific asterism. The secondary and tertiary Daśā systems also follow the same principle of proportionality and sequence as in Mahādaśā system. We have already discussed these principles before in relation with Viṁśottarī Daśā calculation. Many astrologers follow short-cut methods for arriving at the same results. One such method is described below to give the rule of the thumb in this regard. These methods are based on Viṁśottarī system. The total period of planetary rulership under this system is 120 years and different planets have their duration of Daśās as follows: Sun 6 years, Moon 10 years, Mars 7 years, Rāhu 18 years, Jupiter 16 years, Saturn 19 years, Mercury 17 years, Ketu 7 years and Venus 20 years.

During their Antardaśās the planets have the same relative duration, the proportion to the total period also remains the same. For instance, Sun has its Daśā of 6 years during the total of 120 years of Viṁśottarī period. It implies that it covers 6/120 or one-twentieth of the total duration. Sub-lordship of Sun during its own main period will be one-twentieth of 6 years. It will therefore by equal to 3 months 18 days[1]. A shortcut to this calculation is to multiply the total duration of both the planets under consideration and multiply by 3 the last digit of the resultant thus obtained. This gives the number of days, while the earlier digits indicate the duration in months. In the present

1. In this system only 30 days comprise a month and a year consists of 365 days.

case, Sun's rulership is 6 years. So 6 is the rulership period of the planet under which the sub-lordship of Sun is being calculated. So one multiplies 6 by 6, which gives 6 × 6 = 36, the last digit 6 is again multiplied by 3. It gives 18, which represents the number of days, while the earlier digit 3 indicates the number of months. The sub-lordship of Sun in its own main period is thus arrived as 3 months 18 days.

Let us take another illustration. The period of Moon is 10 years in the total of 120 years of Viṁśottarī system. It makes Moon's period of rulership as 10/120 or one-twelfth of the total. Moon's sub-period within Sun's main period which lasts for only 6 years is worked out as one-twelfth of 6 years which gives 6 months. Short cut method is to multiply 6 by 10, which gives 60. The last digit of 60 is zero (0)which suggests that the number of days in this period will be nil, the earlier digit being 6, the sub-lordship of Moon within Sun's major period of rulership would be only 6 months.

The method suggested above can once again be repeated as follows. When the duration of the main period of a planet is multiplied with that of another for working out the Antardaśā, the resultant is separated in two sections: the last digit multiplied by 3 gives the number of days while the previous digit or digits give in month for the planetary sub-period within the main period of a planet. The period of sub-lordship of say, Mars during the major period of Venus is obtained by multiplying 7 which is the duration of the rulership of Mars under Viṁśottarī system with 20 which is the total rulership period of Venus under this system. The resultant is (20 × 7)or 140. The last digit is separated from the earlier one. In this case, the last digit is zero (0), which multiplied by three (3) gives zero, the previous digits namely 14 signifies the duration of 14 months or 1 year 2 months. It shows that the sub-period of Mars in the main Venus Daśā period will be only 1 year 2 months 0 days.

The sequence of sub-lordships of different planets is the same as in the case of Viṁśottarī Daśā. The planet under which the sub-lordship of planets is being worked out gets its own initial secondary planetary period, as in the Viṁśottarī system. The first sub-period under Sun's main *Daśā* will be that of Sun itself, in the case of Moon's major period, the first Antardaśā will be of Moon, and in the case of Mars, the first sub-lordship will be that of Mars and so on. The sequence of the secondary rulership is also the same as under Viṁśottarī. The circularity of the sequence is the same: Sun-Moon-

Mars-Rāhu-Jupiter-Saturn-Mercury-Ketu-Venus. The chain of sequence is disturbed only at the initial stage : whenever any planet takes control over an individual for its major Daśā, the secondary Daśā begins with this very planet and the sequence starts from that planet till the circle is over. This rule applies for the secondary as well for the tertiary Daśās. It implies that the initial secondary Daśā under Sun will be that of Sun itself, and the tertiary Daśā under Secondary Sun will be that of Sun. But during the Moon Secondary Daśā under Sun, the first tertiary Daśā will be of Moon, and not of Sun. Similarly, when Jupiter's secondary period begins, say, under Moon, then the tertiary Daśā under Jupiter's secondary Daśā will begin with that of Jupiter. While the sequence remains the same, this special feature of the circularity of the system should be well recognized.

As mentioned earlier, the Moon at birth is not necessarily at the very commencement of an asterism. It may be several degrees ahead of the beginning. The planet qualifying for the initial rulership (as under the main Daśā calculation) is not entitled to the full period of its rulership. One has to be very careful in working out the first sub-lordship of the planet. The first antar in such cases may not necessarily be that of the ruling planet itself. In such cases, one has to work out the beginning of the primary rulership period from the very commencement of the asterism and find out the planet which would have qualified for rulership by virtue of Moon's location at the specific longitude. A person born with Moon at 20°00' will be born in Bharaṇī Nakṣatra qualifying Venus for the first rulership. Bharaṇī starts from 13°20', so half of the Venus Daśā is already over. At 20°00' in Aries, Venus had already crossed half of Bharaṇī, so it had begun its 11th year of rulership. The sub-lordship of Venus at its initial period should have been that of Venus itself and the subsequent sub-lordships would have followed seriatim. Jupiter's Antardaśā under the main Daśā of Venus starts after 9 years 10 months. That is, 10 years minus 9 years 10 months or, 2 months of Jupiter's sub-period is already over at the time of the birth. The individual is now entitled to only 2 years 6 months out of the total period (32 months) of Jupiter's secondary Daśā. ($20 \times 16 = 320$. 32/0, of which 0 multiplied by 3 gives 0, so only 32 months remain) Once this initial Daśā of Jupiter is over, which would be after the end of 30 months, Saturn will have its full duration of 3 years 2 months:

($20 \times 19 = 380$; $0 \times 0 = 0$; 38 represented 3 years 2 months) in the Venus main period. The individual born at 20°00' in Aries in this way will be able to have the major rulership of Venus at the beginning of his or her birth for 10 years but will begin the sub-period of Jupiter lasting only for 2 years 6 months. Once the main Daśā of Venus is over, other planets will have their full entitlements. The period, which Venus could not enjoy at the beginning of the individual's birth, will be available to the person after the end of Ketu main period if he survives that long. It will happen in this case if the individual could live for another 110 years.

II. Main Daśā Results

Every planet has its unique characteristics. These attributes fructify during its main, secondary as well as tertiary rulership periods. They produce their results at different levels during their different levels of rulerships. The planets produce their general features based on their horoscopic configuration during the entire life of the individual. But these are different from what they produce under their Daśās and Antardaśās. The basic results of the planets and their position in relation with other planets in the natal horoscope are experienced throughout the life of the individual by way of his general status or his general temperament. During their main Daśā period, the planets produce their results in a very concentrated manner at a specific level of the individual's personality. During their main Daśā period, the planets accentuate the results they are likely to produce as a result of their position in the natal horoscope. They influence the physical features, temperaments as well as the individual's social and family status. They affect the permanent features of the individual's life. The major Daśā of a planet leads to important fluctuations, which generally occur at the physical level, which are easily observed objectively. They produce such changes, which are often described as tides of life. They lead to such important changes, which are often described as twists and turns in one's life. Such changes occur at different times in one's life and every planet during the course of its main Daśā generates such changes. Their impact depends upon their position in the natal horoscope. The changes in the general fortune, so to say, of the individual varies according to changes in the main periods of different planets. Often these changes are very important. They completely and radically alter the life style of the person. But there are several other changes, which are also concrete and easily discernable. They also contribute to the general upheaval in the life of the person. But they are of short-term duration. They can be experienced at the personal level of the individual. The general public or the society at large is not much affected by them. The planets working at the secondary and tertiary levels produce these events. Those planets, which operate during the *Sūkṣma Daśā* or at the tertiary level, affect the psychology or the mind of the individual. The planets working at the main, secondary and at tertiary levels have their distinct roles and levels to operate. The secondary and tertiary periods of different planets act at the subtler or the psycho-mental levels of the personality while the main Daśā period impinges on grosser aspects of life. The effects of secondary planets though act at the psycho-mental levels, lead to certain general results also. One has to be very careful in prognosticating such results.

These roles of the different planets complicate astrological prognostications. It has been observed that several powerful horoscopes with many promising features often fail to actualize their potential. Such experiences lead a novice to bewilderment. It causes to frustration to those who believe in the efficacy of powerful planets. Under such conditions, it is necessary to evaluate the natal and planetary periodicity at different levels very carefully. A prosaic person engaged in intricate industrial management problems might at times be seen engaged in artistic pursuits and even taking part in painting competitions. Such contradictions can be resolved by studying the deeper implications of planetary Daśās and the rationale of planetary sequence. These questions are related with esoteric astrology, which relates the cosmic forces with egoic evolution of the individual. But at present we are not concerned with it. We accept here that there are two distinct levels at which the planets operate: one relates with the external, general and concrete changes pertaining to the individual, and the other with his personal, psycho-mental and inner changes. In order to prognosticate the subjective changes we need the knowledge of different principles and of the various sheaths constituting the individual. At present we will not go into the details of these questions. We may however, emphasize here that there is a difference between the nature of the natal horoscope and the planetary periodicity, which guides everyday events in an individual's life. The former represents his potential and the latter the possibility of actualization of the latent qualities. The potential is actualized only during the planetary rulerships of different planets. Unless the appropriate planets assume control over the life of an individual, their benefic or the malefic effects cannot be experienced. This divergence between the potential and the actual is the cause of several frustrating experiences. The timing of events based on planetary periodicity resolves this contradiction in the understanding of the deeper nature of stellar impulses.

The general as well as special contribution of the planets must be taken into account in order to avoid such contradictions. This precaution will even save astrological prognostications from disrepute. It is for this reason that planetary periodicity assumes importance and timing of events becomes valuable tool for astrological forecasting. Vedic astrology requires astrologers to work out planetary relationships at several levels. At least three such levels of their operation known as the main, secondary and tertiary periodicity, also known as *Daśās, Antar* or *Bhukti,* and *Sūkṣma Daśā* are essential for precision in astrological predictions. The planets during their main Daśās influence the individual in a general way. Their influence is felt on the general surrounding. A kind of subjective change also begins to take place. Consequently, the psychology of the individual, his attitude to various aspects and events of life also alters. Gradually, many favourable and adverse situations begin to appear. They provide him opportunities to react to them according to his newly acquired mind-set. Even the responses and opinions of other persons around him change. The indwelling inner spirit begins to react to the external conditions of life according to the basic nature of the ruling planet at that time. The change is evident in the aura of the person. These changes take place very slowly and gradually. They take place progressively and continuously over a period of time. Ordinarily, most of them attain culmination during the middle of the planetary rulership and then they gradually fade off having stabilized the important constituents of the personality. During such periods, the planets prepare the individuals to receive planetary impulses expected during the succeeding period. Some planets however are different. Their impact, as in the case of Mars is sudden and overpowering. The effects of Saturn and Rāhu stretch over their entire duration. They become very strong towards the end of their rulership. While judging the results of any planetary Daśā, these features of different planets must be taken into account. The planets actualize the potential at the personal level when they take control at secondary and tertiary levels of rulerships.

Every planet has its own primary characteristics, colour, nature and other features. It however, accommodates other planets during their secondary and tertiary rulerships in such a manner that it produces new situations for the individual. The changed conditions must be understood from the standpoint of the egoic growth and its unfolding. Every planet permits other planets to contribute their special uniqueness to the special needs of the person concerned. No planet loses its distinctive features, its nature and special attributes but each of them is accommodative of the others. The planets at secondary level seem more powerful than the one at the primary level. This discrepancy is merely apparent. The sub-lords produce concrete or physical results. The finer cosmic forces directed by the main Daśā planets operate at subtler levels but in a general way. They produce fundamental changes. They set the parameter within which physical or concrete results can take place. Such interfusing takes place during secondary and tertiary periods of planets. Difficulties in taking an integrated view of such interblending greatly complicate and confuse the final judgement of the resulting events. In such situations it is important to keep in mind that the primary planet sets out the general background and creates the magnetic field. The sub-planets operate on such highly surcharged cosmically electrified stellar field. The major planets orient the psychology of the individual, his physical preparedness and the immediate environment that sensitize the individual to absorb and respond to sub-planetary impulses. The response of sub-planets to subtler impulses of the main planet expresses itself as the immediate conditions of the individual, his relationships with his surrounding and family relations, the availability of different kinds of resources and other necessary wherewithal needed for tackling the various demands on his life. Major lords and sub-lords operate according to their own characteristics and dispositions and thereby contribute favourably in trying conditions of life. The final effect on the individual is experienced or prognosticated as an interblending of all these combined forces. This leads to complexity of the final outcome. Even the situations confronting the individual under such complicated situations are often baffling. A man of great fortitude may at times experience moments of intense discouragement. Insecurity and mental confusion may surround him. The immediate reaction of the individual results from an amalgam of secondary forces while the primary planetary impulses express the guiding routes marked out by the planetary deities for the individual to enable him to attain his final destiny.

The tertiary planets are related with concrete results. The physical impact on an individual is related with tertiary planetary relationships.

A prosaic person engaged in an intricate industrial programme may sometimes find himself in an artistic pursuit and he may even participate in such activities as painting competitions. The physical action namely, the artistic involvement will be the result of the planet at the tertiary level. The actualization of an event very much depends upon the nature, disposition and strength of a planet at the tertiary level. Unless the planets operating at *Sukṣma Daśā* or at the tertiary level are strong and favourable, good effects of benefic planets at the main and secondary levels cannot fructify and be effective. No straight forward or well defined results can be defined for different planets operating at all the three levels. Astrologers succeed well in predicting results of tertiary planets because they produce concrete results. Deeper implications of such occurrences can be comprehended only when the main and secondary forces operating on the individual is well understood. The impact of planets depends upon their disposition and on the special combinations in which they are placed in the natal horoscope. Their specific placements in a horoscope affect the individual importantly during their secondary and tertiary levels of rulerships. They very much influence the concrete results of the stellar forces, which are evident in everyday life of the individual. The basic nature of planets conditioned by the natal horoscope is manifest at the different levels during their periods of control but they have their distinct role also to play at primary, secondary and tertiary levels.

Various subjective influences of different planets working at different levels are difficult to precisely prognosticate. Such predictive efforts are often misleading. Sometimes they can be dangerous too. Each individual has a very special path to follow during the course of his or her egoic evolution. The astrologer has to be an adept or at least a clairvoyant seer to comprehend the direction to which the hands of destiny are propelling the individual to proceed. Any prediction that does not harmonize with this goal and give wrong ideas to the individual might encourage him or her to exercise contrary will-power. This might immensely complicate his or her life. The planetary forces operating at various levels must therefore be carefully examined and thoughtfully predicted.

The difficulty arises from several factors. Every planet produces its effect at its appropriate level. The events do not produce identical or similar results at all levels of the individual's existence. This can be better illustrated with the help of an example. Suppose a combination under appropriate planetary Daśā leads to the death of one's wife or her husband. Such a loss is certainly important for the individual. The incident has several ramifications. The loss occurs mainly due to some adverse planetary affliction of the 7th house. When the afflicting planet importantly takes control over the individual during its secondary or tertiary rulership, it would be physically unsettle the individual. Under some situations, the planetary affliction can cause loss of marital felicity due to divorce and/or infidelity. In another case, serious illness of the partner may produce marital unhappiness. In all these cases, the final outcome occurs due to the affliction by planets related with the 7th house but the occurrence of the event is guided by the secondary and tertiary Daśā periods. The implications of this frustrating experience would however be experienced at several levels. The death of an ailing wife from some incurable disease will have a different repercussion on the individual than the death of a person who had been immensely helpful and a great support to the person's business enterprise. Death of a wife or husband with a large number of incumbent offsprings who have to be nursed and cared for after the death of the spouse will not be the same as the one in which the living partner was contemplating divorce and to marry someone of his or her choice. These are various implications, which are involved with a simple occurrence of the affliction of the 7th house. It is doubtful whether by considering only the planetary periodicity without taking into account the general framework of the life's unfolding can provide any straightforward answer to such complicated situations. This requires a thorough analysis of the natal chart. The basic horoscope and the planetary periodicity have to be studied together in spite of the fact that the natal chart shows the potential and the periodicity of the planets shows the possibility of actualization. The actual event may be the same but other psychological, mental and spiritual background of the person make a vital difference in the understanding of the significance of any event howsoever insignificant it may seemingly appear to be. It is for such reasons that ad-hoc predictions are misleading. The results of primary, secondary and tertiary planetary periodicity should be considered as important tool for discovering the process of inner unfolding. The relationship of different planets with various principles of the individual and his life-long goals are the essential background conditions on which the task of planetary periodicity should be accomplished.

Major Planetary Influence

Sun

During the major period of Sun, its primary characteristics are evident in the change of general atmosphere around the person. Normal conditions of everyday life around him alter adding to his eminence, creative opportunities and power to exercise much political and spiritual authority. These features produce significant influence around him giving him a sense of satisfaction, happiness and authority. They arise to provide him the necessary wherewithal to proceed securely towards his abiding destiny.

Sun provides tremendous energy, spirit of independence, confidence and positive approach to life. It is considered the central planet around which all other planets revolve. It is the central core of human beings that imperceptibly guides the outer personality towards its ultimate destiny and fulfillment of the purpose of its existence. During the main *Daśā* of Sun, these features of the planet become very active. The everyday conditions of the life of the individual begin to align themselves in such a way that the basic goal of the individual begins to be actualized. The individual begins to attach greater importance to enduring aspects of life. Subjective reality becomes much more significant to him than the superficial external objectivity conditions. The primary impulse of the Sun directs his attention towards the Reality, the Eternal Being and the all-pervading Spirit. Such a psychological orientation in the attitude of the individual affects his demeanor and his general approach to life and its problems. There is pronounced change in his personality make-up. The Sun irradiates the inner spirit that guides the individual to his destiny. The basic influence of Sun is so great that the fullness of the individual's potential is never realized unless its main *Daśā* is available to him.

The major period of Sun is always important. It provides tremendous energy, spirit of independence, confidence in one's own self and creative approach to various problems of life. The Sun makes the aura of the individual scintillate with bright colours. During the main period of solar periodicity the inner life-essence begins to glow and the stellar magnetic field around the individual is intensely surcharged with spiritual attractive force. The individual begins to exhibit the stately grandeur of the inner ruler immortal. People get unconsciously attracted towards him. The stately grace of the person attracts obeisance, surrender, obedience and servitude from others. He receives honor from the state and from governmental authorities. He moves towards the centre of power. His mind becomes sharp and intuitive and other faculties become very active. He gets insight into basic features of things and relationships. His intelligence moves directly to the central essence of existence at different levels. The periodicity of Sun bestows immense power and very high social status. The basic impulse of Sun produces inner radiances. It secures for the individual power, respectability, freedom and creativity.

The Sun is the most important planet that affects every person in a very important manner. Unless the main period of Sun is available to a person, it is not possible for him to achieve the acme of his strength and fullness of his personality. Sun brings forth the best and the most intrinsic qualities of the person. It irradiates the inner spirit of the person. Such unfolding of the inner qualities is vital for him so as to guide him to his ultimate destiny. Sun takes the ego nearer to his final destiny and develops in the individual those qualities and strength which could equip him for this task. It is for such reasons that the major period of Sun is greatly important.

The intensity of solar influence depends upon its locational strength, its placement,, its exaltation, ownership, friendship and so on. These characteristics based on the position of the Sun in the natal horoscope determine the degree of its strength and the quality of its radiance. Adverse locations as a result of its association with malefic planets like Saturn and Rāhu stall, stymie and sidetrack the solar effulgence. They impede the glow likely to irradiate the inner being and impart the stately grandeur. Malefic afflictions debar the individual from deriving the satisfaction of exercising his or her inner strength and power. Adverse zodiacal relationships and associations reduce the intensity of solar radiance. The distressful malefic planets put a filter against its glow that interfere with its light reaching the individual. If the invigorating influence of the Sun is not available to him during the Sun's main Daśā, he feels weak and suffers from many handicaps, ailments and loss of status. The individual feels absence of requisite energy to meet the impending challenges of life. It will put him in the vale of shadow with little hope for redemption. On the other hand, if the Sun is strongly placed, the individual will be effectively led towards his goal. There would be lessening of materiality in his approach to life. He will feel as one with the life around him and with the world at large. During the main period of Sun, the Ātmic Principle establishes closer links with the personality but it would be greatly disturbed if the planet is weak and adversely situated.

Moon

Moon acts on the *Buddhic* plane. When it takes sway over the individual, its effulgence illumines his *Buddhic* consciousness. The man is exposed to a vastly expanded realm of existence. A mirror symbolizes Moon. This cosmic reflector enables the human individual to comprehend the subjective glory of Ātman. The Moon reflects the radiance of the Sun. It also enables the individual to absorb the prismatic rays of the central source of life on the earth. Moon also has enormous protective power. During its main Daśā, the cosmic mother protects the individual, sustains him in his efforts to grow, expand and enjoy the material existence. At the same time, it also makes the individual powerful enough to comprehend his true mission in life and to securely proceed to fulfil his destiny. On the physical plane, during its main period, the Moon imparts to the individual those capabilities that are necessary for serious and deep thinking, meditation; emotional upsurge, dynamic movement and intellectual growth. The stability and changeability experienced during the Moon's main period is very much similar to Mercurialness of the planet Mercury, which is mythologically supposed to be its son. In fact, both, Moon and Mercury are intimately linked. Everything connected with mind, intelligence, comprehension, exploration and the desire to find out meaning of one's everyday experiences can be studied only with the support of Moon and Mercury.

During Moon's major period, the *Buddhic* principle in man is energized. It links the consciousness of man with the universal mother principle. It accentuates the understanding of the evolutionary impulse. It operates on the inner subjective plane. Consequently, the consciousness of the individual expands. Everything assumes a new significance for him or her. The sensitivity of the person gets heightened. The person under the influence of Moon is capable to register changing relationship very clearly and accurately. He becomes sensitive to ever changing human relationships and emotional upsurge around him. His consciousness is able to respond to different levels of existence, he can even establish rapport with denizens of subtler world.

Under adverse situations of Moon caused by its location or association, the consciousness and mental horizon of the person gets greatly restricted. It makes the individual miserable and forlorn. A favorably placed Moon under its major period heightens the sense of enjoyment. It so happens especially as a result of expansion of consciousness and unwrapping of one's subjectivity.

The general effect of Moon's rulership is significantly adapted according to its different placements and the degree of strength resulting from its association with other planets. In the first house, Moon makes the individual graceful, easily impressionable, and quick to adjust to changing conditions of life. When Moon is posited in ascendant, its effects are greatly accentuated, the mind of the individual is greatly energized. He becomes capable of reaching great heights in his meditation. Such a person is very emotional, affectionate and caring for the sentiments and feelings of others. With adverse situation of Moon, the stability of the person becomes uncertain.

The second house in a natal chart is related with wealth, family relationships and speech. When Moon is favourably placed in this house, the individual becomes primarily a family man, sensitive to the needs and emotions of his associates and others. He is provided with conveniences of life and has adequate financial support. As Moon is susceptible to quick changes, one has to be careful in dealing with such persons. These individuals themselves have to be watchful of their fluctuating tides of fortune and fickleness of human emotions. If Moon is in the second house, the main Daśā of such a Moon affects the personal life of the individual and his immediate surroundings. There is a possibility of serious changes in his personal life during this period. If the location of the planet is favourable and its strength satisfactory, these changes would be to his liking, otherwise there could be great whirlpool in his mind, emotion and personal relationships.

If Moon is placed in the third house, its main period can destabilize the individual's relationships with his siblings and colleagues. He may experience emotional strain arising from competitive rivalry from such persons. In case, some one has got Moon in his fourth house, the impact of the planet will be felt on his emotional life. His life would be full of emotional experiences and intense sensitivity. He would become highly "touchy" to every slightest remark and responses of others. But there are other dimensions of this feature as well. It makes the individual susceptible to intonations coming from the cosmic depths represented by the fourth house in a horoscope. Unless the individual has attained psycho-mental stability as a result of yogic austerities, the period would witness much cataclysmic changes often affecting the very foundation of his life-style as well as his mental balance.

The fifth house Moon becomes intensely creative during its rulership period. Mind of the individual becomes creative, his intellect becomes very sharp and his intuitive faculty is made acute so as to comprehend in a flash the deeply buried facts and relationships. Such a person during this period just knows what others could try to fathom after much investigative studies. If other non-luminaries are supportive to the fifth house, the Moon Daśā could be fruitful for concretization of abstract principles and abstruse concepts.

The position of Moon in sixth, seventh and eighth houses give warning signals during its main period. It produces conditions leading to mental disturbances, lack of marital security and sudden upheavals. Those who are striving after yogic attainments, they could take advantage of this period for intensifying their efforts. The chances of their securing favourable results during this period is great.

During the rulership period of the ninth house Moon, the understanding of natural laws and urge for righteous living become pronounced. The Moon's inherent susceptibility to rapid fluctuations however makes the individual unable to confirm to his own high ethical urges. The period is therefore marked by contradictions between one's understanding and its actual practice, between one's profession and action. When Moon occupies the tenth house, its main period brings rapid changes in one's professional career and life-conditions. Every situation confronting the individual during this period is intended to unravel and maintain new aspects of understanding and experiences pertaining to one's latent capabilities.

During the rulership of eleventh house Moon, one cannot be sure about the general attitude of the person. His mind-set is tethered to gross materiality. The person is ever eager to draw material benefit and sensual gratification from every situation and every person he comes across. In the rulership period of the twelfth house Moon, the individual becomes very sensitive to his sensual urges and he desires to indulge in them with much attachment and intensity. But it is also possible that under certain situations he may receive intonations from the other side of life. He may have many unusual psychic experiences.

The Moon could bestow clairvoyance and psychic *siddhis* during this Moon Daśā. It opens the individual to forces emanating from the non-physical realm.

In this way, the general impact of increased awareness and heightened sensitivity associated with Moon's influence can be observed in different aspects of one's life according to its placement in the natal chart. The central feature of this influence is expansion of consciousness, unravelling of sensitivity to subjective experiences and increased linkage with cosmic depth known as *Anima Mundi* in ancient occult literature or *Hiraṇyagarbha* in the *Vedas*.

Mars

The main daśā of Mars produces so much vitality in the person that it overflows in his every activity, almost in every aspect of his life. During this period the slumbering images or the latent ideas in the *Buddhic* consciousness struggle to surface and externalize at the physical plane. The inner vitality gushing for objective expression makes the individual full of animal passion, animated to achieve physical results and make a place for himself under the Sun. It aims to objectify its subjective content. Mars represents the very life force, the *Prāṇa* or the breath, which makes an individual alive and moving. Mars is the primordial creative impulse. It provides the impulse to manifest at all levels of creation. The main daśā of this planet charges the individual with vitality, electrical fluid, energy-on-move, animal passion, and extra-ordinary creative initiative. Whatever may be the age, status or profession of the person, the Martian period is full of dynamism, activity and ever changing relationships.

When Mars assumes the primary rulership over an individual his physical conditions become fluid, ever changing and forming new alignments and adjustments. Every change during the period provides new creative opportunities generating fresh *karma*. During this period, the individual becomes active, restless, impulsive, creative, and struggles to achieve a goal. Under its impact the inner life-essence struggles to externalize itself, the subjective tries to objectify itself, that which lies under the earth's crust or is hidden within the physical sheath is brought to the surface. There is growth, movement, destruction of the old and formation of the new and production of new situations. Under the Martian impact, the individual's interests change, his relationships alter, his surroundings shift and he may even move from one locality to another or from one country to another. When Mars is weak and located adversely, these changes lead to much loss, immense suffering, physical injuries and spilling of blood. These concrete results are primarily the results of the secondary and tertiary planetary impulses operating at that time.

When malefic planets are operating at the secondary and tertiary levels, the Martian daśā can be abundantly filled with accidents and other damaging consequences. On the other hand, if these planets are favourable and strong, the main Dāśā of Mars can prove to be highly auspicious and excitingly dynamic. It is for such reasons that one finds different types of events such as scientific discoveries, explorations of new geological finds, war-like engagements, bloodshed, accidents and angry explosions very common during the period of Mars.

Mars is basically a planet, which links the subjective, or the inner being with objective or the physical level of activities. The former is unseen and is often difficult to discern. It can be recognized as psychological agitation, restlessness and impulsive outbursts. The latter is markedly noticeable in actualization of subjective agitation and whirlwind in one's mind. The Martian externalizing nature is often expressed as bloodshed, abortion or childbirth, animal passions, impetuous sexual advances and angry explosions in one's personal relationships. The Martian impact is greatly dependent upon the placement and the degree of strength it enjoys in a natal chart. Its disposition and its strength in affecting other planets are very much modulated by the quality of its outflow of energy and the channels through which it flows.

Mars is the reservoir, rather the means for channelising the latent life-force. It is an embodiment of the cosmic creative energy. The divinity of man rests on such creativity. It highlights the auspicious disposition of the planet. In Hindu astrology, even the name of the planet-Maṅgala-means that which is auspicious. The placement of Mars in creative houses strengthens its auspicious characteristics. Mars in first, fifth, sixth and tenth houses is highly significant. Such locations give to it extraordinary capability: the individuals under such situations are bound to create an impression on the society in which they live. In the fifth house, Mars awakens in the individual interest in military science, mechanical engineering, atomic explosion, surgery, mining and in geological and seismic excavations. In case, the disposition of Mars is blemished, during its rulership, the mind of the person would work on destructive lines. Adversely associated Mars in the sixth house makes the individual suffer from diseases connected with blood, hostile relationships, litigation and discord in his social relationships. Strong and auspicious Mars in sixth house is very desirable for spiritual aspirants. During its planetary rulership, such individuals can hope to attain higher degrees of yogic siddhis, exploration of the latent faculties and acquisition of much spiritual power. In the tenth house, Mars bestows special possibilities. It may raise the social and official status of the individual, which may involve him or her in intense activities and earn him enduring rewards.

While prognosticating the results that are likely to occur during the Daśā of Mars, it is important to remember that Mars represents the creative impulse of the solar-will. Mars is intimately related with the Sun. The basic impulse of Sun is to provide the individual the motive-force that could direct him to his ultimate destiny. Representing itself as an important agent for this solar power, Mars operates like the divine-will to manifest. But it is neutral so far as the channel through which this will is exercised and channelled. The latter depends upon the strength and disposition of the planets operating at the secondary and tertiary levels. Mars is therefore often described as the reservoir of brute or invincible force. One even considers it blind energy that can function only through some other medium. The actualization of its results is available only through the nature, strength and position of other planets. The association with materialistic planets makes Mars lead the individual towards selfishness, self-centeredness and excessive involvement in sexual pursuits. Therefore in all astrological prognostications Mars should be considered primarily as the reservoir of divine -will to manifest. It is expressed as the life-breath that is ever engaged in externalizing the internal state, powers, situations and bring them to the surface. During the main period of Mars, the individual discovers many of his hidden and unseen qualities. It is a period of tremendous activities and achievement of one's goal in life.

Rāhu

Rāhu acts very deeply and its impact is enduring. Rāhu is not a concrete planet like other planets. It is considered a shadow planet. It is merely a very highly sensitive astronomical point whereas other planets are physical entities, seen physically and identified among the other shining stars. In spite of shadowy nature of this planet, it has been assigned a very significant role in Vedic astrology. Its main Daśā is considered very important for the inner development of the individual. It is described shadowy because its impact is felt on subjective nature of the individual. Externally one may feel that he is constrained by forces beyond his control, but he cannot specify the precise nature of these restrictive forces. The individual may feel that the events occurring during this period are not the results of his own actions, nonetheless these are overpowering forces on his life. Other planets are decisive, positive, having special disposition of their own, and their results can be identified on the physical plane. Rāhu on the other hand, is different. It operates as if some one else, whom no one is able to identify, is directing it to function in a particular manner and to produce certain results. It is a kind of law or dispensation, which acts behind the screen. It is a silhouette, a dark shadow of something hidden behind the screen under a lighted background. The potrait in the backdrop incessantly works on the individual, but during the planetary rulership of this shadowy planet the influence of the unseen image is greatly strengthened.

When Rāhu takes sway over the individual, events happen to him in such a manner that they cannot be ordinarily explained. These events draw him towards his ultimate goal, the image slumbering in the stones. These are the forces, which are coming to him from his hoary past, which cannot be denied. They have to be worked out. These are the forces that reveal the hands of his destiny. They are inevitable and invincible. They have to be borne with patience and fortitude.

Rāhu represents an aspect of the *Law of Karma*. Along with Ketu, it does the churning operation. It curdles the nebulous destiny of the individual lying hidden in his hoary past but always struggling to actualize and transform him into mighty cosmic creative energy. Rāhu's impulses are like the vulture, which looks for the corpse, swallows the decomposed dead material and finally transforms it into life-giving energy. Rāhu unravels the matured or the *Sañcita Karma,* makes the individual undergo the trials and tribulations necessary to counteract the past acts. Rāhu works out the forces of omission and commission, which are anti-evolutionary in character. It finally converts the pains and sorrows of these experiences into mellowed understanding of Divine Wisdom. During the main Daśā of Rāhu, the karmic forces operate in full vigour. These forces are difficult to comprehend-they make the events very elusive. One fails to understand the significance of these events but one can be sure of only one result about them. Rāhu will inevitably produce enduring results. The period is generally very difficult to endure. It inculcates the virtue of fortitude. But the end of the period ushers a new dawn of inner understanding. When the sorrows and frustrations, depression and dejection have ended, when the karmic retribution is complete, the individual is stronger and has come to a better realization of the working of nature. This is the primary mission of Rāhu, which it attains during its main daśā period.

Rāhu and Ketu are always linked together. The experiences and understanding gained during the main period of Rāhu show their impact on the consciousness of the individual during the main period of Ketu. The daśās of Jupiter, Saturn and Mercury that intervene in between the periods of Rāhu and Ketu actualize and ripen the lessons learnt during the shadowy Rāhu. It is for this reason that the results of Rāhu can be understood only on the basis of special configuration of Ketu. The two shadowy planets namely, Rāhu and Ketu represent the positive and negative polarities of planetary churning operation, which brings to the surface latent jewels or qualities embedded in one's inner depths.

Rāhu is such a powerful influence that one cannot escape it. During its control, its psychological impact is very intense and inescapable. Its results are dreaded because the dematerialization effects of these forces are often expressed as some deep-rooted malady difficult to diagnose and elusive to deal with. During this period, one often experiences loss of prestige and excruciating pain accompanied by intense mental anguish, theft, loss of wealth, abandonment by near and dear ones, bereavement, disappointment and such other conditions. They confront the individual without any hope of their early redress. The actual form and conditions of distress depend upon the nature and disposition of intervening *antar* and *sūkṣma daśās*. Rāhu's impact is primarily felt as the inescapable deep scar on one's psyche resulting from the events, which occur during its period. During the daśā of Rāhu, the individual may fall prey to bad company, begin to indulge in undesirable social activities. But these are the superficial expressions of the operation of past karmic forces. They should be understood and tackled in an intelligent manner if they are to be effectively managed. They aim at making the individual thoughtful inducing him to ponder over the deeper significance of one's everyday occurrences. A change in the astro-mental approach of the individual is the primary aim of various influences and events perpetrated during the period of Rāhu. Often it is observed that Rāhu does not only produce sorrows and frustrations during its main period of control, but it even produces unexpected opportunities for enjoyment. They receive different kinds of luxuries, friendships and honour from the state and reputed organizations. Means of transportation, palatial buildings, births of children, acquisition of new clothes and ornaments, and recognition of one's merit in distant land are also possible during the Rāhu period. These expressions of the working of the Law of Karma are related with subsidiary planets. Rāhu is primarily concerned with unsettling of the physical and psychological framework of the individual making him more thoughtful and introspective. How this objective is achieved is the concern of subsidiary planets.

The detailed results of the rulership of Rāhu are examined in its relationships with the ultimate goal of the person. The placement of various events is done with a view to providing the most appropriate conditions for the individual's psychic development. At a certain phase of one's egoic evolution karmic forces generated during the past are accumulated. They have to be worked out. Under such circumstances, sometimes it is considered helpful to provide the ego with abundance of material affluence so that the individual can take an objective view of their significance and develop complete detachment from them. In cases, if there are auspicious karmas already in store for the individual, even the Lords of Karma cannot wipe them out. They arrange them in such a manner that the individual understands their futility. These results can be obtained only through one's psychological orientation. The Lords of Karma arrange the meritorious deeds of the past in such a manner that Rāhu produces the karmic fruits, makes the individual avail the fruits of his past deeds but from them he learns the enduring lesson necessary for his soul's growth and development. Rāhu represents the Law of Karma, the results of good and bad actions done in the past appear to the individual during the main period of Rāhu. The externalization of the results occurs when the karma of the individual has ripened and he has matured enough to take advantage of the retributive justice. Very little can be done either to postpone or to deflect the results of Rāhu. The remedial measures against such afflictions are of little consequence. Only psychological adaptation in consonance with the objectives of Rāhu for the individual can effectively reduce the sting of this planet.

Rāhu produces radical changes in the astro-mental sheaths of the person. The shadowy planet is however engaged in achieving something higher, which can be attained only with a radical orientation in the constitution of the individual. Rāhu has a dual role to perform. It materializes the Divine impulse but in this process it acts in a manner as to teach the individual the Divine Wisdom. Only through an understanding of the mechanism of divine manifestation one can rise above the trammels of materialistic bondage. Rāhu tries to impart this lesson of detachment in many ways. It sometimes intensifies material conditions around a person so as to disillusion him with regard to such acquisitions. Sometimes it immerses him in materiality but does not produce disillusionment. In the latter case, the individual has to undergo severe pain later on to experience the results of such attachments. The method may differ from one individual to another depending upon his past but basically the aim of Rāhu is to inculcate dispassion in the individual and to lead him towards an understanding of the inner reality.

Jupiter

Jupiter is Deva-Guru, the preceptor of gods. Its function is to guide the *daivic* or the godly forceṣ. The *devas* are ever engaged in supporting, fostering and directing the manifestation. As a preceptor of gods, Jupiter has the arduous responsibility of assisting the terrestrial evolution. This role of Jupiter is abundantly evident during its main daśā period.

As a matter of fact, Rāhu, Jupiter and Saturn, all the three are intensely engaged in moving the individual rapidly in his or her evolutionary path. Their methods of operation are different from one another. Jupiter differs both from Rāhu and Saturn. Both of these, namely Rāhu and Saturn, produce enduring astro-mental orientation at deeper levels, which enables the individual to perceive the inner Reality. Psychic changes under their impact are vertical, that is, under their impact consciousness of the individual is turned inwards, towards the centre of existence. Jupiter on the other hand, produces horizontal expansion of consciousness. The individual under the Jovian impulse expands in the realm of physical manifestation. When the horizon of experiences and expectations has extensively increased, the desire to attain greater power, higher status and egoic expansion intensifies. It is based on the assumption that the inner reality of material affluence or disenchantment with it can be revealed only after the individual's direct experiences in this regard. Jupiter expands the horizon of experience and expectations whereas Rāhu and Saturn impart the necessary wisdom and detach the individual from them. Jupiter primarily impels the individual to spread out, grow and multiply in the realm of manifestation. Jupiter enables the individual to participate abundantly in the realm of manifestation. This is the process by which Jupiter assists the gods in their manifestated responsibilites. This is the main influence of Jupiter during its daśā period.

Rāhu is concerned with psychological adjustments whereas Jupiter produces festivals, display of learning, performance of rituals, conferment of royal honour, public decorations and felicitations. There is expansion of material affluence. Such physical beneficence induces the individual to involve him in the growth process. During all these festivities and *yajñas,* religious celebrations and scholarly studies, Jupiter's main thrust is to arouse the individual's interest and aspiration to come closer to divine forces. The Jovian impulse makes the individual philosophical and leads him to expand his mental horizon. He is more attuned to supernatural powers. It orients the astral sheath of the person so as to enable him to absorb greater degree of spiritual vibrations. Jupiter does not open the inner-eye, it does not lead to occult perception, it does not reveal the esoteric knowledge to the individual but it brings him nearer to occult hierarchy and the divine beings. It does not ordinarily let the individual know that the attention of higher forces is directed towards him.During the rulership of Jupiter, the individual experiences delight in material affluence and social eminence. He is sometimes made to feel that the material gifts to him are the rewards for his meritorious deeds.

During the main daśā of Jupiter, the pleasant experiences of the individual release him from the cocoon of his self-centeredness and make him associate with his fellow beings, social organizations and philanthropic activities. These involvement lead to the horizontal expansion of his personality. The astral nature of the individual however remains deeply entrenched in material things. He remains attached to material conveniences and personal relationships, but he begins to think that his outward conditions are merely the outer crusts of his inner spirituality. Jupiter invariably brings this kind of contradiction in one's life and a false feeling of spiritual eminence. The individual remains at the superficial level of spirituality. Jupiter never allows the individual to move away from material existence. This is a feature of Jovian impact, which is well evident during its main daśā. The Jovian period is packed with physical changes and mental preparations in order to prepare the individual for his future psychic changes (which are likely to occur during the main period of Saturn).

The rulership of Jupiter is full of auspicious events such as celebrations, festivities and pilgrimages. The individual gets a feeling of elation. His family thrives during the period and his children prosper. Expansion and protection characterize the main period of Jupiter. The most auspicious results of Jupiter come to fruition during this period, specially if the planet is situated in a trine house namely, the ascendant, fifth or the ninth house. The skill of the individual gets greatly enhanced. His respectability increases. He gets many opportunities for intellectual pursuits, study of religious scriptures and hearing of religious discourses. He may even come in contact with holy order of beings and receives blessings from saints and sages. The placement of Jupiter in trine houses is highly fortunate whose actualization is experienced during the planetary rulership of the planet. Even when the individual is confronted with unhappy situations during this period, the dangers pass off easily without producing serious damage to the person. In adverse houses such as sixth, eighth and twelfth, Jupiter helps the individual in an extra-ordinary manner. Under this situation, there could be some mental anxiety, occurrences of unexpected and sudden spell of misfortune, incurring of heavy expenditure resulting in loss of money, but from all such experiences Jupiter produces something helpful which the individual could not have otherwise got. Jupiter protects permanent loss of money and property, it saves the prestige and reputation of the person. The middle and the end periods of Jupiter daśā recover the loss and towards the end of it the Jovian periodicity produces happiness, bestows royal favour and much importantly deeper faith in divine benediction. Details of these depend upon the secondary and tertiary rulerships of the planets and the placement of Jupiter itself. Basically the Jovian impact is felt on the expansion and intensification of the results of the house in which it is located. Jupiter leads to the expansion of one's personality and the area of one 's influence. The benefic nature of Jupiter is based on these results which abundantly occur during its main daśā.

It should be noted that Jupiter is primarily a benevolent influence. It makes the individual god-turned. Every event occurring during this period represents the God's grace and the individual under its influence is protected in such a manner that no danger of enduring nature takes place. Whatever happens to the individual during the main period of Jupiter, he can rest assured that he would ultimately be protected and preserved and spiritually oriented. Jupiter is closely related with spiritualizing forces but it acts in a very pleasant manner. It makes the personal surroundings of the person, his family and social conditions oriented towards godly forces. It paves the way for Saturn to make its full impact during its own main period, which immediately follows the Jovian daśā.

Saturn

Saturn is the veil of ignorance and an envelope over meritorious deeds of the individual. It does not permit the individual to enjoy happiness from his worldly gains and affluence. Saturn is concerned with providing deeper insight into the working of the divine process. It aims at producing such changes that promote spiritual insight. Its results are produced the hard way. The individual under its impact has to pass through the vale of shadow. His eyes are full of tears and his heart bleeds before his eyes are opened to the inner reality of things. Saturn represents *Yama,* the Death God that makes the rulership period of Saturn very dreaded. It is so because Saturn veils the future and does not permit the past karmas to fructify. Saturn completely isolates the individual from every emotionally satisfying impulse.

The main period of Saturn is therefore very bewildering. The individual feels marooned, abandoned and forsaken. During this period, no ray of hope reaches him, he does not receive any encouragement from any quarter. He is emotionally dried up. The general milieu of helplessness surrounds him, he us unsupported from all sides and is without any guidance. That is the way Saturn produces self-confidence and faith in one's ultimate redemption. That is what Yama also does: death is a situation in which the past is obliterated from the view of the individual and the future is not yet disclosed. Death is the realm of immense darkness. No one can stand this vastness unless the Inner Light illumines his mind and strengthens his heart. This solitude is the domain of Saturn. During its rulership, it creates such a situation for the individual. Its intention is the same as that of Yama. Under its impact, the individual is completely precluded from all those factors that make an individual cheerful, optimist, happy and a good-mixer. These conditions arise because Saturn impedes the divine downpour in the vastness of the unknown and the bewilderment of the loneliness. Under this weight, Saturn however releases the inner fortitude of the individual. Saturn's primary objective during its rulership period is to stir up this latent power of the individual. Actual experiences arising from the dual impact of Saturn's control namely, the insulation of the individual from every external support, and the awakening of one's divine insight makes its main period very stressful and vexatious. The objective of rekindling the Inner Light is the keynote of Saturn's daśā towards which all pleasant and melancholic incidents happening during this period are directed. Various types of events occurring during this period are scum and spume of karmic retribution, which are employed to actualize this central objective.

The main daśā effects of Saturn cannot be realistically deduced merely from its location. During its primary rulership, the auspicious and inauspicious results both could follow even if the planet is situated in the so-called inauspicious houses. Saturn when placed in sixth, eighth or twelfth house from the ascendant is ordinarily expected to produce apprehension of poisoning and injuries from weapons, loss of status, separation from family relations, worry on account of wife and children and persecution from the state. But there have been instances when such placements led to pleasant experiences of overseas travel, exoneration from litigation and false allegations, such placements even elevated the individual to spiritual heights. The planet bestowed on the person honour from the state, renown, money and wealth, and appreciation from various international organizations. These are not very auspicious houses but the impact of Saturn when it is placed in one of these houses during its daśā has been quite heartening. It shows that the planet during its main period is concerned with something else for which it is generally dreaded.

The various events occurring during the main period of Saturn are not important by themselves. They are important because they lead the individuals to some psychological orientation that could enable them unfold their inner strength and develop their spiritual insight. Under the influence of Saturn one even develops the skill in surgery, comes in contact with different types of people and travels to many foreign countries, but these are not the primary impulses that the planet generates. These are merely the means by which the planet attempts to produce deeper insight into the working of the nature.

During its secondary and tertiary periods, Saturn provides the necessary and befitting support to the main planetary lord for the expression of that planet's objectives. During its own main period, Saturn's role is distinct and widely extensive. It operates as the tool in the hands of Yama, the lord over Time and Vastness of the Unknown. It creates that bewilderment that ensues from the dissolution of materiality of existence. This bewilderment is difficult to bear. So the main period of Saturn is often dreaded.

Saturn helps the Lords of Karma to use whatever exists in the karmic reservoir of the person for the development and strengthening of his inner faculties and for guiding him towards his ultimate destiny. Such a planetary period comes during the lifetime of only those persons who have earned sufficient spiritual merit and are on the threshold of attaining *yogic siddhis* and accelerated growth.

Saturn is a great liberating influence. It liberates the individual from temporal bondage. Under its impact, a person becomes a great thinker, a radical philosopher, and even a die-hard nihilist. In case the lessons imparted by Saturn have not matured and the individual is still unprepared to struggle and overcome his material shackles, the major period of Saturn would find him still indulging in anti-social activities, destroying established codes of behaviour, and transgressing all moral principles. These propensities are crystallized during Saturn's main period so that they are effectively destroyed and eliminated from the life of the person. It is the desire for such material gifts, the thirst for sentient gratification that is destroyed by Saturn during its main period.

There is nothing to fear during the main period of Saturn provided the individual is able to recognize the special qualities the planet attempts to generate in the individual. Saturn aims to eliminate the material veil from the inner eyes of the person. The turning of one's gaze inward reduces and very often removes the sting of misfortune experienced during the Saturn's main period. At the early stages of one's evolutionary path, Saturn functions like a veil against the divine downpour but later it removes the impediments against the downward flow of heavenly forces. What had so far been vague and undefined in the life of the person now becomes clear and externalized. His inarticulate qualities get expressed and strengthened. What had so far been obscure and unrealized is made distinct and concretized so as to operate effectively in times to come. The individual creates a niche for himself during the main period of Saturn. Under such conditions the past forces generated by the individual hover around him. They are often kept in abeyance by this planet if they are not needed for the imminent task. But they are released as soon as these are expected to be useful for the person, and the individual gets the benefit of his past meritorious deeds. Under the impact of Saturn the past karmas in this way are concretized and made useful for the individual. In a way this function of Saturn relates it with vulture which uses dead matter for securing life-giving energy out of it by digesting the dead matter within itself. Saturn's main period of rulership is important for psychological transformation of the individual and for spiritual preparations. It pulverizes the existing mental stuff so that the seeds for new understanding and new insight can sprout and take roots at appropriate time. Saturn paves the way for effective action of Mercury at deeper levels.

Mercury

Mercury is related with the mental faculties of the individual. Its primary role is to comprehend the intonations from *Buddhic* consciousness. It also operates to derive the lessons from various mundane experiences. Mercury sharpens the intellect and energizes the mind principle. It activates the thought process. The man becomes logical and analytical. Such a mind can move from the highest to the lowest, from the most abstract to the most mundane or concrete thoughts. Mercury enables the man to delve into the sublime as well the most crude. Nothing is beyond the comprehension and reach of Mercury. Mercury has no special preference for any specific subject for investigation and observation. Whatever comes within the purview of the individual, he can study effectively and minutely under the impact of Mercury. It makes him curious to know about others, to study the unknown, and to investigate the hidden. In the Hindu mythology, Lord Gaṇeśa is worshipped as the lord of intelligence and mind. He is assigned a mouse as his mount. The quality of a mouse is to pry on unexpected nook and corners of a place. It can go everywhere without any difficulty and without any let or hindrance. Such a character of Lord Gaṇeśa and thereby to human mind principle is to indicate that intellect has the capability of watching and exploring into every kind of situation. During its main daśā, the individual can express these qualities effectively.

During the rulership of Mercury mind becomes alert and intellect becomes sharp. This orientation makes the individual adaptable to every situation. Mercury is adaptable to every situation, which is expressed in many different ways. The understanding of the conditions of different persons coming in his contact and the appreciation of different situations confronting him enable a person with a strong mind to overcome his various personal prejudices. Mercury destroys the personal angularities of the individual. He easily adapts himself to every new condition of life. Mercury also exposes the individual to polarization of thought. Duality in the personality of the individual often makes him see both sides of an argument or of a situation. It also leads to instability in one's mind. Mercurial individuals are not always able to take a firm stand. This kind of instability is greatly accentuated during the Mercury main period which makes the common people feel that the person under the influence of Mercury has no personality of his own and is indecisive in character.

Mercury sharpens the intellect but it does not indicate the special area in which this faculty would be employed. The selection of the area of inquiry depends upon the configuration of planets in one's natal horoscope. Mercury reveals the quality of the mind and this aspect of one's personality is active during the main period of Mercury. The secondary and tertiary planets operating at that time guide the selection of subjects. If the secondary planets during the period are strong and well placed, the mental strength of the person could be expressed through those subjects that are related with those planets. Mercury would only assure that the intellectual attainments of the person would be appreciable during this main period. Credit or ignominy received during this period depends on other features of the horoscope. Mercury's main period only indicates that the intelligence of the person will be activated and the mind principle will be expressing itself in an intensive manner.

Absence of support or the lack of areas where the individual can use his mind will make him very ordinary. The period of Mercury's rulership in such cases will not therefore, exhibit any marked prominence. The right judgement resulting from Mercury during this period will be of no avail. Under favorable conditions, Mercury can enable the individual to obtain much monetary, social and literary rewards. Favourable mental disposition provided by Mercury during its main period can lead the individual to profitable business partnerships. Mercury makes the individual swift footed and a good traveller. During the period of Mercury's main daśā, the individual may visit several countries and strike good business proposition. If

Mercury is afflicted, its main period will lead to adverse results and makes the individual unable to take right decisions. By itself, the major period of Mercury results in manifestation of logical mind, intensity of comprehension, eagerness to know and exemplary skill in intellectual arguments. These are some of the qualities needed for attorney, chartered accountants, legislators and professors. For persons in these professions, the period of Mercury's rulership is always beneficial and effective in earning prolific rewards.

Ketu

Ketu is a planet of disillusionment. Its major planetary rulership enables the individual to comprehend the reality underlying the various forms of manifestations. Esoteric knowledge of temporal existence bewilders the mind, makes the individual disinterested in mundane relationships and eliminates attachment. These are by no means pleasant experiences. Ketu reduces all materiality to nothingness. It makes the individual disenchanted with all possessions whether material or psychological. These conditions do not produce happiness. Those individuals who live in the eternal and whose consciousness has transcended the limits of transient existence cannot be happy in the ordinary sense of the term. The perception of underlying reality behind the world of illusion, social pretensions and acquisitive human propensities often make a person extremely unsettled, sorrowful, frustrated and bewildered. These impressions are at times so alarming that they frighten him from facing the unquestionable realities of life. These psychological tensions and a sense of detachment from materiality and from all emotional attachments result in loss of hope and certainty about the future often making a person mentally unbalanced. It is likely to lead to psychological aberrations, create emotional knots and push the person towards the psychiatrist's table. But these are not necessarily the results that one always expect during the main period of Ketu. This planet is an embodiment of Divine Wisdom, insight into the Truth and Reality. By itself, Ketu does not bestow anything except wisdom, occult knowledge and spiritual enlightenment. There is no material aspect to Ketu through which it may cause any suffering. The troublesome consequences of Ketu can be traced through the discordant note sounded by other planets taking sway of secondary and tertiary rulerships.

The awakening of oneself to Truth or to the reality of a situation arises through one's confrontation with one's past actions of omissions and commissions. They are presented once more before the individual when he has gained greater knowledge and wisdom to evaluate them from a wider horizon of consciousness. He is also make to counteract the discordant notes already produced so as to restore the natural harmony. The physical events present during the main period of Ketu depend upon the planetary composition in the natal chart. If the stars are favourable for spiritual experience, Ketu opens the portals of hidden mysteries. The individual may even qualify for initiation into higher aspects of life. Otherwise, for a person of worldly nature, Ketu produces mental aberrations, psychological instability and emotional distortions. Producing sorrowful experiences and eliminating all zest for life. It isolates the individual from his compatriots and friends and makes him introspective.

Ketu operates like the alchemists' crucible. All experiences are processed therein and they are tested. Their underlying essence is extricated during the rulership of Ketu and made a part of the individual's understanding of the life process. Unless one passes through this gruelling epoch in one's life, he remains under the thraldom of ignorance and illusion. He does not come face to face with basic realities of life around him. Ketu is like a mirror, which reflects all impressions without any distortion. Ketu's main period is full of diverse experiences, which are directed towards revealing some deeper truths of life. Unless a person experiences the main period of Ketu, he is not exposed to the immensity of existence beyond the ken of physical perception.

The period of Ketu is much dreaded. It is based on the erroneous conception of the results of Ketu. The central impulse of Ketu is highly desirable for the growth and unfolding of one's deeper awareness. The opening of the third eye or the portals of hidden realities of life is, in fact, a moment of great rejoicing. This stage of inner development marks an important stage in the inner growth of the individual. Those who are entrenched in materiality and are reluctant to give up their life of illusion have every reason to feel skeptic about the period of Ketu. Those who are contented and comfortable in their ignorance may feel that the period of Ketu would destroy their zest for life and take away from them the joy of sensual gratification. Otherwise, Ketu's main period can be considered as the time when the diamond is chiselled to bring out its intrinsic radiance. Ketu ushers in the period of enlightenment and initiation into the mysteries of existence.

Ketu produces eminence and earns royal favour. Ketu's period can be highly propitious if it is posited in a quadrant or a trine house. Especially if Ketu in such a position is associated with or is aspected by auspicious planets, royal attention will be drawn to the individual. It will bring forth much royal and public honour. His social status may be elevated and he may travel to many countries and earn laurels for his wisdom.

Ketu placed in the third, sixth or eleventh house thwarts the disturbing conditions produced by other planets and helps the individual in maintaining his mental equanimity. He even secures much material prosperity and physical possessions. Ketu in second, eighth or twelfth house, specially if it is associated with or is aspected by malefic planets may lead the individual to pass his days in the company of depraved and undesirable persons. It may even lead him to imprisonment, experience humiliation and suffer from mental agonies. Whether in favourable or in adverse circumstances, Ketu in both the cases leads to dispassion, objectivity, clarity of understanding, disillusionment and enlightenment of the self. Ketu's major rulership lays the foundation of spirituality, occult yearnings and purification from the material drudgery. The process by which these qualities are developed depends upon the secondary planets while the main period of Ketu opens the individual to disenchantment and realization of esoteric truths.

Venus

Venus produces harmony. It produces photosynthesis in the context of social relations. It heightens physical sensation, intensifies sensuous gratification, immerses the individual in material bondage and perpetuates manifestation in these aspects till final redemption.Such changes have wide ramifications. The main daśā of Venus is therefore full of events, favourable situations producing pleasant experiences while the period of adverse placements creating serious afflictions and miserable existence.

During the main period of Venus, the individual gets decorations from the sovereign, ornaments from relations and friends and physical comforts and respectful position in his profession. In everyday life, the individual can expect sensual and sexual pleasure and delicacies of food. When Venus is related with the lord of ninth or tenth house and is placed in the fourth house, it bestows during its rulership period real estates, luxurious dwelling and special benedictions from religious organizations. As lord of the second and seventh houses, Venus is not very auspicious. Under such a situation, it produces mental unhappiness and physical agony. The individual during this period feels that his life is dissipating and life force is ebbing out of him. Venus has the special feature of greatly magnifying the feelings and sensations of the person. During its rulership, sensitivity of the individual is greatly accentuated, which can be evident from his poetic expressions and love relationships.

Venus is a planet of wish fulfilment. An individual can expect material gift during its rulership if the planet is favourable. Unless it is adversely associated or it assumes the lordship of second and/or seventh houses, the period of Venus is marked by abundance of material affluence and pleasant events. There is a tendency towards sense gratification and luxurious living making life of the person enjoyable in various ways. Venus does not necessarily intensify sexual pleasure and enjoyment of permissive relationships. Under appropriate conditions, it induces sensitive creative expressions revealing empathic experiences of the person. He develops the capacity to identify himself with the world and its inhabitants around him. The main period of Venus may lead to one's involvement with fine arts, painting, poetry, dancing, sculpting and such other activities.

Secondary Planetary Influences

Planets concretize their results during their secondary and tertiary rulership periods. The main rulership of a planet produces the general conditions or the *milieu* in which the secondary and tertiary planets precipitate the actual events. The planets in their *Antardaśās* and *Sūkṣma Daśās* yield precise results, which can be observed objectively. The effect of sub-planets depends upon their basic characteristics, their relationship with other planets in the natal chart as well as on their location in relation with the major planet. Prognostications based on these relationships are difficult and are only probable expectations. Astrologers venturing to make predictions based on such broad generalizations have to use their ingenuity in identifying the actual event that might occur at any time. But the classical texts have given much hints and suggestions on the basis of which it is possible to pinpoint the likely events to a great extent and even to determine the time when they could take place. There are three main channels through which the timing of events are predicted.

These methods are known as Planetary Periodicity which, included Daśās, *Antar,* and *Sūkṣma Daśās,* the *Gocara Paddhati* or the planetary transits, and *Varṣaphala* or the annual or progressed horoscopy. Here we intend to discuss the system of planetary periodicity. It should however be acknowledged that these descriptions are only broad guidelines. The astrologers who study the horoscope of a person with a view to pinpointing the specific events likely to occur during the coming periods should consider these guidelines carefully on the basis of their ingenuity and specific conditions confronting the individual seeking counselling.

Sub-Lordships during Sun's Main Rulership Period

The Sun's major rulership characterized by its general impulse of radiance continues throughout its control over the life of the individual. This general influence is however modified by the sub-lordship of different planets. During the 6 years of Sun's major daśā the first sub-lordship is that of Sun itself. It lasts for 3 months 18 days. Depending upon the strength and disposition of Sun, the general condition of the person during this period will produce greater activity, royal connections, administrative involvement and active pursuit of one's deeper interests. This is not a period of much acquisition of wealth as of power, though the former could take place under other planetary influence. The individual during this period receives more renown than luxuries of life, more inner strength and confidence than physical health. Sun produces inner glow, radiance, brilliance and will-power, it produces self-reliance and expansion of consciousness. It operates primarily on the will aspect of the inner being. Its influence on physical life is only indirect and as such it does not deny them though it is not primarily directed to them. Other planets connected with different *bhāvas* in the natal chart produce the physical results concerning those houses especially if these aspects of life are under the control of those planets, which operate at secondary and tertiary levels.

During the sub-period of Sun within its own major period, it is possible that the individual may feel tired, lose health, suffer from fever and may even have eye troubles. These troubles however will not be very pronounced even if the Sun is not well-placed in the natal chart. In fact, no planet shows its full favourable or adverse results during its own sub-lordship. Sun waits for the period of other adverse planets to actualize even its own malefic results. Generally speaking, one would find that Sun's sub-lordship during its own major period is often without any significant event.

Moon:

Sub-rulership of Moon during the Sun's primary rulership lasts for 6 months. Moon reflects the radiance of the Sun and transmits it to earth for the growth and sustenance of human and other terrestrial beings. Moon is the cosmic mother while the Sun is the repository of the cosmic principle. The Sun contains within it the destiny of every form of creation towards which it is incessantly moving. During the sub-lordship of Moon under the Sun's main period, the mission of every person is carefully impressed upon him and appropriate conditions for the attainment of the same are laid down. Powerful Moon during its sub-period bestows elevated status and leads the individual to much joyous feeling. The location of Moon in a quadrant or in a trine house specially if it is aspected by a benefit planet like Jupiter is very productive of wealth, joyous festivities and all round affluence. Addition of conveyance, house, ornaments, clothes, births of children and grandchildren as well as achievement of success in all enterprises occur during this period. Moon's *antar* during Sun's major period leads to tremendous psychological exaltation. Weak Moon placed in sixth, eighth or twelfth house either from ascendant or from the Sun makes a person suffer from mental worries and leads him to unprofitable wanderings in distant places. This is usually a period of physical ill health. The individual feels that life force in him is ebbing out. The trouble is intensified when Moon is associated with the lord of the second and the seventh houses.

Mars:

Sub-period of Mars during Sun's main daśā lasts for 4 months 6 days. It reinforces the natural radiance and power generated by Sun and directs the same to the individual to activate him in vigorous activities. During this period, the individual becomes active with enormous vitality in material pursuits. Depending upon location and general disposition of the planet, the individual displays much initiative for physical activities, engagement in extractive and manufacturing programmes, agricultural innovations and intense scientific investigations. Strong Mars placed in a quadrant or a trine house leads to successful completion of every activity undertaken by the individual. The individual frequently undertakes short travels. Mars is highly propitious for inculcating skill in surgery. During the short period of Mars during the Sun's major period, the individual gets renown, opportunities for constructive enterprises and his skill is much recognized. This is a period when many unexpected pleasant events suddenly happen. Mars associated with the lord of ninth or eleventh house, leads to immense satisfaction, happiness from brothers and colleagues, peace of mind, victory over one's enemies, and to success in one's business enterprises. During this period the individual may acquire landed property and he may even do well in real estate business. Mars placed in sixth or in the eighth house has the potential of inducing physical and psychological tension. Exhaustion, intrigues, accident, litigation and unpalatable conditions arising during this period often produce much mental agony. Loss of blood can be expected during this period, which can occur either as a result of accident or by surgical operation or as a result of some ailment. Strong and auspicious Mars leads to acquisition of gems and jewelry, success in mining exploration and in military expeditions while weak Mars enhances the chances of physical injury, loss of prestige, acute mental pain and even of sudden death. Increased sexual activity is generally evident during the secondary rulership of Mars under the main period of Sun.

Rāhu:

Rāhu casts shadow over the solar rays. It produces very troublesome time for the individual during its 10 months and 24 days of its antar in the Sun's main period. It makes the individual suffer from vague sorrows, mental depression and intrigues. It makes him lead a very secluded life, engage in surreptitious deals, and be constantly apprehensive of unexpected misfortune. Suicidal tendency, loss due to theft, dangers from poisoning, separation from wife and children and tiresome wanderings are usual occurrences of this period.

Rāhu aspected by Jupiter produces many auspicious events. It provides opportunities for the development of the individual's personality. It opens for the individual many new lines of serious studies. One may also expect renown from unexpected quarters, especially from distant lands. Rāhu placed in third, sixth or eleventh house from the ascendant or from Moon and occupying a favourable sign can be highly propitious. Such stellar combinations enable the individual to receive honour from the sovereign. This position of Rāhu provides the individual valuable insights in life. It also leads to auspicious celebrations. There could be construction of residential mansions and birth of children and grandchildren. Being an agent of the Lords of Karma, Rāhu produces before the individual auspicious or adverse conditions. These events aim at his psychological and spiritual transformation. Physical, psychological and spiritual events occurring during this sub-period create very deep and radical changes in the life-style of the person. Rāhu placed in eighth or twelfth position from Sun produces acute suffering. It can lead to imprisonment, loss of property or to diseases difficult to diagnose and almost impossible to cure. Placed alone with the lord of the second or the seventh house, Rāhu leads to separation from wife and it may even bring about death of the person.

Jupiter:

The secondary rulership of Jupiter during the main lordship of Sun augments and intensifies favourable opportunities expected from the Sun. This secondary rulership lasts for only 9 months 18 days but it is full of many festive celebrations. The individual receives opportunities for religious and joyful celebrations such as marriages in the family, birth of children, occupation of stately mansions and even beginning of educational activities. During this period religious heads honour the individual. He participates in many important *yajñas*. The Jovian impulse arouses the feeling of joyfulness, spiritual growth and self-development. This is a period of overall expansion. The individual and his family members are surrounded in an atmosphere of happiness and contentment. The individual even receives success in his professional life and elevation in his social status. He upholds the traditional values and adheres to ancient religious traditions. Jupiter placed in sixth or eighth house from the Sun during its antar however leads to illness, increased opposition from adversaries and to mental worry. Jupiter is primarily a protective influence, which gets strengthened during this period. Concrete results from Jupiter can be experienced only through the inculcation of general religious disposition in the individual. People and the state may shower their benedictions on him but any thing pertaining to health, money, service conditions should be prognosticated only on the basis of its relationship with other planets. Jupiter mainly adds its auspicious influence to other planets and makes their action favourable to the individual.

Saturn:

The secondary period of Saturn during the planetary rulership of Sun lasts for 11 months 12 days. This is a period of much hardship and acute mental pain. Saturn is a bitter enemy of Sun. It absorbs the rays of the Sun and deflects them for its own purpose. The primary objective of Saturn is to insulate the individual from all external support. The absorption of solar rays by Saturn makes it powerful to precipitate its own influence. This interaction between the two planets during the secondary rulership of Saturn in the main daśā of Sun is very disturbing.

Saturn in a quadrant from the ascendant qualifies it to bestow auspicious results. This is an unorthodox view, which should be rightly understood in order to convey the precise nature of this influence. Saturn aspects third, sixth, ninth and twelfth houses if it is placed in quadrant houses. The aspect of Saturn has the propensity of destroying the nature of the house it aspects. When it aspects a malignant house, the malevolence of these houses is to a great extent reduced as a result of this aspect.

During the main period of Sun, Saturn removes all obstacles from the path of the individual and secures for him victory over his rivals and adversaries. Under such a benefic influence, the individual may obtain wealth, accumulate fixed assets and have many joyous celebrations in the family. Saturn in strength even draws the attention of the sovereign to the individual, makes him successful in obtaining laurels from the state and acquiring wealth, decorations and status. In adverse relationship with Sun, specially if it is placed in sixth or eighth house from it, Saturn makes the individual suffer from acute physicalz pain, intense mental torments and excruciating emotional sorrow. Under such a situation the person faces all round obstructions especially if Saturn is weak in the natal chart. Saturn in association with the lord of the second and/or seventh lord may even cause death either to the individual or to his near relatives. Essentially, Saturn during its sub-rulership under Sun's main period thwarts all vitalizing forces radiating from the luminary and casts a shadow of gloom and depression around the person.

Mercury:

The antar of Mercury during the main period of Sun lasts for 10 months 6 days. Mercury requires a base for its operation. A powerful Sun energizes Mercury and enables it to cast its influence effectively and in the best interest of the individual. The basic impact of Mercury is felt on one's intellect and mental activities. During this period, the individual gets engaged in deep intellectual pursuits mostly metaphysical. Mercury also leads to swift movements, commercial transactions and socialization with elite and intellectual. It also makes the individual acquire some important personal possessions.

Well-placed Mercury during its antar in Sun's main period attracts the attention of scholarly persons to the individual. The state, high authorities as well as many organizations of repute honour him for his intellectual achievements. During the period, the acquisition of means of conveyances, recognition of the individual's literary activities and intellectual creations become important. This is a very propitious period for successful commercial transactions. Mercury located in adverse relationships with Sun as for example in twelfth from Sun or posited in sixth, eighth or twelfth house from the ascendant, makes the individual suffer from ill health, fever, dishonour, unprofitable and exhausting travels, transfers in one's career and family troubles. Mercury is basically the power of the mind, which receives smooth flow of solar energy. Its results during its secondary period in the Sun's daśā depend upon their mutual relationships and the strength of Mercury. Strong Mercury that is harmoniously posited in relation with a strong Sun is highly auspicious and inclined to give beneficial results.

Ketu:

The sub-rulership of Ketu in the Sun's main period lasts for 4 months 6 days. Basically, Ketu is a counterpart of Rāhu and it works as a karmic agent. Ketu generally produces physical exhaustion, psychological humiliation and mental torments. The beneficence of Sun is so much disturbed during this sub-lordship that the individual loses his anchorage. His mental balance is lost and his actions and reactions are uncoordinated, clumsy and ungraceful. His relationship with his family relations, associates and superiors becomes unnatural. The psychological disturbances experienced during this sub-period produce chain reaction, which make him humiliated and suffer from whirlwind at different levels in his mind. When Ketu is adversely located in relation with Sun, or is placed sixth or eighth from it, physical diseases, ulcers on cheek, problems related with teeth, urinary troubles and even some death in the family may take place. Placed in twelfth from Sun, Ketu can lead to unnecessary expenditure, futile foreign travels and disturbing allegations against him. In spite of these adverse results, if Ketu is placed in third, sixth, tenth or eleventh from the ascendant receiving beneficial aspects of favourably associated planets, it may be possible for the individual to receive glorifying results of Ketu. It has the unique quality of promoting remarkable uniqueness of the individual. Ketu has the extraordinary power of bestowing exceptional honour and stupendous success in the realm of abstract thinking and metaphysical philosophy. Fortune smiles for the individual with Ketu's vibration on favourable wavelengths with Sun. Unexpected latent faculties develop in the person during this period. He even gets opportunities for entry into higher orders of mystic teachings and receipt of initiation or *Dīkṣā* as it is generally described in Eastern religious scriptures. Ketu related with the lord of second or seventh house from the ascendant may lead to one's death.

Venus:

Venus is a benefic planet always prepared to lead the individual to sensual enjoyment, joyous living and artistic involvement. It heightens the sensitivity of the person and brings him in harmonious relationship with different persons around him. It has a long period of its antar during the main daśā of Sun. His antara lasts for a full one year. During this period the person is exposed to material attractions which he greatly enjoys. An important feature of this antar is accrual of wealth, honour and prosperity. In spite of such favourable situations, the individual for some unspecified reason may on occasions be unable to enjoy his luxurious conditions of life. It happens if Sun in the natal chart is placed in signs owned by Saturn. During this period the person may attain his desired objectives, may even get the association of important persons and move in elite societies, eat delicious food, dress well with gems and jewellry. Yet all these will seem to have an aroma of artificiality to him. There will be a feeling that these luxuries do not actually belong to him. He may display enthusiasm in life yet deep down in him he will recognize a kind of contradiction. With all these liveliness there will be a profound sense of disappointment within him. He will often feel that something undefined is missing from his life. In adverse relationship with Sun or with the ascendant, the sub-lordship of Venus is likely to expose the person to professional unhappiness, financial difficulties and even to venereal diseases. His female associates will bring to him much disrepute. Venus is often a death-inflicting planet during its sub-lordship.

Sub-Rulerships during Moon's Primary Period

Moon:

The antar of Moon during its own main daśā lasts for 10 months. During this period, the person is induced to lead a pious, comfortable and satisfied life. He attends to his religious duties and pays proper obeisance to gods, elders and teachers. He devotes considerable time to his family and to the goal of property acquisitions. During this period he is primarily concerned with family matters and with securing a good status for himself, his offspring and for his family relations. Under the secondary rulership of Moon, the person is much concerned with his repute, his family dignity and with continuation of established propriety. Adverse placements of Moon, however, makes him suffer from several diseases. Malignancy of Moon vitally affects the physical well being of the person. Weak Moon produces physical ailments, royal displeasure, mental instability and many frustrating travels. Weak Moon makes him unable to harness the life giving energy from the Sun. Absence of solar influence and its distortions under the lunar influence can critically restrict the growth and sustenance of the person. During the secondary period of Moon, if the psychic body of the person is rightly prepared and properly attuned to receive the finer forces of nature, Moon becomes highly effective in producing super-normal sensitivity and clairvoyant faculties. Under this impulse, the person displays unusual flight of imagination. A strong Moon is desirable both at the primary as well as at the secondary level, while a weak Moon can be very devastating.

Mars:

The secondary rulership of Mars lasts for 7 months. During this period the person becomes very active. Mentally he becomes very alert. His ambition gets greatly motivated. During this sub-period of Mars, the person realizes his desires and ambitions. Favourably placed Mars in a quadrant or a trine house leads to the achievement of one's most difficult goals in life. The interaction between Mars and Moon is such that the astro-mental principles of man receive much encouragement for articulating the subconscious desires and aspirations and for bringing them within the realm of possibility of achievement. Martian results are sudden and unexpected. They are basically achieved by the person's own efforts unaided by any external help. Martian sub-rulership during the main period of Moon strengthens self-reliance of the person.

Acquisition of landed property, success in underground explorations, finalization of laboratory investigations, victory over adversaries, favourable outcome in litigation and conferment of exceptional honour are the predictable results expected during this period.

Such results are however rare. In a large number of natal charts Mars is unfavourable either in relationship with the ascendant or with the Moon. It restricts the favourable impact of this planet. Accidents, murderous attack, physical injury, loss of property and tension in personal relationships are common results which occur during this period. Unfavourable relationship between Mars and Moon gives rise to increased mental tension, rise in blood pressure and tendency towards accidents. It is difficult for a common man to maintain his mental health and emotional balance during this perio. Such eqlibrium can be maintained only when both, Mars and Moon, are strong and well posited.

Rāhu:

The sub-lordship of Rāhu lasts for 1 year 6 months. Much hardship is expected during this period. These difficulties arise primarily at the psychological level. Rāhu incapacitates the Moon and veils its benefic influences. The nourishing influences flowing from Moon are not allowed to permeate to the person. Rāhu increases his mental tension. He suffers from depression and often experiences strong suicidal inclination. He suffers from diseases which are difficult to diagnose and quite often unresponsive to medication. Loss of mental balance, involvement in intrigues and litigations, suspension and demotion in professional career usually occur during this period. The person leaves his country and goes to a foreign land, encounters unfriendly environment, takes untimely and deleterious food and loses his sleep.

Rāhu under the main period of Moon can however, lead to significant occult attainment if potential for it existed in the natal chart. Rāhu in third, sixth, tenth or eleventh houses along with favourably inclined planets and aspected by beneficient ones leads to acquisition of much money and immovable property. The person attains kudos and receives unexpected wealth from some high authority particularly from south-west regions or from west directions. Some influential persons from western countries may help him in many ways and bestow upon him lasting favours.

Jupiter:

The sub-lordship of Jupiter during the main period of Moon lasts for 1 year 4 months. This period is highly propitious for overall growth and expansion. Jupiter has very friendly relationship with Moon. It enables both of them to grant their choicest beneficence to the person. During this period, the person begets children, acquires means of transportation, resides in large mansions and receives favours from elders and religious persons. Jovian impulse harmonizes well with that of Moon. Favourable association between the two secures much happiness and expansion of personality and the area of one's influence. Happiness experienced during this period is *sāttvic* and harmonious in nature. It makes the person righteous, socially oriented in his relationships and charitable in disposition. They make him noble, altruistic and public-spirited. The social and professional status of the person rises higher. He acquires new vehicles that signifies elevation in his social hierarchy. He gets abundant clothes and acquires costly ornaments.

The period is auspicious for begetting children and for moving to a new residence. During this period the individual acquires property, vehicles and respectability. He also comes in close relationship with religious teachers and holy order. Unfavourable Jupiter produces long-drawn illnesses.

Jupiter produces favourable *milieu* for the individual to participate in religious discourses and in philanthropic activities. These activities at the initial phase are induced by a desire for securing personal respectability but gradually the psychological orientation begun at this time leads him to inner purification and psychological upliftment.

Saturn:

The antar of Saturn during the Moon daśā lasts for 1 year 7 months. The period is generally full of agonizing events. The person suffers from mother's illness, damage to one's own reputation, intrigues from unfriendly persons and attack of paralytic strokes. These afflictions destroy the person's peace of the mind. While producing sufferings, Saturn directs the person's gaze towards spiritualism and to basic realities of life. Saturn placed in the sixth or the twelfth house, which are adverse houses or in its debilitation due to its occupation of Aries, leads the person to religious places, impels him to follow purificatory austerities and participate in rituals. They are intended to remove him from material attachments. The possibility of revealing supranormal powers such as clairvoyance or receiving messages from the unknown sources cannot be ruled out during this period. Such experiences however do not absolve the person from passing through a very dreary life. Saturn may very well push the person to the veil of shadow so as to make his life desolate and full of excruciating pain from which it can seem difficult to extricate oneself.

Saturn is not an unmitigated evil. Sometimes Saturn transcends the power of all planets in producing remarkable material results. The auspicious results of Moon are changeable and short -lived while Saturn produces abiding gifts to the person. Often fortitude and indifference practised during the period provide inner strength to the person that proves immensely advantageous in times to come. Several, so far hidden faculties of the person are revealed as a result of gruelling experiences of the period. Strong Saturn posited in favourable signs confers many tangible assets and relates the person with multinational organizations with remunerative employment. The most important feature of this period is its impact on intellectual and philosophical orientation of the person.

Mercury:

The sub-period of Mercury during the main period of Moon lasts for 1 year 5 months. It produces mental expansion. Moon provides favourable *milieu* for intellectual growth. The intellectual faculties related with Mercury are accentuated and come to fruition during this period in an important way. During this period many opportunities occur for participation in seminars, conferences and workshops where eminent persons participate and the individual gets the chance to display his own intellectual superiority. Publications, authorship and exposure of his skill in writing and speech occur in profusion during this period. The person undertakes many professional travelling. His business expands and he secures profitable commercial contracts. Acquisition rather than generousity characterizes this period.

Placed in a quadrant or a trine house from Moon or in the eleventh and second house from ascendant, Mercury produces festivities like marriages in the family, religious rites and charitable deeds during its sub-period. This is the time when the person draws attention of the state and persons at high offices towards his pleasing manners and intellectual qualities. Personal merit is recognized, kudos is offered and the person is felicitated for his personal and intellectual contribution to the society. The period even leads the person to indulge in joyful celebrations where much liquor is poured. Only when Mercury is placed in the sixth, eighth or twelfth house from Moon an individual experiences loss of property, legal persecution, marital discords and troubles from children. Weak and ill placed Mercury during the main daśā period of Moon does not assure either mental equanimity or physical well-being.

Ketu:

Moon is closely related with mental serenity while Ketu disturbs it. Ketu's sub-period during the main period of Moon is characterized by whirlpool in the person's astro-mental field. Ketu's sub-lordship within the main period of Moon lasts for only 7 months but this short period is full of mental storms intensely disturbing the mental self-control of the person. Ketu is concerned with mental agitation, psychological tension, physical illness and personal humiliation. Ketu produces personal unhappiness and psychological humiliation in order to induce the person deeply entrenched in materiality to turn his gaze towards deeper aspects of life. Ketu brings forth disillusionment with every kind of material and emotional life. Every impact of Ketu during Moon's main period depends upon the past karmic forces of the person. The basic objective of Ketu is to provide real and deeper understanding of the life-process. Whenever any contradiction arises between a person's thoughts and feelings and his final goal or whenever any impulse is generated which violates the attainment of deeper comprehension of the life-process, Ketu intervenes and pulverizes the psychological frame of the person. It greatly upsets his whole being. This procedure adopted by this shadowy planet is therefore greatly dreaded. Humiliation experienced during this period although aims at preparing the person towards occult initiations in deeper mysteries of life is not very pleasant to experience. Moon is very supportive in such missions. Ketu takes advantage of this characteristic of Moon and strengthens its efforts in inducing substantial impact. But this is so only from a superficial mundane standpoint. If the person is not yet spiritually mature, the various repercussions of Ketu in dissolving the human psyche and in producing excruciating pain and sorrowful events will be very difficult to bear. Such tortuous experiences however make the person introspective, which in due course prepares him for entry into the portals of Truth realization. It is therefore not always realistic to associate Ketu with hard life. In some cases enlightenment and Truth realization emerge from the tormenting experiences under Ketu.

Ketu sometimes bestows wealth, renown and pleasures of wife and children but in doing so its aim is to show the fleeting nature of these relationships. Ketu produces many desired material objects and relations. It happens so when Ketu is located in a quadrant, trine, or in third or eleventh house in a natal chart. Moon has the task of making the psyche of the person crystal clear wherein Ketu reflects the abiding truth in it. It plants therein the necessary seeds for the emergence of occult knowledge. People in general are not prepared for this kind of spiritual awakening. So the impact of Ketu is generally dreaded and thought to be the producer of deprivations of material comforts and humiliation of the person. Ketu breaks the egotism in man. It happens in many ways during the sub -lordship of Ketu in the Moon's main period.

Venus:

Venus and Moon are both benefic planets. The antar of Venus during the main period of Moon lasts for 1 year 8 months. Venus has special relationship with Sun, which importantly affects its relationship with Moon as well. The maximum distance of Venus from Sun is never more than 48^0. It implies that the proximity of this planet with Moon will assume the nearness of Moon to Sun as well. When sun is close to Moon, it very much reduces the beneficence of the latter. In such cases Venus does not produce favourable results during its sub-period within the main period of Moon. Venus contributes to *Adhi Yoga,* which is constituted by Mercury, Venus and Jupiter occupying in any way sixth, seventh and eighth signs from Moon. It is generally assumed to produce affluence and happiness. Even if Venus is in this position, its impact during its sub-lordship in the main period of Moon is not trouble-free.

Favourably placed Venus in relationship with Moon leads to affluence, sensual gratification, affability and increased popularity. The family life of the person becomes pleasant and satisfying. Adverse Venus gives rise to diseases connected with generative organs and vital fluid. Its association with the lords of second and/or seventh houses, especially if Moon is weak in the natal chart, may inflict even death.

Sun:

The antar of Sun during the main period of Moon lasts for only 6 months but this short duration is very important for the career of the person. Sun represents the Will of the Ego, the very *Ātman* which constitutes the essence of the being. Moon has the portfolio of reflecting this message of Sun for the individual. During the period of the lordship of Sun in Moon daśā, prompting of the eternal message for the person comes into fruition. The sub-lordship of Sun leads to extraordinary results for the person provided he is suitably attuned to higher influences. This period could be propitious both for material attainments as well as for spiritual enlightenment. This is generally a period of glorious achievements and remarkable social prestige.

During the sub-lordship of Sun, one can expect almost regal status with enormous meaningful activities and creativity at different levels. During this period one can expect recovery from physical diseases, defeat of enemies, happiness and joyous family relationships and all round prosperity. Even lost property can be recovered. Meritorious deeds of the person are recognized and he may receive rewards for the same. Decorations for his extra-ordinary achievements are conferred on him. During this period the person becomes friendly with those who are in influential positions. Even politically he gets importance. He may receive diplomatic responsibilities.

Adverse relationships between the luminaries lead to sloth, illness, high fever and even loss of money. Whatever happens to the person during this period, the result brings him nearer to his final destiny in an important manner.

Sub-Rulership During Mars' Primary Period

Mars activates the indwelling spirit that energizes the person. Its basic impulse is to externalize the inner potential and to express it through various external channels. Often its explosive outbursts are so powerful that the individual finds them uncontrollable. They express them in different ways. The Martian forces that result in accidents and other calamities, particularly those where blood is spilt, are expressions of the same externalizing process. Impulsive behaviour, passionate infatuation and feverish involvement in business activities are different aspects of the same revelation. Whenever any planet intervenes during its secondary rulership in the main period of Mars its characteristic impulse impinges upon this basic nature of Mars. Some differences however arise in their manifestation. Astrologers concerned with day to day mundane predictions expect that the antar of Mars in its own main period would enable the person to make money through the sale or manufacture of fire-arms, by engaging oneself in vending war materials among the rival groups or by undertaking military expeditions. Medicines, trickery, fraud, deception and cruel acts are also connected with Mars. All these can be clearly perceived as manifestations of some inner trait of the person. During the period, one can expect the person to suffer from fever due to morbid state of bile and blood-defects. The individuals are likely to associate themselves with women of easy virtue. These individuals also incur wrath of senior persons and elders. The Martian impact may so much exhaust and depress them that they are unable to enjoy good food and sound sleep. But these are manifestations of some inner current of vital energy with which the planet is closely connected. The basic impulse of the planet is to make a person active and engage him in dynamic activities with all vigour and emotion. Martyrdom is a feature of the same trait. This characteristic takes different forms on the physical plane according to the nature of the intervening planet and the general disposition of the natal chart.

Mars:

The antar of Mars in its own main period lasts for 4 months 27 days. The first few weeks of this period is devoted to psychological preparations which enable the person to adapt himself to the influx of the new impulse. The impending changes in the life of the individual are subject to intense strain arising from rapid changes without providing any intervening respite. These changes occur suddenly and unexpectedly. As the entire period of 7 years under Mars is likely to be full of such unexpected events, the secondary rulership of different planets have to work on this psychological preparations made by Mars during its secondary rulership.

Favourable Mars leads to influx of wealth, favour from the state, elevation in one's official status and recovery of lost property and position. These events happen unexpectedly and suddenly. In understanding the nature of these events, a clever astrologer can relate them with inner changes taking place during the period. *Rucaka yoga* is formed with Mars in exaltation or in its own sign occupying a quadrant house either from Moon or from the ascendant. It leads to renown, honour, foreign assignment, overseas travel and professional elevation. If Mars occupies this situation, the impact during its sub-lordship are inspiring and highly beneficient. Even otherwise, strong Mars during its secondary period leads to acquisition of landed property, wealth, vehicles and fulfilment of one's cherished desire. Only when the planet is weak, ill-placed and badly aspected that the persons suffers fever, dislike of friends, annoyance from brothers, displeasure of the ruler, loss in business and even bodily injuries.

During the sub-period of Mars, some important past karmic forces are externalized which expose the person to many unexpected situations. In all such situations, whether they bring honour or disgrace, it is some act of the person that arouses these reactions from different quarters. The antar of Mars during its own main period is characterized by externalization of the inner to the surface, the past into the present and the desires and aspirations of the individual on the objective plane of achievement.

Rāhu:

The sub-period of Rāhu in Mars's daśā lasts for 1 year and 18 days. It introduces important psychological changes. As Rāhu is a planet which operates as an agent of karmic forces, whatever changes it produces are very abiding and significant. Often the impact appears at the first instance as intense depression. It arises as a reaction to some unexpected events or to some actions of another person. Once the psychological strain is absorbed and suitable lessons learnt from them, the beneficence of Rāhu can be recognized. Strong Rāhu occupying an auspicious position makes the person a deep thinker. As an intellectual he associates himself with unorthodox groups and agnostic religious organisations. He may often denounce the well-established practices. Rāhu makes the person thoughtful. The individual broods over abiding human relationships and the essential nature of things. Rāhu makes the person to work diligently and leave an imprint on the coming generation. Adversely placed and aspected Rāhu leads the person to company of depraved persons. He indulges in ungraceful sexual relationships and debauchery. He is even prepared to commit murder. The sub-period of Rāhu placed in eleventh house induces the individual to undertake illegal means of income. Placed in eighth or twelfth house, Rāhu spoils the peace of the mind and produces complicated and fatal diseases. Lower-blood pressure, scandal, intrigue, loss of money, humiliation and even imprisonment characterize Rāhu's sub-rulership in Mars' daśā. Rāhu and Mars generate contradictory malefic influences, which makes the period full of tension.

Jupiter:

The sub-rulership of Jupiter under the main period of Mars lasts for 11 months 6 days. It produces the most auspicious religious atmosphere. The person associates himself with traditional, philanthropic, ritualistic and religious organizations. He becomes highly popular for his social activities. It is also a period of recovery from long-drawn serious illnesses and celebration of joyous festivities. The person during this period may be advised to take precaution against ear-diseases and phlegmatic disorders. This sub-period provides the individual opportunities for marriages of children and grandchildren as well as for new additions to the family. An atmosphere of religious festivity, joyous anniversaries and all round prosperity surrounds the person. But there may be less of tangible results and more of expectations and psychological exultation.

Saturn:

The secondary period of Saturn in the main period of Mars lasts for 1 year, 1 month and 9 days. Saturn is related with veiling of the real while Mars tries to objectify the hidden. These two planets generate opposing forces. They operate at all levels and churn the physical, emotional and mental make-up of the person. The period is full of stress and strain. The person feels caged and confined in every way. His initiative gets curbed, his mind gets disturbed and he suffers from heat and bilous complaints.

The individual travels to a foreign land, meets with basically dishonest and hypocritical persons and acquires wealth and power. In spite of such material gains, which many persons may covet, the person may not be psychologically carefree and clear headed to face his difficulties. The period may witness death of one of his close relations. If Saturn is associated with the lord of the tenth house, there may be suspension or dismissal of the person from service. Whatever else happens during this period, the person gets serious surprise, which completely unsettles his life-style.

Mercury:

The sub-period of Mercury lasts for 11 months 27 days. During this period, the person is put to serious unpredictable changes. His attitude to various problems of life is tested and the genuineness of his approach determined. Impediments may arise in his place of work. Relationship with his brothers and friends becomes cheerless. Physically, the person becomes engaged in tiresome and arduous activities. Strain arises because the impending work demands quick action whereas a veil of sloth and laziness surrounds him. The inner urges and outer disinterestedness to actively tackle the work in hand complicates the life of the person. It happens both at psychological and physical level. The person becomes very impulsive and his response to the situation is not totally in conformity with the dictates of his mind. Whenever he takes any quick decision it is often without adequate consideration. He is thus put to conflicting and contradictory situations from which it becomes difficult for him to extricate him without any psychological injury.

Unless Mercury is well protected, favourably placed and well aspected, the period inevitably witnesses loss in business. Strong Mercury during its sub-period provides many remunerative opportunities for literary work. The basic impulse during this period represents intense conflict between mental thoughtfulness and emotional impetuosity at the physical level. This results in physical strain, psychological indecision and difficulties in business activities.

Ketu:

The antar of Ketu in the main period of Mars lasts for 4 months 27 days. It produces philosophical thoughts. It induces the person to be a recluse and isolated from the mainstream of life. Depending upon its placement, especially in relation with Mars and ascendant, Ketu produces humiliation, physical injury, disease and social estrangement. Divorces occur during this period. The person gets trapped in scandals and blackmail. Psychologically, it is a very trying period. The best possible way out of it is deep thinking and undertaking of serious yogic austerities. If the person adapts himself to the impulses coming from Ketu, his inner faculties can be laid open and he may even receive unusual honour and recognition.

Venus:

The secondary period of Venus during the main period of Mars lasts for 1 year 2 months. During this period, Venus is capable of inflicting even death or death-like injury to the person. There is likelihood of the person getting into passionate physical intimacies with young ladies. Infatuation arises under its influence. But soon afterwards such relationship results in abiding sorrow. The person may however acquire substantial amount of money, jewels, costly clothes, furniture and such other items of material luxuries. Adverse Venus produces loss of face, humiliation, property, absence of domestic support, personal help and trouble in the eyes. Strongly placed and auspicious Venus on the other hand, enables the person to acquire almost every item of material comfort. It is a period primarily concerned with materiality and sense gratification.

Sun:

It is a period of intense activity and success in enterprises. The period lasts for only 4 months 6 days but makes the person engaged in intense hard work. He receives his well-deserved reward for his efforts. He also receives extra-ordinary offers for professional betterment. During this period decorations from overseas, honour from the sovereign, recognition of merit from intellectuals, and respectability from the society are expected. Adverse Sun leads to loss of money, trouble from administration, and suffering from high fever. Adverse Sun during the period can seriously harm the father of the individual who may even meet his end. Such a situation also strains the relationship of the person with his superiors.

Essentially, the Sun brings out inner radiance and accentuates will-power of the person. Impediments in their actualization lead to difficulties. Expression of will-power leads to initiative and enthusiasm. These are the traits greatly encouraged by the Martian impulse. The lack of appreciation of the individual's capacities and his hard work can bring him in confrontation with his superiors. The primary feature of this period is initiative, hardwork, intense egotism and desire to receive appreciation from one's superiors. In case, they are not forthcoming, the individual can feel greatly discouraged and he can even become cruel and regressive in character.

Moon:

The secondary period of Moon during the main period of Mars lasts for 7 months. It makes the person home sick and interested in his domestic affairs. Agricultural improvement, internal decorations and cultivation of special hobbies become the person's primary pastime. Scientifically oriented persons find this period highly propitious for laboratory investigations and mining explorations.

In case, Moon is adversely located either in relation with Mars or with ascendant, the person suffers from mental strain, domestic worries, loss of property and physical weakness. He becomes impulsive and loses control over his emotions. Generally speaking, this period leads to acquisition of wealth, jewellery, social status and prosperity. The influence of Moon during the main period of Mars is felt suddenly and unexpectedly. No abiding results are however expected during this period. Whatever happens is of short-term nature.

Sub-Rulership During Rāhu's Main Period

Rāhu produces abiding results that are very distressing. It brings to life the results of omissions and commissions of past lives. It happens primarily to counter-balance the disturbances that were created in the natural harmony as a result of individual's indiscretions. The process is inevitably painful. The people are afraid of these disturbing consequences. So they are afraid of Rāhu. The unhappiness and sorrow caused by Rāhu is only from the short-term viewpoint. Rāhu aims at producing suitable psycho-mental conditions which spiritualize the person. Rāhu has the lasting happiness of the person as its goal, which arises from understanding the life process and not born out of the availability of material conveniences of life. During this period a person is dematerialized and put on the path of inner unfoldment. Secondary planets contribute their impulses in this main task and assist Rāhu in its spiritualizing process.

Rāhu:

The secondary rulership of Rāhu during its own main daśā lasts for 2 years 8 months 12 days. It is a distressing period. It produces illness through poison and water-born diseases. It often happens that the person during this period sights some long black serpent either actually or in dreams. His sexual morality is also low. Such persons often commit adultery and are separated from his near and dear ones. He keeps company of depraved persons. His mind is confused, his intellect becomes dull and he wastes his wealth. He wanders aimlessly in foreign land and suffers from intense emotional pain. In case, Rāhu is placed in Cancer, Scorpio, Virgo or Sagittarius sign and is aspected by an auspicious planet, it may confer honour and decorations from the state and lead to acquisition of ornaments, vehicles and good clothes. The individual may undertake some profitable undertaking. He may travel towards the West. Only when Rāhu is placed in eighth or twelfth house from the ascendant and is associated with or aspected by a malefic planet that its sub -period is likely to produce theft, boils, displeasure from superiors and suffering of wife and children. The period is primarily a period of mental pain and emotional disturbances.

Jupiter:

The sub-period of Jupiter during Rāhu's main daśā lasts for a period of 2 years 4 months and 24 days. It produces enormous patience and orientation towards ritualistic observances. During this period an important journey is made towards south-west or towards western direction. It is possible that the person at the place of his sojourn is granted an audience with the head of the state and his desired objective is realized. If the person is spiritually inclined he may get initiated in secret mysteries. A common householder receives much beneficence from Jupiter during this period. There is all round happiness for him. He develops respect for gods and for learned persons, he gets freedom from diseases and has the pleasure of meeting charming women. If Jupiter is weak and adversely located in the natal chart, there may be worry for him. He even incurs loss of property and wealth and faces impediments in his enterprises. The last few months of Jupiter's antar may create troubles for his elder brother and produce difficulties for his parents.

Saturn:

The secondary rulership of Saturn during the main period of Rāhu lasts for 2 years 10 months and 6 days. During this period, a kind of whirlwind is created in the mind of the person. It insulates him from all beneficient powers flowing through other benefic planets. He feels emotionally dried up, psychologically a recluse and mentally very confused. Everything that is commonly considered personal is destroyed. He gets solace only when he is oriented towards philanthropic and public service or when his material expectations are completely eliminated. An ordinary individual under this period of Rāhu-Saturn cannot attain satisfaction in any of his personal relationships. A feeling of disenchantment dawns upon him. It makes him lethargic, listless and recluse. Servitude and residence away from homeland also characterize the period for a common man. Saturn during Rāhu's main period leads a person to smuggling, drug peddling, shady transactions, intrigues and sufferance from incurable congenital diseases. No remedial measure is ordinarily effective in these cases. These are Karmic results of past sins of omissions and commissions which intensely affect the person and make him learn the lesson of life by the hard way. If Saturn is placed in eighth or twelfth house and is any way related adversely with other planets, these results are intensified.

In some cases, the sub-period of Saturn produces extraordinary results. Saturn works on a very extensive scale and Rāhu is very intense and both of these aim at transforming the life-style of the person. If the person has sufficiently strong natal chart with powerful combinations, the period can prove highly propitious. The educational achievements in regard to deeper scientific investigations, mechanical engineering, business management and even in medical profession specializing in chronic and oldmen's diseases can be extraordinary. Favourable disposition of two or three planets related with Saturn and Rāhu can raise the person to great heights. They can relate him with international organizations and even bestow upon him much money and material gifts.

If he already has meritorious deeds in his karmic reservoir and is egoically evolved, he may receive during this period, opportunities for working on extensive global scale. He will learn the lesson of disenchantment from every material situation confronting him. The period will destroy in a basic way his self-centeredness and put him on the path of global consciousness.

Mercury:

The sub-rulership of Mercury lasts for 2 years 6 months and 18 days during the main period of Rāhu. Mercury by itself is a neutral planet. Its results depend upon the support it gets from other planets. If it secures the slightest backing from any other planet, its sub-period can prove to be very propitious. The person can travel extensively, participate in learned discourses and qualify even for initiatory rites. It can happen specifically if Mercury occupies third, ninth or tenth house from Rāhu. Mercury's placement in sixth, eighth or twelfth house from Rāhu is considered adverse. It leads to humiliation, scandal, unmerited accusations, ill luck, theft, mental instability, displeasure of superiors and agonising sorrowful expenditure. During this period brothers create agonizing problems, children fall sick or die and one's wife suffers from devitalising and distressing ailments. Weak Mercury placed in second or seventh house from Rāhu specifically if it is adverse, proves highly injurious, even fatal, for the individual.

Ketu:

The sub-period of Ketu lasts for 1 year and 18 days. Ketu is a karmic agent as is Rāhu. Ketu's sub-period in Rāhu's main daśā invariably produces loss of wealth, damage to family happiness and ill health to oneself. Ketu produces disenchantment, a thought process that is induced by the conditions produced by Rāhu. Ketu is not concerned with physical happiness or material prosperity. It arouses Divine Wisdom and inculcates in the person the temperament of a recluse. The person under its influence becomes a wanderer without any well-defined goal. He meets different types of persons each of whom gives him some special spiritual message. Each of these persons unravels some secret law of life. Spiritually inclined persons observing austerities, purity and psychological self-inquiry and inward contemplative mind find this period very illuminating. He becomes intuitive and gets flashes of higher wisdom.

Ketu's association with benefic planets provides physical comfort, wealth, honour as well as festive occasions in the family. These conditions are produced in order to lead the individual to deeper understanding of the life-process. Ketu related with the lord of the ascendant enables the individual to attain his desired objectives while placed in a quadrant or a trine house it provides material wealth. Only when Ketu is placed in the eighth or twelfth house that illness, separation from parents, troubles from brothers and mental anguish are anticipated. Ketu acts on consciousness of the person and intensifies the thinking principle induced either by the abundance of material gifts or by their deprivations.

Venus:

The sub-period of Venus in Rāhu daśā lasts for 3 years. It is a period of material affluence and sensual gratification. Venus immerses the person in transient existence and makes him deeply entrenched in ephemeral pleasures. When the individual realizes that the sensual gratification experienced by material attainments is transient and that the reality of existence eludes him, Venus enables him to proceed to higher rungs of spiritual evolution. During the sub-period of Venus in Rāhu daśā, the person gets access to vehicles, new mansions, royal honour and social recognition and other kinds of conveniences in life, but all of these aim at showing him that real happiness lies beyond material conditions. Strong Venus leads to enjoyment of comfortable living conditions, servants, good meals and pleasant social relations, expansion of one's business and extraordinary favour from the state. Venus placed in a quadrant, trine or in the eleventh house from Rāhu makes the individual a leader of his community and provides him ample opportunities for participation in musical festivals and cultural programmes. He also receives decorations and honour from administration. Venus becomes troublesome when it is associated with Mars, Saturn or Rāhu in the natal chart. This tendency is emphasized when it is located in the sixth, eighth or twelfth house in relationship with Rāhu. This combination results in the persecution of the individual for different kinds of offences. He is disappointed with his family relations. His wife troubles him, he indulges in extra-marital relationships, suffers from venereal and blood diseases and is tormented by mental agony.

Sun:

The sub-period of Sun in Rāhu daśā lasts for 10 months and 24 days. It is a period full of contradictory influences and much dissatisfaction. During this period the person is induced to perform several charitable acts. He attempts to resolve his psychological conflicts. At the mundane level, he even receives much administrative power. These exceptional results arise in direct proportion to the strength of the Sun and the disposition of other planets associated with it. Ordinary configuration of planets accentuates the contradiction between Sun and Rāhu producing troubles from adversaries, dangers from poisoning, fire and deadly weapons. The person may be physically as well as psychologically incapacitated. Dishonour, mental agony, litigation and pessimism are some basic features of the period.

Moon:

The sub-period of Moon lasts for 1 year and 6 months. It is a very agonising period comprising futile wanderings, psycho-mental depressions, and aberrations in the thinking process. Loss of wife, quarrel with one's near and dear ones, mental agony, failure in agricultural and business enterprises and danger from water are usual results of Moon's sub-period in Rāhu main daśā. These maleficent results can be overcome if Moon in strength occupies its own sign or the sign of its exaltation and is associated with benefic planets. Even its placement in the eleventh house in a natal chart nullifies the adverse results of its planetary periodicity. Under these conditions Moon proves to be auspicious. It may even elevate the status of the person. He may acquire power and enjoy high status in life. He may even receive honour and respectability. His health may be good and his family relations pleasant.

Moon has special impact on one's house and real estates affairs, which under its auspicious placement produces favourable results. During the sub-period of adverse Moon, a person may suffer from abdominal troubles, theft and loss of wealth. During this period health of the person requires special attention. This impact is accentuated if Moon is placed in adverse relationship with Rāhu.

Mars:

The sub-period of Mars in Rāhu daśā lasts for 1 year and 18 days. Mars produces sudden and unexpected results. The unexpected nature of any trouble arising during this period is acute. One also expects persecution as well as professional setback during this sub-period. Dangers from fire, thieves and weapons are also possible. Typical results of Mars antar are accidents, injury to one's limbs, loss of blood, separation from wife and unexpected failure in every enterprise. These results are severe specially if Mars is weak and adversely placed either in relation with ascendant or with Rāhu. Strong and beneficial Mars resulting from its placement in a quadrant, trine, third or eleventh house from ascendant or from Rāhu bestows auspicious results. These results provide optimism and inspire the person to hard work and achieve official elevation. These are karmic gifts of the planet to the person. They are always prolific. During this period one may even expect the retrieval of lost property, expansion of one's business and addition to one's real estate. The individual embarks on a very profitable journey, gets an audience with the head of the state, attains elevation in his professional status and receives tremendous encouragement in his enterprises. He is ever ready to take initiative in new ventures. He even becomes head of a multinational organization. Mars placed either in the sixth, eighth or in the twelfth house from Rāhu produces unexpected troubles. In the second or the seventh house from Rāhu it affects the individual's physical well-being.

Planetary Sub-Rulership in Jupiter's Main Period

Jupiter is a planet of expansion and beneficence. It provides ample opportunities to secondary planets during its main period to exert their full power. Jupiter supports them in their natural impulses as long as they are helpful for the growth and unfoldment of the latent qualities of the individual. Jupiter is a benefic influence under which all beneficence thrives.

Jupiter:

The secondary period of Jupiter in its own main period lasts for 2 years 1 month and 18 days. Jupiter's modesty makes it abstain from manifesting its own results during its own main period. It provides an atmosphere of well-being and gradually bestows wealth, vehicles, apparel, royal favour and purity of heart, power and knowledge of scriptures. It envelops the individual in an atmosphere of religiosity and spiritualism. During the secondary period of Jupiter in its own daśā one has good luck, receives high esteem and social status, begets a son and receives honour from the state. His ethical suceptibilities are heightened. He receives many opportunities for creative activities, forges close relationship with his preceptor and gets company of pious men. During this period one becomes an ardent student of scriptures, meticulously follows one's social traditions, and becomes a pious observer of religious rituals. His philanthropic activities increase.

Jupiter deepens the faith of an individual in higher beings. He adores deities, obeys elders, respects teachers, follows the scriptures and showers favours on his subordinates. Response of others to him also gradually becomes very respectful. He receives veneration from others, attains respectability and gets social esteem. Jupiter radically transforms the milieu around the person and he gets greatly enthused to work for society and for the general welfare. An inspiring atmosphere in which there is faith, respectability and spirituality than any actual achievement in any concrete manner surrounds him.

Saturn:

The sub-period of Saturn lasts for 2 years, 6 months and 12 days. Jupiter is liberal in granting freedom to other planets to generate their own special impact on the person irrespective of the fact whether they are in accordance with their own disposition or not. Saturn also gets this privilege and imparts its own special influence. The sub-period of Saturn in Jupiter daśā induces the individual to associate himself with women of easy virtue, with persons of depraved character and low morals and to experience sickness in one's family. Saturn in such situation also leads to loss of property and wealth. Saturn produces exorbitant and unprofitable expenditure and psychological irritability apart from mental worry and pessimism.

During the antar of Saturn, the individual lives in a gloomy atmosphere where natural buoyancy of life remains absent. The placement of Saturn in its exaltation or in its own sign, in a quadrant or in the eleventh house in a natal chart ameliorates the difficulties to a considerable extent. It may even lead to increase of favours from superiors, acquisition of ornaments, apparels and wealth, possession of vehicles and expansion in real estate. Under this situation one may be honoured by the Administration. Generally it is observed that Saturn leads the person to those things which are blue in colour. It makes him travel to the west. Adverse effects of Saturn are experienced when the planet is weak and unfavourably located.

Mercury:

The antar of Mercury lasts for 2 years, 3 months and 6 days. Mercury and Jupiter do not vibrate harmoniously to each other. Mercury activates mind of the person who becomes critical of religious and traditional values. It does not awaken ethical and righteous behaviour. The Mercurial impulse during the daśā of Jupiter magnifies the individual's attraction for women, gambling and drinking. These traits over a number of years destroy his physical health. In spite of these shortcomings, Mercury period has its brighter side as well. It accentuates literary sensitivities of the person who produces some of his best pieces during this period. He succeeds well in his business enterprises as well.

Ketu:

The antar of Ketu in the Jupiter daśā lasts for only 11 months and 6 days. During this period the individual receives good as well as adverse karmic results. These results are the carry-over of past actions that cannot be avoided. They appear to the individual during this period to teach him certain important lessons. During the usual course of events they are primarily intended to arouse religious sensibilities. The various distressing experiences of this period however completely change the temperament of the person and orients him towards the spiritual path. He therefore needs a different kind of teaching which Ketu effectively inculcates during this period.

Favourably placed Ketu specially if it is located in the fourth, tenth, ninth or fifth house from Jupiter bestows much benefic results. It bestows chauffeur driven vehicles, which marks a distinct stage of social respectability. He possesses much property and many luxury items. His enterprises succeed well and he attains elevation in his professional career. In case the chart supports spiritual evolution, the secondary period of Ketu provides great encouragement in this direction. Acquisition of pearl and coral ornaments, pilgrimages to holy shrines, addition to wealth and sufferance for the sake of elders and the wise also take place during the period. Adverse Ketu produces wounds caused by a weapon, misunderstanding with one's subordinates, estrangement with one's wife which may even lead to separation, divorce or her death. The individual experiences extreme degree of mental distress. During the sub-period of Ketu, the mind of the person is activated, distressed and impelled to strive towards spiritual enlightenment. It is a period of spiritual discontent.

Venus:

The sub-period of Venus in Jupiter daśā lasts for 2 years and 8 months. During this period the individual is likely to get immersed in material abundance. He acquires vehicles and other assets, which makes him to belong to the elite group of the society. His status gets elevated and he finds himself in the company of young women. He secures professional advancement. His wife someway assists it. Important celebrations in the family also takes place. During this period, the individual's own marriage or that of his children gets solemnized and new household goods are bought. Artistic interests of the individual also intensify. Journey towards eastern direction is expected to be undertaken. The period is generally characterized by events related with much sociability, sensitivity and development of artistic faculties. In spite of such pleasant atmosphere around the person, psychologically he may feel the absence of an abiding goal in his life. It leads to some kind of inner contemplative search and dissatisfaction with one's philosophy of life.

Sun:

The sub-period of Sun in the Jupiter daśā lasts for 9 months and 18 days. During this period the status of the individual gets elevated and there is inner growth. There is expansion at the material level as well as at that of his consciousness. His business expands, his contribution to the society increases and he gets renown, honour, reward and wealth. The fame of the individual reaches its zenith. He gains control over a large number of persons, acquires much property, vehicles and establishes his residence among the elite of the country. He displays regal splendour. Adverse location of the Sun leads to physical illness and loss of honour which gets much controlled and greatly minimised if the Sun receives favourable aspect of the Jupiter.

Moon:

The sub-period of Moon during Jupiter daśā lasts for 1 year and 4 months. During this period the sensuous nature of the individual gets sensitive. He associates with young females and forms close intimacies with them. He gains much money and receives extraordinary yield from agricultural cultivation and trade in agricultural products. His fame increases. He takes much interest in religious and social celebrations. Moon in adverse location will however make him to wander from place to place with much physical fatigue and loss of money.

Moon's antar in the Jupiter daśā is generally a period of acquisition of property, expansion of business and enjoyment of family comforts. Suffering experienced during this period is insignificant unless Moon is adversely placed.

Mars:

The sub-period of Mars in Jupiter daśā lasts for 11 months and 6 days. Jupiter and Mars are harmoniously related with each other. The period consequently results in much creative activities. Natural recklessness of Mars however leads to some minor injuries or to some social problems. Mars makes an individual attracted towards the opposite sex, which leads to unusual intimacies. Such relationships lead to social complications and mental worry for the person. For an average individual, this is a period of satisfactory family relationships, addition to wealth acquired by one's own efforts, expansion of land, real estate, industrial machines and equipment and engagement in charitable activities. During this period the individual also earns much kudos for his chivalry and courage.

Rahu:

The secondary period of Rāhu during Jupiter's main period of rulership lasts for 2 years, 4 months and 24 days. It is a period of much inconvenience and trouble. It is full of psychological pain and suffering unless favourable planetary conjuncture is present. In that case, one may expect increased activity on global scale with much close contact with different classes of people. Under such circumstances the individual is likely to get fruitful opportunities to help those who are disturbed in their mind, waylaid and engaged in large-scale industrial concerns.

It is a time for karmic forces to surface and get dissolved. Difficulties during this period may arise mainly for those who are strong enough to confront them and to derive the lessons they have to learn from these experiences for their ultimate life's mission. The period becomes significant because of its dual role. On the one hand it produces troubles and on the other it strengthens the individual inwardly so that more onerous responsibilities can be borne by him. During this period the individual is confronted with distressing events on account of family relations. He suffers from excessive mental anguish and from unhappy consequences of theft and diseases. These incidents take place primarily to counterbalance the disturbances caused by the past karmic omissions and commissions. The person may also have to face scandals of serious kind. He may have setback in his business. Once the karmic debts are over, the individual begins to experience divine beneficence. He is invited abroad, his guidance is greatly sought for, he is showered with honour and felicitations are organized for him. He goes to holy places and performs many religious rites. He participates in many auspicious and joyous celebrations.

Rāhu's sub-period during the main period of Jupiter is always very special for the spiritual growth of the individual. One may experience sorrow or joyous celebrations but in both these cases the emphasis is on inculcating disinterestedness with the physical events and expansion of spiritual awareness.

Sub-Rulerships during Saturn's Primary Period

Saturn restricts. It is a veil of shadow. Often it makes a person pass through the vale of sorrow. It creates impediments so that the creative impulses of the person do not operate as before. It blocks the creative urges and directs the accumulated energy to burst forth in a new direction. The process is painful. The life of the person seems completely dissolved. An indirect result of this kind of sorrowful operation is concretization of the accumulated forces. It transforms the subjective or the spirit-like energy into physical forms. This makes the impact of Saturn very intense. The sorrowful experiences felt during Saturn's main period can arise in numerous different ways but the basic direction of these events is the same. It concretizes the inner subjective feelings and urges into physical forms and provides the source material for spiritual experiences. At a later stage, this very impulse destroys the material attractions of the individual and puts him on the path of spiritual awakening. Finally, the latent spirit-like energy of the person begins to mingle with the cosmic energy. The whole process produces very excruciating pain but that is the easiest and surest method adopted by Saturn to take the individual by the shortest route to his goal. The process is certainly much dreaded which the outer man wants to escape but the inner being cherishes. Saturn is the most powerful spiritualising influence of the stellar world and every other planet contributes to Saturn their might in this task in the most exceptional manner.

Saturn:

The antar of Saturn in its own main period lasts for 3 years and 3 days. During this period Saturn produces diseases and sufferings of different kinds. It intensifies sorrows, arouses the understanding that materiality cannot give enduring peace and happiness and in this way sows in the person the seeds of spirituality. Saturn accentuates envy and pride and leads the individual towards sorrow and dispassion. It exposes him to the rapacity of others. It deprives him of his wealth and property. Under favourable conditions, it may however improve the individual's earnings, augment his property and increase his income particularly through the help of labour class, friendship with old women and resort to unrecognized and unapproved trade practices. Saturn makes the individual lazy, sinful and antisocial. The individual under its impact becomes very selfish. He is likely to refrain from spending his money but will like to cover his miserliness from the gaze of others. He will like others to believe that he is very generous. These are some of the effects of Saturn if it is not exalted or it does not occupy its own sign with favourable aspects on it.

A favourable Saturn makes a person a philosopher, a deep thinker renowned for his learning and industrious nature. Saturn even leads to the accrual of much wealth, foreign assignment and honour from overseas.

Mercury:

The sub-period of Mercury lasts for 2 years, 8 months and 9 days. Depending upon its auspicious placement it enables a person during its secondary rulership to go on a pilgrimage and take a dip in holy waters. It makes a person interested in scriptures and in deep philosophical discourses. His learning enables him to acquire material riches. His sexual morality becomes permissive. He may adopt suspicious and deceptive tactics to attain his objectives.

Mercury acquires an extraordinary disposition when it occupies the sixth, eighth or twelfth sign from the ascendant or from Saturn or if it is debilitated and is in association with malefic planets like Sun, Mars or Rāhu. Such a situation enables Mercury during its sub-period to bestow decorations and honour on the individual from various large and learned organizations as well as much wealth and control over a large number of persons. At the beginning of its secondary influence, such a situation of Mercury enables it to give auspicious results which however follow during its middle and end period through diseases, impediments and mental worry. The distressing impulse continues till the very end of the period. Saturn and Mercury are friends but that does not qualify Mercury to bestow unqualified gains and happiness.

Ketu:

The antar of Ketu in Saturn daśā lasts for 1 year, 1 month and 9 days. The period is very distressing for the individual. Strong Ketu located in a quadrant or a trine house from the ascendant and associated with benefic planets destroys the well-established mode of life. There is loss of status, loss of money and wealth, there is danger of imprisonment, separation and even upset in family relationships and conflict with one's superior. The person may even move out of the country. If Ketu is associated with the lord of the ascendant, the secondary rulership of Ketu can produce wealth, enable the individual to follow the path of holiness and take him to holy places. During this period the individual can get initiated into mystery schools. Similar results follow if Ketu is located in a quadrant, trine and third or the eleventh house from Saturn. Adverse results take place when Ketu is in the eighth or twelfth house from the ascendant or from Saturn.

Venus:

The sub-period of Venus during the main rulership of Saturn lasts for a period of 3 years and 2 months. It is a period of unique results. Saturn and Venus are both friendly to each other but the results of Venus during this period fail to produce the expected auspicious results. Venus is widely acclaimed as the planet of comfort, pleasure and sense gratification. Usual expectation is that Venus will lead to enjoyable association of friends, wife and family relations. It will increase wealth, produce success in business enterprises and enable the individual to travel overseas, acquire power and experience elevation of status and widespread renown. A powerful Venus in a natal chart is considered an asset for bestowing happiness and prosperity. Even a strong Saturn gives unusually auspicious results cherished by individuals. However, the relationship between the two is fraught with intense suffering especially during their antar and daśā periods. It is specially so when both of them are strong. Taken singly, each of them can produce auspicious results but when both of them are strong, there is exceptional misfortune. There is happiness only when their strength is not equal. Venus placed in a quadrant, ninth or eleventh house from Saturn leads to happy consequences. Under these conditions the individual receives many honours from the authorities, success in his enterprises and attains his desired objectives. He involves himself in charitable and philanthropic activities and undertakes religious pursuits like pilgrimage, scriptural discussions, literary production and listening to discourses. Illness of different kinds arises if Venus is located in the sixth, eighth or twelfth house from Saturn.

Sun:

The antar of Sun in the Saturn daśā lasts for 11 months and 12 days. It is a difficult period. There are contradictory forces at play, which make the life of the individual full of conflicts and produce much mental strain and physical trouble. There is apprehension of death or fatal injuries from enemies. There is likelihood of sickness to elders, disease in stomach and eyes, loss of money and failure in enterprise. During this period the person may experience a sinking feeling in his heart. He will be vulnerable to all such complications that arise due to obstructions to the downpour of divine energy and benediction.

When Sun is situated in the eighth or twelfth house, the unhappy events isolating the individual from every beneficial influence greatly increase. It may manifest by way of ill health, heart ailment, eye trouble, general debilitation, acute mental distress and failure in business, separation from wife and children and death of near relations. The period is highly unfortunate for father who may suffer from fever, devitalization or may even die.

Moon:

The antar of Moon in Saturn daśā lasts for 1 year and 7 months. It produces acute suffering. During this period one apprehends loss of one's wife, danger to one's own life, trouble from friends and relations, exposure to diseases, and unexpected bad news. It is a very distressing period for business transactions, commercial and speculative deals as well as for frustration in social activities. One can hope some redress if Moon receives the benefic rays of the Sun and the strengthening aspect of Jupiter. Under such favourable conditions, Moon can bestow some protection from enemies and favours from elders and protection against accusations from administration. The intensity of these difficulties is increased if Moon is weak, malefically aspected and situated in the sixth, eighth or twelfth house from Saturn. Sloth, pessimism and lack of enthusiasm are the characteristic results of Saturn-Moon period.

Mars:

The sub-period of Mars in Saturn daśā lasts for 1 year 1 month and 9 days. Mars does not produce favourable influence during this period. Initiative, enthusiasm and dynamism of Mars are coldly wrapped up under the veil of Saturn. The individual is paralyzed. He becomes ineffective. Depending upon the location of Mars, the individual experiences loss of status, feels emotionally marooned, finds demoralizing servitude and humiliating work experience. He develops misunderstanding with his family members. He suffers from acute diseases and loss of money. Distress on account of brothers and property may occur during this period. Strong and auspiciously placed Mars suddenly bestows on the person honour and property. Adverse Mars produces boils, arthritis, gout and such other diseases.

Rāhu:

Rāhu attains its secondary rulership during the major period of Saturn for 2 years, 10 months and 6 days. It exposes the individual to malignant influences of the worst kind. During this period the general psychology of the person gets perverted. He becomes corrupt. He carries surreptitious business, becomes a drug addict, visits houses of ill name and wastes his money. He suffers from complicated ailments that are difficult to diagnose and cure. During this period there can be devastation caused by thieves and marauders. One can experience mental torments. One deviates from the accepted moral code and established norms of social behaviour. Attacks of congenital and venereal diseases are not ruled out during this period. The danger of being exiled is also there.

If Rāhu is well fortified by its exaltation or otherwise and is favourably placed in relation with Saturn, the early phase of Rāhu sub-period may produce some good results. The individual may undertake religious pilgrimages, meet devout elderly persons and attain some property and wealth but during the later phase of the antar troubles arise. Rāhu in Aries, Virgo, Cancer, Taurus, Pisces, Sagittarius and Leo in the natal chart during its secondary rulership period produces beneficial results providing happiness and wealth to the person.

Jupiter:

The antar of Jupiter in Saturn daśā lasts for 2 years, 6 months and 12 days. The spiritual aspirations of the person get suppressed during this period. He feels contented merely with the exoteric religious practices. He is pious and visits holy places regularly but the craving for the realization of the inner secrets of esoteric philosophy is not permitted to grow. The individual takes delight in performing ritualistic rites. He even attracts the attention of others by such behaviour and earns social esteem. During this period, the individual lives in his own house and passes his time happily with his wife and children.

If Jupiter is well fortified and has the association of the ascendant lord, the period becomes very pleasant and capable of enhancing his social status. Weak Jupiter placed in the sixth, eighth or twelfth house in a natal chart, during its secondary rulership creates much distress making the individual take long and tiresome journeys and separating him from his near and dear relations. There can even be physical hardships and personal life may get disorganized. During such a period, the individual incurs displeasure of his superiors and experiences serious setback in his professional career or in his business enterprises.

Sub-Rulerships during Mercury's Primary Period

As we have indicated earlier, Mercury is concerned with the mind principle. It awakens the discriminatory abilities and expands the intellectual power. Through its impetus, the mental horizon of the person widens. But by itself Mercury is neutral. It requires some support for its operation. Unless any other planet is supportive, its power becomes non-operative. During its main period, the results of Mercury are observed only through the influence of other planets.

Mercury:

All planets during the secondary rulership period in their own main period remain reserved. Much is not expected from them during this period. So is the case with Mercury as well. But this period of secondary rulership of Mercury is fairly long. It lasts for 2 years, 4 months and 27 days. During this period, Mercury gradually orients the individual to absorb the influences of other planets. The development of mental power makes the individual critical, enabling him to analyze and go deeper into every situation confronting him. Such a mind does not create feelings of delight. It sobers the person. It leads him to a strange feeling of dissatisfaction. It produces neither happiness in the performance of religious rituals, nor in the enjoyment of luxuries of life though it awakens attraction for the both. Essentially Mercury strengthens the quality of the prying mind which gets intensified during this period.

Auspicious and strong Mercury leads to the acquisition of sea-born wealth, profit from commercial transactions and gain even from writings, speeches and intellectual activities. Adverse Mercury produces hostilities and differences with one 's brothers and colleagues.

Ketu:

The secondary rulership of Ketu during the main period of Mercury lasts for 11 months and 27 days. During this period, Ketu tests the mental fibre of the individual. It puts him in trying situations so that he can learn to maintain his mental composure. In the process it deepens his power of contemplation. The thinking principle at this stage gets activated through creation of circumstances misery, sorrow, confusion and dispute with others. In the case of favourable locational position and auspicious aspects of benefic planets, one may expect physical pleasure, acquisition of wealth, gainful travels, educational attainments and renown during this period. Placed in the sixth, eighth or twelfth signs from Mercury, the planet makes the person perverse, depraved and mentally unbalanced.

Venus:

The antar of Venus in Mercury daśā lasts for 2 years and 10 months. Venus is a benefic planet friendly with Mercury. Venus produces physical conveniences, sensual enjoyment and association with social elites. As a result, the individual gets to feel an extraordinary delight. Venus also produces refineness, artistic talents, and increased sensitivity. These qualities get greatly sharpened under the Mercurial impact. Depending upon the strength and position of Venus, the individual secures during this period benefiction of gods, gifts from elders, profitability in business transactions, refinement in artistic skill, enjoyment in the association of charming girls and a feeling of delight in the company of intellectual persons. He lives during this period in luxurious residential houses. Only when Venus is weak and placed in the sixth, eighth or twelfth sign from Mercury that one apprehends heart ailments, humiliation and mental worries.

Sun:

The sub-period of Sun in Mercury daśā lasts for only 10 months and 6 days. The period produces auspicious results. It enables the individual to acquire gold, coral, vehicles, property, status and a well furnished house. During this period the individual begins to feel confident of himself. As a result he expresses his ideas freely and effectively. If Mars aspects Sun, the individual, during this period, acquires much landed property, mining rights and becomes extrovert taking active part in social activities. The aspect of ascendant lord on it produces all round success and elevation in one's status. Intense pain is experienced if Sun is associated with Saturn, Mars and Rāhu and is placed in eighth or twelfth house from the ascendant. The period proves troublesome if the luminary is placed twelfth from Mercury.

Moon:

The secondary period of Moon during the primary daśā of Mercury lasts for 1 year and 5 months. If Moon is weak and adversely placed in the natal chart, the period turns out to be difficult. It produces much mental worry. There is loss of status and wealth. Strong Moon with favourable aspects from Jupiter and other benefic support makes the most significant influences on the person. Its secondary period becomes the most momentous period in one's life. During this period, the individual can hope to acquire a new residence, pleasures of good social parties and musical entertainment. He may develop interest in serious studies. He can undertake gainful journeys to distant countries (situated particularly in the southern direction).

If Moon is placed in a quadrant, a trine house or is in third or eleventh sign from Mercury, the individual at the very outset of the period embarks on a fruitful journey to religious places, meets scholarly and learned persons and forges new and profitable business partnerships.

Mars:

The antar of Mars in Mercury daśā lasts for 11 months and 27 days. Mercury and Mars do not vibrate harmoniously with each other. Mars acts to acquire and to achieve while Mercury impels the individual to think and to enjoy. Rarely they work in a well coordinated manner with each other in order to achieve anything productive. Whenever they adapt themselves to each other they produce exceptional results, which can be highly effective and helpful to the society and intensely intellectual.

During this sub-period of Mars, the individual may initiate activities on many different fronts but hardly reaches finality in any of them. While engaged in the work, he hardly gets the opportunity to enjoy the work or its fruit. He gets impulsive, often facing chances of dangers from fire, and injuries to his body. Others may swindle him. He may have to face suspension in service. He may associate himself with perverse persons and commit cruelty to others. Such results however do not occur in all cases. Mars in strength located in auspicious houses from the ascendant and favourably located in relation with Mercury reduces these difficulties to a great extent and the period may even prove to be good for him. It may also bestow fame and reward for his charitable deeds. The person may have unexpected gains from his various enterprises.

Rāhu:

The antar of Rāhu in Mercury daśā lasts for 2 years, 6 months and 18 days. When Rāhu is placed in adverse relationships with Mercury, it produces intense pain, ill health, bad company and differences with others. During this period, the individual suffers from mental, abdominal and eyes troubles. He faces dangers from fire, poison and water. Otherwise, when Rāhu is located in Cancer, Aquarius, Virgo or Taurus and occupies a quadrant, trine or eleventh house from ascendant, it produces during its secondary rulership many auspicious results. The state and trade union workers honour the individual. There is an inflow of wealth and downpour of divine benediction. The person takes a dip in holy waters, visits holy places and engages himself in philanthropic activities. He respects elders. This period is usually marked by many fruitful long journeys.

Jupiter:

The antar of Jupiter in Mercury daśā lasts for 2 years, 3 months and 6 days. It produces mixed results. It generates a protective force for the individual. It inspires him to perform religious rituals and engage himself in philanthropic activities. It does not encourage him to think deeply. Weak Jupiter puts the individual to strained relationship with his friends and relations. Otherwise, Jupiter is likely to relieve the person from his persisting sicknesses. It destroys enemies, ends fear and leads to self-knowledge. On attains deep knowledge of religious scriptures and adheres to religious and moral duties. During this period the individual receives special honour from the state.

Jupiter invariably gives many occasions for auspicious celebrations and festivities and it bestows extra-ordinary self-satisfaction.

Saturn:

This planet has its sub-rulership for 2 years, 8 months and 9 days. During this period, the thought process of the individual gets concretized. Favourably placed Mercury and an auspicious Saturn makes the period very joyous. It kindles enormous enthusiasm, bestows honour from overseas, general public and from the working class. Acquisition of a large mansion to live in also materializes. The period can be auspicious even spiritually. The individual may proceed on a pilgrimage to holy places and participate in some important rituals. He becomes a free thinker and a philosopher, though his personal life may be at variance with what he professes. Placed in the eighth or twelfth sign from Mercury, Saturn causes much damage to the person socially, financially and ethically. His thinking gets distorted.

Secondary Rulerships during Ketu's Primary Period

Ketu is a planet that causes much mental distress. When its primary influence begins to affect the individual, his life and mind gets disorganized and disturbed. His judgement gets strained. He becomes afflicted with many diseases. His approach to life becomes perverted. He begins to associate himself with depraved, unsociable and discarded sections of the society. He himself becomes a recluse and is cut off from the main stream of the community. These traits however show many variations during the 7-year period of Ketu. Depending upon the configuration of planets in the natal chart, Ketu affects different persons differently. Even during the period of its secondary rulership in its own main daśā, many modifications in its basic impulses can be deciphered.

Ketu:

During Ketu's own secondary rulership which lasts for 4 months and 27 days, there is much distress to the individual resulting from death of wife, quarrel with enemies, litigation in courts, humiliation from near and dear ones, and perversity in sexual relationships. Fever and may be complicated diseases will affect his health. Imposition of others on his personal life upsets him greatly. Well placed Ketu in the natal chart and in auspicious relationship with the ascendant lord, lord of the fourth house, lord of the ninth house and that of the tenth house leads to much acquisition of material wealth, pleasure of wife and children as well as honour from the superiors. There may however, be mental distress and the person may not be able to enjoy any of the conveniences available to him during this secondary rulership of Ketu.

Venus:

Venus has its secondary rulership of 1 year and 2 months during the main period of Ketu. It seriously affects the sociability of the person. There is likelihood of misunderstanding with his wife. Relations even with his near and dear ones may get strained and unpleasantness with superiors may happen. He may have to suffer from fever and dysentery. But there may be birth of a daughter during this period. The person may encounter humiliating experiences. These are the general results of this sub -period, which get modified according to the conjuncture of planets in the natal chart.

Strong and favourably associated Venus, particularly with the lord of the fourth house, can make the period very pleasant. Under this situation, the individual can expect some lucky beginning in his career. If Ketu is associated with the lords of ninth and tenth houses, there can be abundance of wealth, retrieval of lost property, attainment of respectable position and opportunities for visiting holy places and taking dip in holy waters. Venus placed in a quadrant, trine or third or eleventh house from Ketu may enable the individual to attain good health, celebrate auspicious events in family and enjoy good food, good apparel and honour from the society in which he lives. Only when Venus is placed in the sixth, eighth or twelfth house from Ketu or when it is associated with a debilitated planet while placed in the sixth or eighth from the ascendant there may be fatal accidents or trouble from others. The individual under such situations may even be afflicted with heart disease, ailments of head and eyes and boils may erupt on his body.

Sun:

The antar of Sun in Ketu's main period lasts for 4 months and 6 days. It produces death in the family, physical illness for the person and unpleasant journey abroad. These results become acute if Sun is placed in the eighth or twelfth house from ascendant and is associated with malefic planets. If Sun is in a quadrant, trine, eleventh or second house from Ketu, the individual secures auspicious results. There may be birth of an offspring, stability of the mind, acquisition of more power and elevation in social and political status.

Moon:

Moon has its secondary rulership for 7 months in the Ketu daśā. During this period the mental anxiety of the person gets greatly accentuated. Unexpected changes occur in his life. During the period he experiences separation from his son and strain on account of wife (for example, laboured delivery producing much sorrow and anxiety).

These results however occur only if Moon is weak and placed in the sixth, eighth or twelfth sign from Ketu. Afflicted Ketu can even be fatal for the person. Strong and well-placed Moon, at least in the beginning of its secondary period leads to gain of riches, honour and physical well-being. Such a Moon even bestows honour from the superiors. Only towards the end of the period, the individual incurs displeasure of the ruler and gets into tiresome and fruitless travels.

Mars:

The secondary period of Mars lasts for 4 months and 27 days. It creates much trouble for the individual. If it is placed in the eighth or twelfth house from Ketu, there can be grave danger to his life, troubles from abroad, displeasure from the state, affliction such as diabetes, urinary diseases etc. and even theft may take place in his house. Only when Mars is strong and well placed and associated with benefic planets that one hopes for the accrual of wealth and real estate. Its association with the lord of the ninth house or when ninth and tenth houses in the natal chart are related with Mars that this period can lead to possession of much landed property. The life of the person generally gets unsettled during this period.

Rāhu:

The antara of Rāhu in Ketu daśā lasts for 1 year and 18 days. It upsets the individual very much. There is sorrow in every sphere of life. He receives setback in his enterprises. The problems confronting him become elusive and difficult to grapple with. He suffers from psychosis. This is a period that greatly disturbs the very existence of the individual and his future well-being.

Experiences gained during this period are vital. They provide the foundation on which his future philosophy of life depends. The problems become acute if Rāhu is placed in the eighth or the twelfth house from the ascendant along with malefic planets. Strong Rāhu placed in a quadrant, trine or a friendly sign or in second or the eleventh house can produce sudden accrual of wealth and favour from overseas. Rāhu's secondary rulership during the main period of Ketu begins with much physical and psychological difficulties but as the period comes towards its end, much goodwill, strength and enlightenment come to the person.

Jupiter:

The secondary period of Jupiter lasts for 11 months and 6 days. During this period, the individual may expect every kind of auspicious result such as accrual of wealth, landed property, favour from superiors, opportunities for religious studies and birth of a son. Gifts from many sources are showered on him. His health improves. These blessings come to him unexpectedly and they relieve him of some long -standing malady or misfortune which are mostly due karmic backlashes. Jupiter placed in a quadrant, trine, third or eleventh house from Ketu bestows on him unusual gifts of clothes and ornaments, invitations to visit foreign lands and honour at home. These benedictions are however interfused with physical illnesses in the beginning and disputes and sudden loss of status towards the end of the period. The impulse of Ketu succeeds in modifying the experiences under the influence of Jupiter according to its own natural disposition.

Saturn:

The secondary rulership of Saturn in the main period of Ketu lasts for 1 year, 1 month and 9 days. This period is full of malignancy. This is a period of intense impact. Saturn placed in the eighth or the twelfth sign from Ketu creates much distortion in the thought process of the individual. His physical health deteriorates. He gets tormented mentally and there is much loss of income and wealth. His subordinates create troubles for him. If he has the responsibilities of industrial management, he may be confronted with difficult labour problems. Saturn forms *Śaśa Yoga* due to its exaltation or ownership of a quadrant. When Saturn attains auspicious disposition in relation with other planets good results of this planet may be possible. Even in these cases, the individual may have to work hard. He may often experience exhaustion and psychological despondency.

Mercury:

The secondary rulership of Mercury lasts for 11 months and 27 days. It produces pleasant results. During this period there may be birth of a very spiritual and intelligent son. The individual may receive appreciation for his literary, commercial or occult studies. Erudite persons may recognize his worth and the superiority of intelligence. During this period, the individual may get opportunities for participating in learned conferences, seminars and workshops. He may receive honours at such congregations. He also gets opportunities for celebrating marriages and other festivities in his family. When Mercury is placed in the sixth, eighth or the twelfth house from Ketu and is associated with Saturn, Mars or Rāhu that some differences arise with his superiors and some loss of wealth and property occurs. There may be trouble from his adversaries, loss of property and difficulties relating to his enterprises.

The period of Mercury's rulership during the main period of Ketu is generally unpleasant and unhappiness clouds the individual's life. Towards the end of the period the individual can however expect some relief from the distressful impact of Ketu.

Sub-Rulerships during the Venus' Primary Period

Venus is a planet of luxurious life and benefic influences. It has the longest period of planetary periodicity. During this period, every planet gets sufficient opportunity to produce its impact. The basic impulse generated by this planet is that of increased sensitivity and intensification of sensual gratification. This impulse provides an overall milieu under which other planets produce their results.

Venus:

The sub-period of Venus in its own daśā lasts for 3 years and 4 months. It fulfils all material desires of the person. During this period the individual gets beautiful clothes, costly ornaments, luxurious vehicles, exotic perfumes and the pleasures of couch. He associates himself with pleasing damsels and establishes intimacy with them. He mixes well with social elites and is widely known for his achievements. Considerable expansion of his personality takes place during this period. He becomes very popular in his social circles. He attains almost everything mundane that he wants. In short, this period of his life is full of joy and material attainments.

Venus is a first class killer as well. Placed in the sixth, eighth or the twelfth house in a natal chart in association with a malefic planet or aspected by it, Venus produces acute mental agony, trouble from wife, humiliation from girls, scandal in the society and failure in his enterprises. The strength of Venus for giving propitious results is greatly enhanced if it is placed in the third, sixth, tenth or the eleventh house from the ascendant.

Sun:

The sub-period of Sun in the main period of Venus lasts for 1 year. During this period the individual is beset with many difficulties destroying his well-established life-style. His vital energy gets sapped and he feels greatly forlorn.

His ambition gets shattered and all his moorings almost vanish. Mental anxiety vitally affects his health. It produces general exhaustion, seminal debility and revulsion from civilized society. Mental imbalance, sense of inferiority and seclusion from all human relationships often characterize this period. The person may change his place of residence in order to escape humiliation and disgrace.

Adverse results of the period are minimized by the favourable placements of Sun. However unmixed happiness may not be expected. Even if the person attains material affluence under the influence of Sun and Venus, he cannot enjoy the same because he does not have an anxiety-free mind.

Moon:

The antar of Moon in Venus daśā lasts for 1 year and 8 months. It vibrates harmoniously with Venus. It makes the mind of the person spiritually inclined enabling him to reflect the reality without much distortion. It makes him peaceful inducing him to engage in religious rituals and meeting holy men and women. The person during this period also acquires wealth to some extent and gets into good company. There is also a possibility of his taking resort near some river or having water resort. He gets the company of respectable girls and enjoys the pleasures of life. Towards the end of the period however, he will begin to feel that all these pleasures are slipping away from him.

Mars:

The antar of Mars in the main period of Venus lasts for 1 year and 2 months. The period is full of auspicious possibilities and great excitement. Unless Mars is placed in the eighth or the twelfth house from Venus and is weak otherwise, the individual is suddenly made active, enthusiastic and chivalrous. He is much sought after by charming women in whose company he gets much warmth and pleasure. The person secures landed property, succeeds in seducing many young females and occasionally gets setback in his enterprise.

The sub-period of Mars often creates troubles like loss of blood and excess secretion of bile. But the period leads to the acquisition of gold, copper and other precious metals. Even with all opportunities for the enjoyment of life during this period, the person tends to experience a sense of missing something which he cannot very clearly identify.

Rāhu:

The sub-period of Rāhu in the Venus daśā lasts for 3 years. During this period the individual attains many coveted things of life but he does not remain mentally happy. He feels as if a poisonous serpent has entered his bridal-suite. He cannot specifically identify the nature of this fear but he would be so much obsessed with it that he cannot extricate himself from it. This fear always haunts him. It even deprives him from the various pleasures at his command. He acquires wealth and elite status, gets married and begets children, receives honour and fame but he remains estranged from his own relatives. He gets disturbed by his enemies, suffers physical illness and mental unhappiness. He experiences loss of wealth and change in the place of his residence.

If Rāhu is placed in the third, sixth, tenth or the eleventh house from the ascendant the first five months of the period is full of mental happiness, enthusiasm royal honour and accrual of other auspicious benefits. Later on, the individual inevitably suffers from acute psychological distress and passes through a period of intense sorrow. Finally the trying period imparts him insight into the abiding principles of life.

Jupiter:

The antar of Jupiter in the Venus daśā lasts for 2 years and 8 months. During this period, the individual performs religious and family duties, becomes pious and ethical, spends much time with his family members, derives satisfaction from his status in life and exercises his power effectively. He receives much appreciation for his activities and abilities. He gets support and assistance from venerable elders who seem to take sympathetic interest in his welfare. In case, Jupiter is placed in the sixth or the twelfth house from Venus, there may be adverse results.

Saturn:

The sub-rulership of Saturn in Venus daśā lasts for 3 years and 2 months. During this period, there is much happiness for the individual provided both Saturn and Venus are not equally strong in the natal chart. Such a situation may enable him to receive honour and appreciation from his superiors, acquire wealth and power through his activities and enterprises and establish intimacy with rich and desirable women who may even be elder to him in age. Increase in his social status and travels to different parts of the world can take place during this period. If Saturn is placed in the eighth or the twelfth house from Venus, the person may be afflicted with sloth and fatigue, expenditure exceeding his income, ill-health of parents, strain on account of wife and children, setback in his enterprises and destruction of property.

If Saturn is favourably placed in the natal chart, the individual exercises much power, especially over industrial workers or his political followers.

Mercury:

The antar of Mercury in Venus daśā lasts for 2 years and 10 months. It produces favourable conditions for the individual. During this period, the individual's own offspring provides him immense happiness. He is very creative with sensitivity transparent in his literary works. He secures renown for his literary genius. His enemies lose their hold over him. During this period, his sociability increases and he remains much in popular demand in social circles. Strong and well placed Mercury provides him rare opportunities of attending to learned discourses on religious scriptures, participate in meetings and conferences attended by eminent scholars and he even associates himself with poets and writers famed for their erotic activities and writings. He becomes a social elite during this period. These results accrue only when Mercury is not placed in the sixth, eighth or the twelfth house from Venus and is free from any malefic aspect or association.

Ketu:

The sub-period of Ketu in the Venus daśā lasts for 1 year and 2 months. During this period, the individual gets mentally tortured. He gets humiliated, often thrown in the company of perverts and suffers from diseases whose infection is difficult to eradicate. During this period, the individual becomes a destitute, suffers from dangers of fire, loses some of his limbs, and associates himself with courtesans. He indulges in unnatural sexual relationships. He gets jilted in love, separated from his wife, and is likely to be deprived of his job. These features of misfortune torment him psychologically and he is likely not to find succor from anywhere.

Tertiary Planetary Rulership

Antardaśā of Different Planets

Some of these have already been considered in the context of the timing of events. The tertiary order of planetary rulership is a reflection of unending wheels within wheels. The working out of minor Daśās within a major one generally depends on the principle of proportionality and their sequential relative positions. As indicated earlier, under Viṁśottarī Daśā system, a total of 120 years is allotted to the complete cycle of planetary rulership. Within this total, different planets are assigned different periods of rulerships. For example, out of the total of 120 years under Viṁśottarī, Sun is allotted 6 years, Moon 10 years and so on. The sequence of these planets is also fixed. Moon always follows Sun. Mars follows Moon and so on. While working out the sub-rulership of different planets during the main rulership of different planets, these principles are adhered to. Accordingly the secondary chain of their periodicity is worked out. It applies to the calculation of *antardaśā* as well as *sūkṣma daśās*. Within tertiary rulership these two basic considerations also apply. Some astrologers continue with this principle of wheels within wheels and even go to the finer calculations of the planetary periodicity. They carry the calculations so minutely that they begin to examine the very inflow of life -essence to the individual. Generally, one works up to the *Sūkṣma Daśā* i.e. up to the tertiary planetary impulses (or rulership). An attempt is made here to indicate the short-cut method for working out the tertiary Daśā periods.

The duration of *Antardaśā* or sub-lordship of Sun in the main period of planetary rulerships under Viṁśottarī Daśā is 3 months and 18 days. Considering this duration as equivalent to 120 years, one has to work out this period as equal to 6/120th part or one-twentieth part of the Antardaśā period. Similarly, Moon's tertiary rulership period during the Sun's sub-lordship is worked out. One has to find out 10/120th or one-twelfth.

Multiply the number of years assigned to the three planets under consideration. That is, multiply the number of years allotted to those planets whose daśā, antardaśā and sūkṣma daśā are under calculation. It implies that the duration of rulership of the main daśā planet is multiplied by the number of years assigned to the planet having the antara daśā and also by the number of years assigned to the planet which is going to have its sūkṣma daśā. Let 40 divide the resultant figure. It gives the period of rulership of the planet at the tertiary level in number of days. In case there is some remainder, it may be converted into number of hours. In case, one desires to have the duration very accurately, one can even refine the result by working out the minutes from the remainder. For example, if the tertiary rulership of Venus in Moon's sub-period under Sun's main daśā is to be found out, one multiplies (Venus's period) × (Moon's period)× (Sun's period). All the periods are taken from the total duration of Virhśottarī periodicity cycle. In the present case, it works out as follows: 20 × 10 × 6 = 1200. Let 40 divides this total, which gives 30 days, i.e. one month. The easiest way to find out these periods is several ready reckoners which are easily available.

CHAPTER#2

Planetary Transits

Planets always move. The planetary configuration at birth is only a snapshot description of the ever-changing stellar relationships. Each individual is mystically linked with the spirit represented by the planet and his evolutionary course extending over several lives. The law of reincarnation and the law of karma are two fundamental principles guiding this relationship. The planetary deities closely watch and guide the operation. They watch the various events confronting the individual and his responses to them. On this basis they regulate the planetary forces so that they can help the individual in fulfilling his allotted task. Every event is inevitably connected with his eternal mission. The ever-changing course of planetary relations reveals the manner in which these forces are regulated so as to pilot the course of his life towards the ultimate mission. Each event, however insignificant and mundane, occurring to an individual is a link in this eternal drama. Planetary transits in this way show the possibilities of occurrences though the common-man is ordinarily not aware of the future or of his ultimate destiny. He may not feel concerned with the significance of the various situations/events confronting him. His interest is mostly restricted to the immediate future. It is the responsibility of the astrologer to reveal to him the course chalked out for him by his guardian angel. On the basis of counselling the individual may suitably be prepared to adapt himself to his destiny. The astrologer must take cognizance of the ever-changing planetary configuration for this and interpret it indicating to the person concerned the significance of the changing configuration. Transits of planets are deciphered by a different set of rules in comparison to the planets at the time of the birth. The way these transits influence an individual is different from the birth time planetary relationships. The effects of birth time planetary positions and the transiting planets are both important for better delineation of the astrological results.

The planetary configuration at birth of an individual represents his inherent potential. These do not always receive adequate opportunities for their realisation. That is why many a flower blushes unseen and many a seed perishes without sprouting. The natal planetary positions describe certain sensitive points, which require activation for the fruition of those qualities. When these points are energised, these qualities begin to develop. During the course of their transits, the different planets fulfil this task. They energise the sensitive points in a natal chart. Some of these changes which are planned to take place at a particular age of the person are studied under Annual Progression of the horoscope. Transits of planets and Annual Horoscopes are two aspects of the same phenomenon.

The inherent disposition of a planet changes during the course of its transits. It is a common experience that Jupiter, which is a benefic of the first order, fails to produce favourable results during its transit over the natal Moon. It inevitably produces unsettlement. During this period the individual either changes his residence, his job or travels abroad with much frustrating experiences. He feels tired, exhausted and worried. Against this, the worst malefic of the stellar system namely, Saturn produces very favourable effects when it transits in the 3rd, 6th and 11th signs from Moon. As a general rule, when a planet transits through its friendly, it's own or its exaltation sign, it bestows its gifts generously. Similarly they are well disposed in *Upacaya* houses namely the 3rd, 6th, 10th and 11th houses from ascendant or the Moon-sign. In *Apacaya* namely 1st, 2nd, 4th, 5th, 7th, 8th, 9th and 12th houses, the planets are inclined to give adverse results. In fact, favourable and adverse effects of a transiting planet depend upon several factors. Three of these are:

(i) The location of the planet itself may change. A planet in exaltation, in its own sign, or in a friendly sign in a natal chart, may later on traverse in its debilitation or in its enemy's sign. Such changes will alter its temporary disposition and affect its capabilities at the time of such transits.

(ii) The changing strength of a planet is measured under *Aṣṭakavarga*, which describes the relative power of a planet in different signs in the horoscope. *Aṣṭakavarga* measures the strength by eight criteria.

(iii) The effects of the transits are at times blocked by presence of certain obstructing planets. The good and adverse effects of a planet fructify when there is absence of such hindering agencies. These obstructing agents are studied under Vedhas.

The criteria for determining the locational strength of a transiting planet are the same as given for the planets in the natal chart. But Aṣṭakavarga and Vedhas are special features of predictive techniques, which need special consideration.

Aṣṭakavarga Preparation

Assessment of the eightfold strength of a planet depends upon the nature of occupancy of the planet in relation with other planets excluding Moon but including Ascendant as a special case. The final table that emerges on the basis of this calculation is an aggregation of seven tables prepared for the seven planets. In each table favourable as well as adverse positions of a planet in relation with others including the ascendant are marked. Dots and dashes represent these, one of them (usually the dots) represent the auspicious influences and the other (usually denoted by dashes) represent the adverse situation of the planet. The dots and the dashes taken together will always total eight. The total number of favourable markings in every horoscope is 337, though their distribution in different houses is not uniform. They vary from house to house.

Sun is auspicious in the 1st, 2nd, 4th, 7th, 8th, 9th, 10th and 11th house from Mars as well as from Saturn. In relationship with Jupiter, Sun is auspicious when it transits the 5th, 6th, 9th, and the 11th signs from it. It is also so in the 6th, 7th and 12th signs from Venus. Sun is auspicious in the 3rd, 5th, 6th, 9th, 10th, 11th and 12th signs from Mercury. In relation with Moon, Sun is auspicious in the 3rd, 6th, 10th and 11th signs from it. From ascendant, Sun is auspicious in the 3rd, 4th, 6th, 10th, 11th and 12th signs from it. Total auspicious dots for Sun in every horoscope is 48.

Moon is auspicious in the 3rd, 6th, 7th, 8th, 10th, and the 11th sign from Sun, It is also so in the 1st, 3rd, 6th, 7th, 10th and 11th signs from itself. Moon is auspicious in the 2nd, 3rd, 5th, 6th, 9th, 10th and 11th place from Mars. With regards to Mercury, the auspicious places of Moon are in the 1st, 3rd, 4th, 5th, 7th, 8th, 10th and 11th signs. With regard to Jupiter, it is so in the 1st, 4th, 7th, 8th, 10th, 11th and 12th places from it. Moon is favourable in the 3rd, 4th, 5th, 7th, 9th, 10th and 11th signs from Venus. In the case of Saturn, it is so in the 3rd, 5th, 6th and 12th places from it. With regard to ascendant, Moon gives favourable results in the 3rd, 6th, 10th and 11th places from it. These favourable points total 49.

Mars has its favourable places from Sun in the 3rd, 5th, 6th, 10th and 11th while from ascendant the favourable places for it are in the 1st, 3rd, 6th, 10th and the 11th signs. From Moon the favourable places are 3rd, 6th and the 11th sign. The auspicious places for it from itself are 1st, 2nd, 4th, 7th, 8th, 10th and 11th. From Saturn, these places are 1st, 4th, 7th, 8th, 9th, 10th and the 11th signs. From Mercury these places for Mars are in the 3rd, 5th, 6th and 11th signs. From Venus they are 6th, 8th, 11th and 12th. The auspicious places for Mars from Jupiter are in the 6th, 10th, 11th, and 12th signs. The total auspicious points for Mars are 39.

Mercury's auspicious points are as follows: 1st, 3rd, 5th, 6th, 9th, 10th 11th, and 12th places from the sign occupied by itself, in the 5th, 6th, 9th, 11th and 12th signs from Sun, in the 6th, 8th, 11th and 12th signs from Jupiter, in the 1st, 2nd, 4th, 7th, 8th, 9th, 10th and 11th signs from Saturn. From Mars its favourable points are in the 8th, 9th, 10th and 11th signs. As far as Venus is concerned, Mercury attains favourable points in the 1st, 2nd, 3rd, 4th, 5th, 8th 9th, and 11th signs from it. Its auspicious points with regard to Moon are in the 2nd, 4th, 6th, 10th and 11th signs. In relation to ascendant, Mercury's favourable transit points are in the 1st, 2nd, 4th, 6th, 8th, 10th and 11th places from it. The total auspicious points of transit for Mercury are 54.

Jupiter is beneficial in the 1st, 2nd, 3rd, 4th, 7th, 8th, 10th and 11th places from the sign occupied by Sun. It is also so in the 2nd, 5th, 7th, 9th and 11th signs from Moon, in the 1st, 2nd, 4th, 5th, 6th, 9th, 10th and 11th signs from Mercury, in the 2nd, 5th, 6th, 9th, 10th and 11th signs from Venus, in the 1st, 2nd, 4th, 7th, 8th 10th and 11th signs from Mars, in the 1st, 2nd, 3rd, 4th, 7th, 8th, 10th, and 11th signs from itself, in the 3rd, 5th, 6th and 12th signs from Saturn. With regard to the ascendant, Jupiter is auspicious in the 1st, 2nd, 4th, 5th, 6th, 7th, 9th, 10th and 11th places from the ascendant. The total benefic dots for Jupiter amount to 56.

Venus produces good results when it transits in the 1st, 2nd, 3rd, 4th, 5th, 8th 9th and 11th signs from the ascendant, in the 8th, 11th and 12th places from Sun, in the 1st, 2nd, 3rd, 4th, 5th, 8th, 9th, 11th and 12th signs from Moon, in the 3rd, 5th, 6th, 9th and 11th signs from Mercury, in the 1st, 2nd, 3rd, 4th, 5th, 8th, 9th, 10th and 11th place from itself, in the 3rd, 5th, 6th, 9th, 11th and 12th signs from Mars, and in the 5th, 8th, 9th, 10th and 11th signs from the sign occupied by Jupiter. Venus is auspicious in the 3rd, 4th, 5th, 8th, 9th, 10th and 11th signs from Saturn. Total auspicious points for Venus are 52.

Saturn is auspicious in the 1st, 2nd, 4th, 7th, 8th, 10th and 11th places from the sign occupied by Sun. In relation to Moon, it is auspicious in the 3rd, 6th and 11th signs from it. Saturn is auspicious in the 6th, 8th, 9th, 11th and 12th places from the sign occupied by Mercury. In relation to Venus, it is auspicious in the 6th, 11th and 12th signs away from it. Saturn is auspicious in the 3rd, 5th, 6th, 10th, 11th and 12th signs away from Mars, in the 5th, 6th, 11th and 12th places away from Jupiter, and in the 3rd, 5th, 6th and 11th places from the sign occupied by itself. From ascendant, Saturn is auspicious in the 1st, 3rd, 4th, 6th, 10th and 11th places. Total auspicious points for Saturn are 39.

The maximum number of benefic dots in any house is 8, which signifies that a planet in its transit of that house will be inclined to impart its most auspicious results. If the planet in the natal chart is not well placed and the transit placement is also not very favourable, its temporary malefic impact will also be reduced to a great extent. If the planet is favourably situated in the natal chart as well as in its transit position and the benefic dots are the maximum possible, the planet will produce the best result at that time of which it is capable. If the favourable dots are only 4, i.e. half of its maximum point, the temporary strength of the planet to do well is much reduced and at the same time its malefic power is also weakened. The benefic nature of a planet is considerably weakened if the dots are less than four and it acquires malefic disposition in that situation. The Aṣṭakavarga numbers represent the scale of the capability of a planet to impart its auspicious results. This capacity is also measured by deducting the inauspicious points from the auspicious points and dividing the remainder by 8. For example, if the benefic dots are 5 and the malefic dashes are 3, so $(5 - 3) = (2)$. Dividing this number by 8, we have $2 \div 8 = 1/4$ or, 25%. Under such a situation, the benefic potential of a planet is reduced to 25% of its capability.

Sarvāṣṭakavarga

An overall picture of all the *Aṣṭakavargas* in a natal chart is known as *Sarvāṣṭakavarga.* The presentation of all the benefic dots on one chart describing the total benefic dots in every house in the horoscope by itself is very useful. It helps in assessing the relative importance of different *Bhāvas* in a person's life.

The average number of benefic dots in a sign is $337 \div 12 = 28.0083$, or 28. Presence of 28 benefic dots in Sarvāṣṭakavarga shows that the aspect of life represented by that house will be very average without any special significance. When benefic dots in a house exceed 28, that house has some significance for the person. If the number is less than the average number of 28, the significance of that house Zis minimal, showing mediocre qualities. More than 30 benefic points in a house points to auspicious nature of that house. Dots between 25 and 30 points show mediocre or commonplace disposition of that house and with less than 25 points, the house is considered inauspicious. An enterprise begins during the transit of a planet in that house where the benefic dots exceed 30.

The distribution of benefic dots among the various houses in a natal chart reveals several other important features of the horoscope. It describes the relative significance of different houses. For example, if the number of benefic dots in the 11th house is more than those in the 10th house while the number of such points in the 12th house is less than those in the 11th house while the ascendant has sufficiently large number of auspicious points, that is more than those in 12th house, in that case the individual will certainly earn handsomely and will enjoy life comfortably with sufficient bank-balance. The number of dots in the 12th house has direct impact on one's expenditure, pleasures of bed, super-sensuous activities and relationship with denizens of non-physical plane. If the number of dots in the 12th house exceeds those in the 11th house, the individual may always experience shortage of money.

Sarvāṣṭakavarga also reveals the most important phase in one's life. The stream of events in the course of one's life do not flow smoothly. There are bumps on the road of life that teach important lessons. On the basis of Aṣṭakavarga calculations it is possible to apprehend the phases when the most important lessons of life can be learnt and the most significant events will be experienced.

It is a general rule of Hindu astrology that the number of planets divided in three groups comprising 1st to 4th, 5th to 8th, and 9th to 12th houses in a natal chart represent the three important phases in one's life namely, childhood period, adult age, and the period of old age. The distribution of benefic dots between these three divisions in the natal chart indicate the period when the individual will experience his most auspicious event of life. In the same way, the division which contains the least of these dots (implying the division which has the most of the dashes) will be full of deprivations and frustrations. A fairly uniform distribution of the dots and dashes over all the twelve houses indicate that the individual will have a smooth life. In most of the cases, even distribution of dots and dashes occur in such a way that the ego has to learn many lessons of every type and a person's life is not yet individualised or specialised in any specific way as yet. Generally, such individuals are either mediocres or very highly evolved.

Planetary transits over a house occupied by Saturn, Rāhu and Mars with a large number of benefic dots produce physical and psychological difficulties associated with the planet. One expects diseases, functional disorders, accidents and psychological depression during the transit of Jupiter over these houses. If the houses occupied by Jupiter, Mercury, Venus and ascendant have such clusters of benefic dots, the transits of benefic planets over them produce the most pleasant years in the individual's life. If the number of dots for benefic planets such as Venus, Mercury and Jupiter etc. taken separately, or added together show more than the average number of dots, one can assuredly predict that the person will have abundance of pleasant experiences.

The Aṣṭakavarga numbers represent the scale of the capability of a planet to impart its auspicious results. This capacity is also measured by deducting the inauspicious points from the auspicious points and dividing the remainder by 8. For example, if the benefic dots are 5 and the malefic dashes are 3, so (5 – 3) = (2). Dividing this number by 8, we have 2 ÷ 8 = 1/4 or, 25%. Under such a situation, the benefic potential of a planet is reduced to 25% of its capability.

Vedhas

Vedhas refer to obstruction points. They arise when a planet occupies a specific house in relation with the Moon-sign. It operates when a planet transits a favourable house in respect of the Moon-sign. Corresponding to every favourable location of a planet there is a house which must be vacant otherwise the auspicious effects of the transiting planet will not materialise. In some cases, certain planets are precluded from such obstructions, that is, even if a specific planet occupies the Vedha house it does not create the usual obstruction. There are two specific instances in this regard. To illustrate, Mars is considered auspicious while it is transiting the 3rd place from Moon but its benefic impact is nullified in case an obstructing planet, known as *Bādhaka* planet, is not present in its *Vedha* house which is 12th house from Moon. In the case of Moon, 1st house is an auspicious transit placement, that is, while it transits over the natal Moon, it produces auspicious results. It happens if no planet is present in the 5th house from it, as the 5th house is said to be its *Vedha* house. The exceptions in regard to Vedha relationships are made vis-a-vis Sun and Moon. It is laid down that Saturn does not produce with regard to Sun, and Mercury does not do so in relation with Moon. It implies that the presence of Saturn in a Vedha house and Mercury in respect of Moon in such a situation while they are inclined to produce auspicious results do not create obstructions.

There is also another exception to this rule. The Vedhas operate only in the absence of any nullifying planet present in a house which is said to counteract this obstructing effect. In other words, Vedhas operate if their power to obstruct is not nullified by a counteracting planet known as *Viparīta Vedha.* [Viparīta = opposite, Vedha = Obstruction]. For example, 3rd house in relation with Moon is laid down as auspicious transit for Saturn as long as no Vedha-producing planet is present in the 12th house from Moon. If any planet other than Saturn is present in the 3rd house from Moon, the Vedha effect of the planet occupying 12th house from it is held back. In essence, it implies that there will be no Vedha for a transiting planet if it is associated with any other planet. While considering the possible effects of transiting planets and various Vedhas operating over them, one has to keep in mind the two exceptions mentioned earlier between Sun and Saturn, and between Moon and Mercury. No explanations for these exceptions are given in astrological texts, but it is generally mentioned that Sun and Saturn, and Moon and Mercury have the father-son relationship. So they do not create any obstructions in between them. This mythic relationship is merely a mask over their highly esoteric inter-relationship. For everyday predictive purposes, this is considered a well accepted exception to the general rule.

The following table gives the auspicious results likely to follow by different transits of the planets. The first numerical indicates the house where the planet produces auspicious results while the figure in bracket against this numerical shows the house which must be free from any transiting planet to enable it to produce its impact.

Auspicious and Obstruction Points (Vedhas)

Sun	3 (9), 6(12), 10 (4), and 11 (5)
Moon	1(5), 3(9), 6 (12), 7 (2), 10(4), and 11 (8)
Mercury	2 (5), 4(3), 6(9), 8(1), 10 (7), and 11 (12)
Venus	1(8), 2(7), 3(1), 4 (10), 5(9), 8 (5), 11 (6) and 12 (3)
Mars	3 (12), 6 (9) and 11 (5)
Jupiter	2 (12), 5(4), 7 (3), 9 (10), NS 11 (8)
Saturn	3 (12), 6 (9), and 11 (5)

Rāhu and Ketu do not have Vedhas.

Vedhas apply also to inauspicious planets in the same manner.

The following table indicates the Vedha Points for their Inauspicious locations:

Sun	1 (1), 2 (2), 4 (3), 5 (6), 7 (7), 8 (8), 9 (10), 12 (11).
Moon	2 (1), 4(3), 5(6), 8 (7), 10 (10), 12 (11)
Mars	1 (1), 2(2), 4 (4), 5(4), 7 (6), 8(7), 9 (8), 10 (10), 12 (12)
Mercury	1 (2), 3 (4), 5 (7), 7 (6), 9 (8), 12 (11).
Jupiter	1 (1), 3 (2), 4 (5), 6 (6), 8 (8), 10 (9), 12 (12)
Venus	6 (12), 7 (2), 10 (4)
Saturn	1 (1), 2 (2), 4 (4), 5(4), 7 (6), 8(7), 9 (8), 10 (10), 12 (12) 136.

Vedhas are also sometimes considered in relation with Nakṣatra. While considering the transit effects of a planet in various Nakṣatras, it is often helpful to ascertain whether its results are nullified by any other planet in a different Nakṣatra. Nakṣatra-wise Vedhas are very selective. The following table shows the obstructing planets and their placements while a planet is transiting certain specific Nakṣatra. The numericals in the table shows the serial number of a planet from the Nakṣatra in which the planet under consideration is transiting. For example, if Sun is transiting Aśvinī, then 9 th Nakṣatra from it that is, Aśleṣā should not be occupied by Rāhu or Ketu to enable it to give its full results. In the same way if it (Sun) is transiting any Nakṣatra the 15 th Nakṣatra relative to it should also be free from the occupancy of any planet.

Planets	*Serial No. of Vedha Nakṣatra relative to the Nakṣatra being transited by the planet and the Planet causing Vedha to that Planet.*
Sun	9th Nakṣatra (Rāhu or Ketu), 15th Nakṣatra (Ketu)
Moon	7th Nakṣatra (Mars), 12th Nakṣatra (Sun)
Mars	4th Nakṣatra (Mercury), 12th Nakṣatra (Moon)
Mercury	5th Nakṣatra (Jupiter), 12th Nakṣatra (Moon)
Jupiter	6th Nakṣatra (Venus), 12th Nakṣatra (Rāhu)
Venus	8th Nakṣatra (Saturn), 18th Nakṣatra (Mercury)
Saturn	9th Nakṣatra (Sun), 12th Nakṣatra (Jupiter)
Rāhu/Ketu	9th Nakṣatra (Moon), 13th Nakṣatra (Mars)

Transit Effects

The planetary locations at the time of the birth show their possibilities for producing their results, while their realisation depend to a large measure on their transits. The capacity of a planet to manifest its effects is determined on the basis of *Aṣṭakavarga,* which shows its eight-fold strength. The results follow unless the planet is held up by *Vedhas* without being nullified by a planet producing *Viparīta Vedha.* In everyday life, all the planets continue producing their results at all times, but the effects of slow moving planets such as Saturn, Rāhu and Jupiter are very marked. Saturn during its 2 and 1/2 year of transit in a sign radically influences the individual's approach to life. This however is a gradual process. Only towards the end of its sojourn one perceiwes the important changes that have taken place in one's life. Jupiter during the course of first few months in a house at first acclimatise's itself before casting its protective influence. Among the other deep acting planets whose impact is invariably noticeable are Sun and Mars, which make their entry known immediately on their entrance in a house. Their action is sudden, unexpected and profound. Even Ketu acts in this way but its effects are mostly on the psychological makeup of the person. Moon and Mercury are not very profound in their impact. They change the general environment in which the individual functions. Their influence is like the soft Moonbeams, which are enjoyed as long as the planet rules the sky. Their impact is felt indirectly on feelings and emotions. Venus always tries to make the life of a person pleasant and enjoyable. It intensifies the sensitivity of the individual. Venus unfolds its benefic results after it has spent sometime in the house. The transit effects of five planets namely Saturn, Rāhu, Jupiter, Mars and Sun are the most important ones for predictive purposes.

Saturn

General: Saturn's sidereal period is 29.46 years, which gives it about 2 and 1/2 year in each sign. Its most inauspicious effects are expected when it transits the 1st, 2nd and the 12th houses from Moon. This period is approximately 7 and 1/2 year and is known as Saturn's *Sāḍe-Sātī* which is much dreaded because of the intense pain likely to be experienced. There may occur death of near relations, frustration in one's undertakings, deterioration in social status, loss of income, increase in expenditure and disturbing psychological isolation. This period repeats every 30 years or so. The first cycle is often intensely painful, the second leads to fruitless travels and the third has the potential of killing one of the parents. During *Sāḍe-Sātī,* Saturn may remove one of the major supports of the individual.

Saturn produces auspicious results during its sojourn in the 3rd, 6th and 11th houses from the Moon sign. During this period, the individual receives material gifts, increased income and a rise in social status. The pattern of the individual's lifestyle changes for the better. Impediments against his creativity are removed, long delayed rewards come through and there is material affluence all through. Other results of this transit are recovery of debts, opening of fresh sources of income, emergence of new alignments in one's life and greater yearning for material entanglements. These results are possible when there is no other planet except the Sun transiting the 12th house from Moon.

First House: Saturn during its transit of the First house restricts the individual in every way. The individual feels physically devitalised, suffers from serious illnesses and he may have to perform funeral rites to get a first hand experience of death. During this period, the individual is separated from his near and dear ones and his familiar and desired objects. "Depression, fatigue, penury and loss of enthusiasm characterise this period. The individual bereft of friends, feeling disappointment in life, suffering from ill health, and tension in professional career is a miserable person immersed in gloom and self-centeredness. Saturn's transit of the first house from Moon makes an individual experience humiliation, bad news, social and financial tension and denial of one's legitimate opportunities for growth and unfoldment as well as material prosperity.

Second House: Disturbs the family harmony, causes loss of property and fixed assets. Energy for creative activities gets depleted. Confusion occurs in the individual's thinking process. He experiences speech impediments and makes gloomy pronouncements. This period of Saturn's transit is not conducive for a stable family life. The person is always on move. He however expects some legacy, which he may receive but it will not make him happy and capable to enjoy it. For spiritual aspirants, this transit is very helpful. Such persons may develop perseverance, inner contemplation and heightened sensitivity.

Third House: A transit of auspicious results. During this period, the individual acquires material gifts with increased possibilities for social affluence. His trials and tribulations of the previous 7 and 1/2 year get over and he is rewarded for his perseverance. His life style changes for the better. Impediments are removed from his creative activities and long-delayed rewards are secured. Recovery of debts, fresh sources of income, new alignments in life and greater yearning for material entanglements, as mentioned earlier are the general results of Saturn's favourable transits during this period.

Fourth House: During this transit, the depressive whirlwind churns the emotional life of the person and his peace of mind and stability of relationships are disturbed. He is made psychologically unbalanced, his behaviour becomes uncoordinated and his official career turns out to be very frustrating. His married life turns sour. Those individuals whose mind is weak and have intense attachment with material objects, find themselves either on the psychiatrist's chair or in a lunatic asylum during this period.

Fifth House: Saturn in the fifth house from Moon stifles the urge to secure a position in the material realm, enjoy pleasures of life and thereby makes the individual frustrated, anti-social, morbid and introvert. The wealth of the individual declines during this period, his children feel upset, his career gets destabilised and his mind becomes unbalanced. His family members desert him. The psychological loneliness of the person becomes very oppressive. Saturn in this position however makes the individual prepared for spiritual awakening.

Sixth House: A powerful situation enabling the individual to show his prowess, conquer difficulties, resist disease carrying viruses, counteract degenerating tendencies and overcome devitalisation of life -force. During its 6th house transit, Saturn effectively blocks the adverse karmic effects of earlier lives, greatly accentuates the fructification of latent faculties and develops new talents. During this period the individual earns good income, augments his fixed assets and prospers socially. Discord in material life gets removed, cooperation from colleagues and relations becomes possible and self-imposed austerities become easy to bear. The individual may occupy a new residence, move to a better environment and attain a greater seat of power. These results are obstructed by the presence of a planet in the 9th house from Moon.

Seventh House: One of the most disturbing transits of Saturn. In case this house happens to be a movable sign of the zodiac, Saturn during its transit of it completely destroys the individual's peace of mind. The person will always be moving from one place to another without any respite and suffer from hunger and thirst. His wife will find living with him difficult. His business partners will consider him inflexible and non-cooperative. He himself becomes morbid, confused, and afflicted with inferiority feeling. He is likely to keep company of depraved persons and suffer from suicidal tendency. This is a period of rigorous testing for those who are treading the path of spiritual development. Once such an aspirant survives the ordeal, he will be eligible for approaching the portals of Divine Wisdom with possibilities for insight into the mysteries of life that lie ahead of him.

Eighth House: During this period of Saturn's transit the individual experiences gloom, loss of money and separation from near and dear ones. He feels as if life is going to dissolve and melt into nothingness. He faces public disapproval, family disturbances, loss in speculation and afflictions of children. With intense sorrow he feels as if passing through the evil of shadow. But the restrictions imposed upon him in various ways are aimed at teaching the person the lesson of patience and perseverance. The *yogis* look forward to this period in order to succeed in their attainments, the *siddhis,* so that they can achieve control over subtler forces of Nature and can discover their own latent faculties.

Ninth House: A period of great uncertainty. The individual loses all his moral support from the elders. He suffers from loss of money, encounters obstacles in his business activities and faces death of one of his elder relations. These events on the physical plane deeply affect his psychological make-up. Occasionally however, he receives physical and financial help at a time when he least expects them. But as soon as he begins to depend upon them, they melt away. During this period the person becomes deeply contemplative. His inner nature gradually changes. On the physical plane of existence he experiences loss of various kinds which make him feel that his worldly moorings are receding from him.This feeling of exasperation kindle spiritual understanding in him and universalisation of his personal psyche.

Tenth House: Saturn transiting the tenth house from the natal Moon makes the person pliable enough to receive the divine message. During this period, the ultimate destiny of the individual flashes to him. The comprehension of one's destiny, listening to one's inner voice and preparation for unification with the universal or cosmic consciousness may still be a distant dream but an humble beginning is likely to be made during this period. Materialism and spirituality cannot exist together. After crucifixion on the wooden (material) frame the spirit is released to soar high in the ethereal realm. The subtle process of delivering the human beings from their material thraldom is carried out continuously for a long time at different stages, before the final result is achieved. The process continues whether the person is aware of it or not. During this period, events happen very swiftly and the individual is caught unprepared. He is likely to be swept by the storm. He does things which he may not do consciously and knowingly. He experiences loss of honour. He is afflicted by acute physical illnesses. But he also begins to get premonitions from the other world. He begins to feel that a future awaits him beyond the veil of shadow. During this period,there may be disturbed life, fall from high status, estrangement with one 's wife and change in one 's existing environment and residence as well as in the place of work. All these occurrences are primarily preparatory ordeals in the impending changes in life.

Eleventh House: Saturn's transit through the 11th house from Moon produces respite from difficulties of life. The individual experiences happiness of all kinds, acquires wealth, achieves professional preference and receives extraordinary honours. Greater opportunities to shoulder social and professional responsibilities arise during this period. It is also favourable for courtship. The transit aims at leading the individual to the universal stream of consciousness and to wider benefic influences which sustain the universe. It is the most beneficent transit of Saturn which markedly gives a new turn to life provided no planet transits the 5th house from the Moon. Such experiences come to the individual to test his spiritual maturity and his preparedness to the next stage of his inner growth. His reactions to these situations determine the next course of his spiritual development. The happy experiences met during this period will enable the individual to march towards the universal stream of consciousness and the influences, which sustain the universe. During this period there is concretisation of one's philosophy and one's everyday life. There is greater emphasis on practicability of a goal rather than on imagination and fantasy. Efforts primarily get goal oriented and the individual very much succeeds in achieving the same.

Twelfth House: Saturn in the 12th house produces physical suffering and material loss. During the period of this transit, the individual may be robbed of his money. His wife and children may suffer from serious diseases. There may be much mental anguish. At this stage God's protective shield is temporarily withdrawn to enable the individual's unconscious and suppressed proclivities to have freeplay. He gets no more supervised and protected by his guardian angel, or his *alter ego.* Unless the individual is spiritually advanced, there can be moral lapses during this period. It brings remorse to the person. The possibility of sorrow arises also from the loss of wealth and destruction of property, deterioration of health, occurrences of theft and such other frustrating experiences. In case the spiritual nature of the person has already developed, the period may be an occasion of individual's spiritual progress. The inner most content of one's psyche begins to establish control over the outer man, which radically transforms the nature of the person during this period.

Rāhu

Rāhu traverses the entire zodiacal cycle in about 18 years and 6 months, always moving retrograde, which gives it about 1 and 1/2 year in each house. It produces certain enduring results during its transit through different houses. It exposes results of one's past karmic forces and dissolves them to make the individual free to proceed speedily on one's evolutionary path. Rahu's auspicious results are experienced in the 3rd, 6th and the 11th houses from Moon, but there are no *vedhas* for Rāhu.

First House: While transiting the 1st house, Rāhu produces great distress to the person. He feels sad, gloomy, unable to generate happiness. He remains greatly concerned with his own safety and security. He is burdened with illusory and self-created responsibilities. He behaves in illogical, anti-social and self-centered manner. His social relationship gets strained and there are chances of separation and breakdown of the partnership in married life.

Second House: The shadow of darkness is cast on one's speech, family affairs, financial earnings and on the desire of the person to go out and mix with others when Rāhu transits 2nd house from Moon. Loss of wealth, strained family life, speech defects and absence of creative urge including repugnance of procreative activities are indications of the period. If the individual is still on the path of materialisation, some kind of depravity will surface during this period. On the other hand, if he is already spiritually inclined, he will be increasingly involved with excessive zeal in social and family affairs.

Third House: Rāhu's 3rd house transit presents before the individual situations in which he will have to display exemplary courage, initiative and perseverance. The mind gets positively energised and special psychological qualities are aroused which become the permanent nature of the personality. During this period the individual may attain success over his adversaries, success in financial ventures and in setting up of profitable enterprises. He attains unusual inspiration from certain unknown and unexpected sources. The individual succeeds in all his ventures during this transit which imparts great self-confidence.

Fourth House: The heart is churned when Rāhu transits the 4th house. The individual suffers intense emotional pain. The mental anguish and painful experiences make him dizzy, unstable, lose his moorings and cut him from the source that sustains him. These experiences are intensely personal. No one can succeed in sharing them. Everyone in his company recognises that he is passing through a period of intense unhappiness. During this period, the individual should guard against his suicidal tendency and heart ailment, both physically and metaphorically.

Fifth House: Rāhu during the course of its transit of the 5th house from Moon, damages the family life of the person. His children fall sick and there is excessive worry on this account. His income shrinks. His intelligence gets blunted. He is denied the right reward of his educational activities, intellectual efforts and creative undertakings. He is ignored, superseded and rejected on all sides. Such humiliating experiences destroy the very sense of I-ness or ego. Weak individuals under these conditions begin to develop many kinds of psychological problems. They do not share their problems with others thereby blocking assistance that would have come to him.

Sixth House: An extraordinary position for Rāhu to bestow good luck on the individual. In the 6th house from Moon, Rāhu harnesses latent qualities of the individual and opens out new avenues of self-expression. Having established a powerful link with reservoir of natural power which the conscious mind is not ordinarily able to tap, the individual becomes exceptionally fit to achieve unusual bits. During this period, the person attains psychological maturity and immense personal satisfaction. He enjoys a sense of fulfilment and experiences command over tremendous power.

Seventh House: A period of intense pain and frustration. During this period many kinds of difficulties arise, some of which may be beyond any relief. Overbearing attitude of a husband drives his wife to dithers and her mentality becomes depraved. Married relationship breaks down. The individual finds that his business partners are also very trying. During this period, the individual gradually becomes isolated and cut-off from his society and feels intensely lonely.

Eighth House: A period propitious for psychic development. Depending upon the strength and disposition of Moon, this transit of Rāhu in the 8th house from Moon, brings to surface many unexpected results. It leads to psychic vision, interest in occultism and develops healing touch. If the individual is not morally developed, the influx of such superphysical energy leads him to sexual perversion, psychological unbalance, emotional disturbances and to every kind of depravity, debauchery, drug addiction and drug trafficking.

Ninth House: A powerful influence making an individual exceptionally straight-forward and morally brave. During the transit of Rāhu in the 8th house from Moon, the individual gets his ideas well articulated, values in life well defined and personally he becomes willing to sacrifice himself for his ideals. His moral philosophy gets much ahead of his time. His conception of Ultimate Reality becomes highly abstract and difficult to grasp but it provides him much enthusiasm to move towards spirituality despite much difficulties entailed in adhering to this ideal. He is determined to mould his life in the ideal pattern that he professes for others. When any planet like Saturn or a sensual planet like Venus afflicts Ketu, his idealism gets tarnished and he deviates from the path of righteousness.

Tenth House: A period of intense psychological distress. The transit of Rāhu in the 10th house from Moon is accompanied by Ketu in the 4th from it. As a result of the combined effect of Rāhu and Ketu together during this period of this transit of Rāhu, the person becomes very impractical with regard to his career. A sense of pride, a feeling of superiority and an urge to be right without the slightest touch of corruptibility weakens his relations with his superiors. He develops strong differences of opinion with them which sometimes results in his suspension or disciplinary actions are initiated against him. The person does not repent whatever is his external suffering. He feels remorse over the whole incident and prefers it the same not to happen again. But once the action is done and its consequences are before him, he does not express any apology for it. Whatever is the justification for the event, this position of Rāhu produces much psychological strain.

Eleventh House: Rāhu in the 11th house from Moon produces the most beneficial results. Those who are materially oriented as well as trying to acquire religious merit gain while Rāhu transits here. Rāhu creates new channels of income, secures gainful social relationships and forges links with influential persons. There is also a possibility of establishing liaison with persons of the opposite sex who may help him or her reach higher echelons of the society. This period may bring windfalls to smugglers, black marketeers and persons engaged in shady deals or in secret services. For those who are traversing the spiritual path, there may be sharpening of psychic perception and repugnance of material attainments. During this period, there may be an intense urge for perfection and realisation of enduring values.

Twelfth House: In this transit of Rāhu in the 12th house from Moon, Ketu transits 6th from it. During this period, there is preparation for the next phase of inner development. In concrete terms it implies that the individual is washed of all his material moorings. In actual everyday life, it suggests serious hardships of different kinds. It creates such a situation that the individual has no pleasure of bed, no happiness of affluent living and no craving for self-glorification. Such a person to be happy and contented can only be an ascetic. A person in this frame of mind to a common man may appear as unpractical, schizophrenic and frustrated. But this attitude of the individual is not necessarily the result of his disappointments. What happens is that the veil of materiality surrounding him is completely sent under the impact of this transit and the inner man now comprehends the Ultimate or the Basic Reality underlying existence. This comprehension may not be absolute at this stage, but a small beginning.

Jupiter

General: Jupiter takes 11.86 years to complete its journey around the zodiac which gives it about a year in each sign. It produces beneficial effects in the 2nd, 5th, 7th, 9th and the 11th houses from Moon. Basically, the Jovian impulse is protective. During its transit through any houses it fructifies the related impact if the house is not directly connected with the house in the natal chart. Jupiter imparts auspicious, ethical and purifying effects. It spreads its beneficence in order to accelerate results relating to the house which for some reason have been withheld or delayed.

First House: Traversing the sign occupied by Moon, Jupiter makes an individual leave his well established residence and go to distant places. He incurs heavy expenditure and becomes malicious towards others. He dreads the change, becomes apprehensive of the future and receives dishonour from his superiors. Trouble develops in his profession and he begins to suffer intense pain and sorrow. Jupiter's occupancy in the Moon-sign destroys the roots of fleeting attachments and relationships without apparently showing its destructive role. Jupiter disturbs the person's existing environment. Seeming adverse consequences of the Jovian transit enable the individual to function efficiently to receive the divine downpour of benefic influences.

Second House: During its transit of 2nd house, Jupiter helps the person to relax and enjoy the natural conveniences of life. He acquires more money, receives social recognition and popularity. Adversaries vanish and the company of pleasant persons becomes available. During this Jovian influence, one may expect abundant inflow of money and wealth, greater renown and professional achievements. This period is highly propitious for speculative gains. However there may be occasional illnesses and a few sorrowful experiences in order the remind the individual of his spiritual responsibilites. During its 2nd house transit, Jupiter arouses compassion and a charitable disposition. It makes the individual's words very inspiring. These effects are however, obstructed by the presence of any planet in the 12th house from the Moon.

Third House: The urge to grow, move forward in the world and engage oneself in philanthropic activities characterise the transit of Jupiter in the 3rd house from Moon. But the individual experiences loss of position, opposition to his helpful ideas, separation from his wife and near relations, non-cooperation from his business partners and also spell of psychological exhaustion, shift from one's established place of residence and changes in affection also occur during this period

Fourth House: The transit of Jupiter in the 4th house from Moon is a period of turmoil specially in one's emotional and home life. The emotional life of the person is signified by divine urge for enlightenment, his heart yearns for spiritual expansion but he receives material affluence and abundance of love and affection from others. The conflict between the inner craving and the outer achievements produces a feeling of indifference and disenchantment with worldly affluence. The person feels resigned and takes no delight in anything around him.

Fifth House: The 5th house transit of Jupiter makes the creativity of the person align with his ultimate destiny. The new alignment of psycho—mental creativity in the most fruitful direction provides experiences at different levels of one's existence which gives great satisfaction, joy and happiness, and a feeling of psychological fulfilment. Apart from receiving increased income, unexpected honour and all round prosperity, the individual during the 5th house transit of Jupiter experiences marked expansion in his personality. Invariably for common individuals this period is associated with a child birth. For intellectuals it is associated with recognition of their mental prowess evident from the publication of a book, scholarly presentation of papers or learned discourses at important conferences. During the transit of Jupiter in the 5th house from Moon, the individual experiences an upsurge of mental creativity, which produces in him a sense of elevation. These Jovian influences are hampered only by the presence of a planet in the 4th position from Moon.

Sixth House: The transit of Jupiter in the 6th house from Moon produces turmoil. The inner-man wishes to control the finer forces of Nature, to devote itself to arduous preparations of thought control and emotional purification but the external conditions produce impediments, temptations and physical inabilities. Increased enmity, unmerited accusations, unusual impediments and hospitalisation with serious illnesses may occur during this period. In some cases, increased income takes place to detract him from his spiritual goal. When an individual desparately and genuinely strives for spiritual growth, Jupiter in the 6th house often produces invincible temptations. The realisation of one's failure to recognise and inability to overcome the same often fills the individual with intense regret.

Such psychological conflict and contradictory situations bring tremendous upheaval in the person, especially in his emotional life.

Seventh House: The 7th house transit of Jupiter is often described in very poetic terms. During this transit Jupiter releases its spiritualising impulses and operates as the spring wind blowing over vegetation, producing new bids, flowers and foliage for the enjoyment of individuals and taking them towards the Supreme Power. In this position Jupiter produces the most pleasant experiences of life almost everything the person can aspire to be attained. The individual enjoys pleasure of t he bed, company, abundant wealth, good meals, flowers and conveyance. The power of speech and the intelligence of the person become extensively recognised. The effects are obstructed by the presence of a planet in the 3rd house from Moon.

Eighth House: During the transit of Jupiter in the 8th house from Moon, its beneficence operates in a mysterious manner. It acts very favourably for those who are treading the path of spiritual development. Those interested in material gifts and involved in everyday mundane existence find that this transit produces much adverse results. Persons attracted towards *yoga,* occultism, *tantras* (methods of redress of personal problems by harnessing Nature's finer forces for the purpose) and other *siddhis* (perfection) can hope for favourable results during this transit. The latter category of individuals who are involved in materialistic pursuits experience unexpected development during this period. A common-man under this transit is found undertaking fruitless journey. He is unlucky in other ways also. He has chances of imprisonment, seclusion from others and sufferance from long-drawn illness. He experiences loss of money. Jupiter's transit of the 8th house from Moon produces in the individual mental unsteadiness, disruption in his activities and strained personal relationships.

Ninth House: The auspicious effects of the 9th house transit of Jupiter are proverbial. Whether the individual is attracted towards material conveniences or is inspired by spiritual ideas, Jupiter provides sustenance and energy for their fulfilment. During this period, the person succeeds in enjoying all prosperity. He also receives Divine Grace. Under this situation the auspicious tendencies inculcated during past lives, called *pūrva-janma-saṁskāras,* get energised and the individual behaves in a gracious manner. He receives very favourable responses from others. He is showered with honour and wealth. Auspicious celebrations take place in the family.

There can be an addition to the family and occasions of festive celebrations, and happy anniversaries in it. The social status of the individual is also raised. Performance of religious rituals, successful completion of purificatory practices and undertaking of pilgrimages to holy shrines or visits to inspiring places or persons are expected during this period. The individual is recognised for the maturity of his thoughts and helpful counselling. The presence of a planet in the 10th house from Moon produces vedha for these transit effects.

Eleventh House: Jupiter bestows much happiness when it transits the eleventh house. The individual receives many gifts and his popularity among his business colleagues increases. During the period he gains in income, improves his official status, receives cooperation from his friends and gains from speculative ventures. Even in his personal life there is much happiness. His married life becomes joyous, family life becomes harmonious and he undertakes pleasant and successful journeys. In the 11th house from Moon, Jupiter produces contentment, happiness and possibly birth of a child in the family.

Twelfth House: Dissolution of material attainments and a feeling of disenchantment characterize the influence of Jupiter's transit through the 12th house from Moon. During this period, the individual experiences a sense of desolation. He is not able to enjoy the pleasures of life as he apprehends their disappearance very quickly. He is confronted with physical illnesses, financial indigence, failure in material pursuits, loss of property and increase of adversary. His residential accomodation gets destabilised. He makes unnecessary movements. He is attracted to increased sexual urge and towards clandestine liaisons. In the 12th house from Moon, Jupiter produces loss of property, which leads to grief and insecurity to the person.

Mars

General: Mars takes a little more than two months to traverse a sign as its sidereal period is only 687 days. This planet is full of vitality. It is always eager to express itself and produce results particularly on the physical plane. Martian impact on the emotional and mental well being of an individual is often indirect. The primary effect of Mars is externalization of latent faculties. Under this impact the seeds break their hard crust, sprouts extend into foliage, and plants begin to bear fruits. Mars is energy on the move. It takes delight in exposing difficulties, grappling and overcoming them. During Martian transits through various signs, these features of the planet are accentuated, keeping in view the special nature of the sign it traverses.

First House: During the course of its transit of the Moon-sign, Mars energises the individual so much that he finds difficulties in controlling and harnessing the impulses in fruitful channels. Uncontrolled, the Martian influx is devastating and upsetting to the person. There arises an excessive heat in his system. He may meet with accidents. There may be blood loss and he is unable to sustain his mental composure. This transit for an average person, leads to emotional instability resulting in frequent outbursts, impulsiveness, fidgetiness and loss of control over his emotional expressions. Even his relationship with his wife, during this period, suffers from hypertension and such other blood diseases.

Second House: Mars in the second house from Moon causes fear, impolite speech and loss of wealth. His family relationships get upset. Misunderstanding with his brothers gets intensified. His children suffer from loss of blood. His father gets afflicted with hypertension. He himself may have to undergo surgical operation. He is often rendered unable to take right decisions. The chances of his association with criminals increase. He may even be persecuted. He may suffer from theft of his properties and injuries from fire. Properly harnessed the energy flowing through Mars can make the individual skilled artist during this period of transit. He may be a painter much interested in painting extremely vibrant fire of hell or he can compose stirring ballads.

Third House: Mars has a natural affinity with the 3rd house, the house of courage, prowess and valour. Placed 3rd from the Ascendant or Moon, its natural disposition towards leadership, physical activity, the spirit of exploration and self reliance gets expressed under this placement. Mars leads to investigative studies, personal initiative, courage to face difficulties and heightened nervous tension. It imparts valour to the individual with enormous amount of challenging and enterprising strength, enabling him to successfully complete any task howsoever difficult it may be. Whether the individual receives money, clothes, real estate, property or honour during this period or not, is not as important as the courage and strength Mars gives to overcome adversaries and difficulties. Any planet in the 12th house from Moon will greatly reduce these transit effects.

Fourth House: Mars in the 4th house from Moon disturbs the mental and emotional balance of the individual. Excessive pride ruins many of his bright chances for recognition of merit. He generally gets beset with many enemies during this period. His hot-headedness strains his relationship with his wife as well. He suffers physically also. There can be stomach ailment, loss of blood, hypertension and fever. He displeases his superiors. There is loss of property.

Fifth House: The destructive nature of Mars becomes evident during its transit of the 5th house from Moon. During this period, the uncontrolled influx of Martian vitality completely inundates the individual's intelligence and creativity, stimulates his sexual appetite and arouses uncoordinated impulsive activities, which damages him in many ways. He is unable to control, harness and concretise the enormous vitalising energy. The period is adverse even for pregnant mothers. They become susceptible to miscarriages. Properly harnessed and its energy effectively directed it is possible to appropriately produce much valuable literary work or attain laurels in sports competitions during this period. If the Martian flow is blocked, it causes serious repercussions on the individual. With favourable planetary configurations with much creative potential, the Martian transit in the 5th house from Moon can provide tremendous opportunities and energy for producing extraordinary results.

Sixth House: Mars in the 6th house arouses the capacity to dive deeply within one's psyche or in difficult physical situations to retrieve and activate hidden forces. The 6th house in the natal chart is very mysterious, containing within it the past karmic forces, which have not yet been worked out. While traversing the 6th house from Moon, Mars acquires special force to severely counteract those impediments which otherwise may have been difficult for the individual to surmount. Such a situation however assumes that there will be plenty of strife and problems in life during this period though the end results of the Martian impulse will be in the favour of the individual. Towards the conclusion of the period there will be withdrawal of adversaries and success for the individual. One can also expect that this period will witness eruption of infectious diseases such as boils, pox as well as inconveniences and difficulties in business enterprises, litigation over property matters and other such disputes. The internal changes produced by this transit will prepare the spiritually oriented in undergoing severe austerities towards inner unfoldment. Such individuals may get valuable opportunities of coming in contact with great seers and saints. They may become psychologically attuned to receive messages from the subtler realms of Nature. But in the case of any other planet traversing the 9th house from Moon, there will be obstruction to this Martian transit.

Seventh House: Mars in the 7th house from Moon disturbs the mind of the person and makes his behaviour ill-adjusted. Even his friends fall away from him. Differences arise with business partners. Women humiliate him and his relationship with his wife gets worse. The physical health of the person deteriorates. He gets stomach ailment and eye diseases. He feels restless, experiences mental storm and is afflicted by neurosis and other psychological illnesses. It is period of material loss and physical devitalisation.

Eighth House: Mars in the 8th house produces fever, anemia and loss of wealth and stigma to his reputation. During this period many unexpected events occur from some secret reservoir which everyone tends to forget. In the 8th house from Moon, Mars produces many situations, which are not necessarily adverse. Unexpected illnesses, sudden accidents causing much loss of blood and money are likely to take place. But the individual during this period has also the possibilities of gain in speculative activities, windfall profits, unexpected glorification and kudos for his unusual bravery and courage. During this period many persons get involved in clandestine liaison. They form secret associations with drug addicts and smugglers. They may get caught doing surreptitious deals and are put behind the bars. During this period one can even meet with accident where much blood is lost or else there may be a surgical operation leading to much loss of blood. The transition to a materialist can lead to estrangement with friends and relations, loss of money, increased amount of tiresome work, besides personal sickness and mental depravity. Those on the path of spiritual unfoldment, may find this transit providing them unique opportunities for undergoing severe penance and voluntarily accepting denials of physical conveniences in order to wrest from Nature its secrets.

Ninth House: During the transit of Mars in the 9th house from Moon, persons receive mental jolt, a kind of psychic trauma. They feel unsettled. These conditions may produce psychosomatic diseases in a person. During this period the individual may feel that his past is receding from him, his friends and relations getting indifferent towards him and he is receiving setbacks even in his profession. There is much loss of his vital fluid that affects his bodily functions and psychological reactions. He moves from one place to another aimlessly and fruitlessly. Those who are very strong inwardly, find this period highly propitious for observing their religious discipline very meticulously. The period may lead the person to enormous expansion in his consciousness. It can lead such persons to establish conscious link with their own higher self as well as with those great seers and saints who constantly guide the occult progress of the humanity.

Tenth House: The transit of Mars in the 10th house from Moon produces tremendous mental agitation and inner dissatisfaction. The restless spirit within the person feels frustrated because he realises that there is enormous latent energy, which remains non-operational. His inner spirit struggling to externalise itself does not find suitable conditions for its expression. The conflict between the inner and the outer self often leads to nervous breakdown. The person gets constantly on move. He changes his job, changes the place of his residence and changes his business partners as well. Those having favourable planetary configuration assuring them appropriate conditions for the expression of their inner strength, energy and ideals, succeed well in achieving their goals during this period. It is a period of vigorous activity for them, both professionally and in their personal life. Familywise, the period proves very auspicious producing elevation in social status. His children do well in life. During this period, under such conditions, one can confidently expect professional preferment, extension of friend's circle and expansion in the level of popularity.

Eleventh House: In its 11th house transit, Mars acquires strength to produce material affluence and to bestow valuable gifts on the individual. From this position the planet sufficiently energises the socialness of the person, making him and his speeches socially popular and agreeable, relationships friendly, courteous and warm. The person becomes centrifugal or outward-turned in attitude and people begin to like him. Financial gain, freedom from sickness, addition to landed property, and expansion of one's social circle also happen during this period. Through achieving success in one's venture and acquiring much wealth and prosperity, the individual begins to feel very happy. Gain in respectability, promotion in career and enhancement in one's status are important features of this transit. The good influence of the individual increases unexpectedly and suddenly in many directions. There is also revival of old interests in life and recovery of lost property. But the transit of another planet in the 5th position from Moon nullifies the good effects of this transit.

Twelfth House: During the transit of Mars in the 12th house from Moon, tension is built up in the individual and he begins to feel frustrated in life. He feels physically exhausted, psychologically drained out and his mind gets into a feeling without any hope. He feels greatly upset during this period. It is so unsettling that he becomes unable to maintain any social adjustment. His sexual life becomes unpredictable as he is likely to get involved in extra-marital relationships. He experiences intense infatuation towards undesirable women through secret liaison. There may be explosion in his family life with possibility of separation from his wife. He gets isolated from his family members and from his social circle. He may face danger to his life during this period. The individual may meet some elderly person during this period who can save him from his turmoil and despair provided he reposes wholehearted trust in him during this period. All impulsive action requires to be eschewed if the individual seeks to overcome his difficulties.

Sun

General: The Sun covers the entire zodiacal belt in 365.25 days which gives it a month for traversing each sign. Its auspicious transit from the Moon sign are through the 3rd, 6th, 10th and the 11th houses. Sun irradiates all the signs it occupies whether auspicious or adverse. Sun does not glamorise but brings the inner glow of the inner spirit to the outer visage of the person. It destroys impediments to its radiation process.

Sun is a deep acting planet. It irradiates the sign it occupies and thereby vivifies the characteristics represented by the sign. The glow of the Sun is so radiant that any impediment obstructing its path gets destroyed. As most of the houses in a natal chart are unable to absorb the solar effulgence fruitfully, the solar transit is considered auspicious in only a few. As it is a deep-acting planet, its impact even during a month's transit is substantial. Its frequency and intensity make the transit very significant. Sun affects the indwelling spirit and makes it more vibrant on the physical plane. It influences the individual to express his individuality in various ways and helps different aspects of life to glow with his unique radiance. The spark however proves devastating during its transit in those houses which are discordant with its basic nature. That is why it is often felt that some of the houses which ordinarily bestow material gifts do not have favourable impact of the solar transit while some of those houses such as the 3rd and the 6th ordinarily related with adverse aspects respond well with solar transit.

First House: The Sun's transit through the 1st house from Moon provides to the individual enormous vitality. It arouses noble thoughts and aspirations in him. The solar radiance is averse to everything material. During the course of this transit Sun is not very helpful even for marital relationship. It also arouses disenchantment with material prosperity, physical pleasures, sexual relationship and mental servitude. The person gets oriented towards spirituality gradually and begins to consider himself supreme in every way. It intensifies egotism in ordinary individuals. During this period, the person suffers from fatigue and loss of wealth. He becomes psychologically irritable especially on account of financial shortages while his aspirations run very high. He often falls sick. He has also to undertake many wearisome journeys.

Second House: The transit of Sun through 2nd house from Moon makes the individual attracted towards his family members, family affairs and their prosperity. But the transit also produces loss of wealth, deceit at the hands of relations and friends and fruitless mental worries. During this period, the individual gets duped, loses wealth and becomes unhappy. In the process however his understanding of the life-process gets clearer and actions determined accordingly. A common man during this transit often becomes obstinate, tenacious and obdurate.

Third House: In the 3rd house from the natal Moon, the Sun leads to improvement in health, removal of obstacles and favours from superiors. During this transit, the individual acquires a new position in life. There is advent of money, experience of happiness and freedom from the feeling of inferiority. The frequency of solar transits in one 's life makes them more supportive of long-term results rather than merely producing transient results of their own. Under the solar transit of the 3rd house, if some decisions concerning service matters, litigation or disputes have been delayed and are overdue, they are likely to get decided in favour of the individual. The most significant result of the transit is to make the individual very confident, self reliant and full of optimism. These results occur when there is no planet transiting the 9th house from Moon.

Fourth House: The fourth house transit of Sun affects the emotional life of a person. His attachment with wealth and property, sexual enjoyment, affectionate personal relationships, and to holidaying get lessened. The individual is restrained from deriving happiness from such activities and relationships. He gets into a feeling of helplessness. Changes in environment, domestic unhappiness, beginning of mental agitation, and occasional flashes of abiding truths are some of the other results of this transit.

Fifth House: The Sun in the 5th house from Moon does not cause the birth of a child during this period. The individual takes delight in abstract thinking under its impact, and he tries to expound such a philosophy. Often for a common man the experience of servitude during this period produces excruciating pain and personal sorrow. The dangers of stomach pain, blood impurities and heart disorder can also not be ruled out.

Sixth House: Like Mars, the Sun is also powerful in the 6th house from Moon. This transit activates the spirit of adventure, specially in the realm of new ideas, exploration in the secrets of nature, courageous ventures in arduous undertakings and dauntless courage for assuming Herculean responsibilities which others can mostly be bound and reluctant to carry out. Solar radiance in the 6th house from Moon dispels sorrow, pessimism. Victory over enemies, successful termination of litigation, and removal of restrictive conditions are the usual features of the transit. The precise nature of the transit results will depend upon the specific task at hand. In all such cases the solar transit provides the necessary motive force for accomplishment of one's goal. The impact of the transit is more in the availability of necessary motive force and energy rather than in the content of the task at hand. The 6th house solar transit releases enormous energy for the individual. But the presence of a planet in the 12th house from Moon nullifies the intensity of the solar transit effect.

Seventh house: The Sun in the 7th house from Moon produces expansion of the ego. It complicates the marital as well as social relationships of the individual. He becomes self-opinionated and unyielding. Psychological pain is inevitable during this period. It is often accompanied by setback in health either of the person himself or of his family members. Business transactions also do not move smoothly. Other effects of the transit are fruitless travels, fatigue and mental ennui. Troubles connected with anal region and generative organs are not ruled out during this transit.

Eighth House: The transit of Sun in the 8th house from Moon is not an unmitigated evil. During this period, hidden recesses of the mind get activated. The sub-conscious becomes much vitalised. Unknown forces begin to pressurise the person to act in a special manner. Other persons do not very well comprehend and appreciate such behavioural expressions. Brusqueness brings disharmony in the person's relationships. But the individual also gets unexpected windfall of money and chances of meeting enlightened soul. He also receives occasional flashes of the Reality. These results are however, very rare and possible only when supported by natal planetary configurations. Generally speaking, only such results as accidents, physical illness, difficulties in personal adjustments, quarrels with friends, royal displeasure, high blood pressure and separation from near and dear ones mark the period.

Ninth House: The transit of Sun in the 9th house from Moon produces a feeling of inferiority. The person at the same time feels self-righteous and presumes himself as the holiest of the holies. The reaction of other persons is often hostile to him. Even when the person is right in his approach, others oppose him. During this period the individual feels tortured and humiliated. He becomes frustrated and disappointed. There may also be danger to his life. He feels alienated from his associates and isolated from his social circle. Physically, he feels let down and run down. However, for those on the path of occult preparations, the period is significant for expansion of spiritual consciousness.

Tenth House: During the 10th house transit, the Sun produces sufficient strength and understanding for the discharge of one's terrestrial responsibilities. During this period, the inner man reminds and inspires the personality towards its ultimate destiny. If the individual is not in tune with his mission of life, there can then be a sense of mortification, urging the individual to orient the self towards the pursuit of ultimate objective. For those having life's mission and profession well synchronised this period usually heralds success, royal favour, divine direction and generosity for one's friends and relations. There may be increased sense of pride and greater efficiency in work. The individual can realistically expect agility in action, sharpness in intellect, leadership in profession and successful completion of difficult undertakings. The period is marked by honour, enthusiasm, pride and recognition of merit, accrual of wealth and other professional rewards. *Vedhas* for this transit arise from the presence of a transiting planet (except Saturn) in the 4th house from the natal Moon.

Eleventh House: A new status, increased income, freedom from illness and disease and a sense of involvement in one's undertakings of importance are some of the results of solar transits through the 11th house from Moon. During this period the individual secures recognition from the highest authority. The individual may not expect fears from anyone, works efficiently, interacts correctly and pays proper respect to others. The people in general speak well of him. Those preparing themselves for higher life, may come in contact with their mentor and guide during this period. They are likely to receive downpour of beneficient impulses from higher sources which can lead them to rapid progress towards their self-unfoldment. This is a very significant solar transit because it leads to the accomplishment of one's goals in life, completion of arduous responsibilities, attainment of new positions and much honour. This is a period of all round self fulfilment. The difficulties in the fructification of these results occur only when Vedha is present due to the presence of a planet other than Saturn in the 5th position from the natal Moon.

Twelfth House: When the Sun transits through the 12th house from Moon, all attractions towards material attainments come to a close. During this period, the consciousness of a person gets linked with the realm of super-physical reality. Dreams, clairvoyance, philosophical ramblings, meditational trances and deep involvement in speculative philosophy are some of the results of this transit. If suitable preparations have already been made earlier and the planetary configurations support, the period can be fruitfully utilised for developing psychic faculties. But for a common man the transit of Sun through the 12th house from Moon is extremely frustrating. A sense of disappointment dawns on him and he feels a sense of irreparable loss of everything -status, wealth, honour, and the sense of direction in life seems gone. The duration of Sun's transit through a zodiac is very short. So these conditions change very quickly and the individual recovers from such a state of psychological whirlpool and begins to prepare himself for challenges of the succeeding transit.

Venus

The sidereal period for Venus is 224.7 days. But it takes about 15 months to complete one round of the zodiac. The average period of transit in a sign takes about three weeks. Its auspicious transits are 1st, 2nd, 3rd, 4th, 5th, 8th, 9th, 11th and 12th houses from Moon. The auspicious impact of the planet in these houses however gets nullified if there is any planet in the 1st, 3rd, 5th, 6th, 7th, 8th, 9th, 10th and 11th houses from Moon respectively. Venus is greatly related with sensual enjoyment, which gets accentuated during its favourable transits. It is a planet of sensitivity and in every house through which it transits this quality of the planet is emphasized. It produces sensitivity, emotional entanglements, luxurious life and sociability in the individual.

First House: The transit of Venus in the 1st house from Moon provides all kinds of sensuous pleasures. There is transient flash of luxurious living and heightened feeling of happiness during the three weeks that the planet stays in this house. The individual feels happy with his ability to enjoy and thinks that the sense gratification is a reward of his past meritorious deeds. During this period, the mind is oriented towards physical enjoyment. He is attracted towards sex gratification. He is greatly vulnerable to seductions of the senses.

Second House: Venus in the 2nd house from Moon makes a person fond of his family members. He spends much of his time with them. During this period, he clothes himself with new clothes, eats delicious food and spends time in the company of his near and dear ones. He speaks pleasing and friendly language. His mind becomes fertile, physical health sound and disposition very affectionate. There is inflow of money and the individual receives many enjoyable social invitations.

Third House: In the 3rd house from Moon Venus produces good relationship with one's colleagues and brothers. The individual during this transit receives kudos and goodwill gestures from his superiors and the state. Women become friendly with him. Better employment opportunities are offered to him but these are the general results of the 3rd house transit of Venus. While providing a sensuous melieu around the individual, Venus also produces different sorts of difficulties for the person during this transit. Unless the planet is propitiously placed in strength in the natal chart, this transit often leads to loss of wealth, increase of enemies and fruitless wanderings.

Fourth House: Venus in the 4th house makes the individual very ease loving. He has pleasures of a comfortable house, pleasant surrounding, luxurious vehicles, and enjoyable company. He gets affection of his mother and love from his wife. The conditions produced by Venus during this period resemble very much the atmosphere that prevails during the period of one's pleasant holidays. The individual during this period also acquires wisdom and participates in learned discussions and seminars.

Fifth House: A period of artistic creativity exists when Venus transits through the 5th house from Moon. During this period the individual reads and enjoys poetry, goes to movies and dances, acts in dramas and spends maximum time with his children and family members. He has a large number of retinue to look after his comforts. He gets sweets and delicious food to eat. He acquires wealth and fulfils his desired objectives. He often receives unusual gifts from his friends.

Sixth House: In 6th house from Moon, Venus produces mental worry, scandal and threat of persecution for embezzlement of money or misdemeanour. He falls sick and may even suffer from venereal infection. It is one of those transits when Venus is least capable of producing auspicious results.

Seventh House: During the 7th house transit from Moon, Venus makes the mind confused. The individual thinks of satisfying his sensuous cravings. He devotes much time scheming for procuring the objects of his carnal passion. He succeeds in seducing young damsels but such situations often bring disrepute and dishonour to him. Drug addiction and venereal diseases are likely to afflict him during this period. He is also liable to be in the company of those persons who are not reputed for their ideals.

Eighth House: During the 8th house transit of Venus, the conditions of life change significantly. The individual does not enjoy his social life, he prefers seclusion, secrecy and isolated living like going to a place where he can remain alone and do whatever he wants to do. During this period the individual will pass his lonely time often in the company of enjoyable women. Some unexpected gifts are also received during this period.

Ninth House: During the transit of Venus in the 9th house from Moon the individual remains centered around his sensual gratification. He however, gets into urges for charitable activities. He desires to visit some religious places and to attend some religious services. He does so not with any sense of guilt but just for experiencing the pleasure of being religious.

Tenth House: The transit of Venus in the 10th house from Moon makes the individual's mind agitated and full of remorse and guilt. He gets seized with some unknown fear. He becomes much worried. He feels that he has wasted his life on useless endeavours. During this period, the individual suffers from physical illness, feeling of being drained out, loss of money, vanishing financial prospects and increase of hostilities from all sides. He becomes scandalized by women, humiliated by friends and frustrated in his professional career.

Eleventh House: During the transit of Venus in the 11th house from Moon, the individual regains his composure of mind. He becomes happy. The general environment in which he lives radiates greater joy and contentment. The financial status of the person improves. He receives valuable gifts of clothes and perfume. He forges valuable friendship and is invited to important parties and social gatherings. He becomes free from worries and receives pleasant news from the persons of his love. He achieves his cherished desire. There is all round happiness, peace and enjoyment.

Twelfth House: The results of the 12th house transit of Venus from the Moon -sign depend primarily upon the natal planetary configuration. Pleasures of bed, sexual happiness, floral decoration and pleasant company are some of the results of this transit. During this period, the individual may receive good news from overseas, or may receive invitations for visiting distant friends. Travel and new friendship are another set of results of Venus in the 12th house from Moon. The natural disposition of Venus is to ensure gifts of desired objects, inflow of wealth and income and invitation to musical entertainment which are abundantly available to the individual during this period. At the same time the individual may however incur excessive expenditure causing debts. He may suffer theft and accidents and there may be impediment to professional activities. The results of the 12th house transit can be auspicious as well as adverse which depends upon the natal planetary configuration and planetary periodicity.

Mercury

General: The sidereal period of Mercury is only 88 days but the planet takes about a year to complete its sojourn around the zodiac. The period of its transit is very short and takes only about two weeks to cover a sign. The effect of the planet is primarily in the realm of thought. Its results are very much affected by the fact that it is always very near the Sun. As such, the proximity of Mercury to Moon is inevitably accompanied by nearness of Sun to Moon, which is a devitalising factor. The transit effects of Mercury therefore have to be defined very carefully. Moreover, the effects of Mercury being on the subjective plane through one's intelligence and understanding, the outer expression of the transit can be experienced only indirectly. They are usually expressed as sociability, literary faculties and conversational skill. All these indirectly influence trading and commercial transactions, speculative activities and political diplomacy.

First House: The transit of Mercury in the 1st house from Moon produces much confusion in mind. The situation makes the individual so vacillating that he is unable to think consistently and take decisive stand on any issue. This results primarily due to the clustering of Sun, Moon and Mercury together, which very much reduces the strength of Moon. Loss of wealth is an indirect result of the configuration. Psychological vacillation is inevitable during this period. In rare cases however this period produces understanding and insight into the inner working of Nature and of the discovery of some important scientific laws, which can be inferred only theoretically.

Second House: The result of the transit of Venus in the 2nd house from Moon depends upon the position of Mercury in relation to the Sun. If Sun is ahead of Mercury, Mercury produces much auspicious effect. It leads to financial gain and family union. The individual makes plans for future action. When Mercury is ahead of Sun, there is setback in work, financial loss and social humiliation. The individual however, makes good speeches.

Third House: When Mercury transits the 3rd house from Moon, the person is brought under cloud. He gets in conflict with his associates and the society for some unknown and unspecified reason. He gets disturbed and is unable to manage his affairs efficiently. During this period his income decreases and adversaries become powerful.

Fourth House: During the transit of Mercury in the 4th house from Moon, it makes the individual unsteady. He becomes torn between conflicting choices. He becomes more social but his social relations do not get established on an even keel. He suffers from love-hate conflict, vacillation between performing a specific task or not. He feels uncertain whether to express his affections and thought or not to do so. Such situations of indecision often confront him. Under such a situation the individual can often be found to increase the circle of his friends but these friends are not steady and dependable primarily due to his own instability and vacillation.

Fifth House: Contrary to the normal expectation, the transit of Mercury through the 5th house from Moon does not lead to much creativity. When Mercury passes through this house the lack of emotional stimulation and indecisiveness in one's approach and the perception of contrary aspects of a problem restrict the creative expressions of the person. He perceives wisdom of both the sides of the picture. During this period, one expects accidental conflicts and disputes, separation from wife and children, lack of family pleasure, fear of death and physical illness. During this short period of Mercury's transit, the individual feels low and incapable of controlling the situation so as to be creative.

Sixth House: The 6th house of transit of Mercury is characterised by sharp intelligence and crafty nature. Friends and associates like the individual during this period and his popularity increases. He is appreciated for his professional skill. He succeeds in outmanuevering his adversaries. The energised mind principle in a common man expresses itself during this period by inducing him to engage in some literary activities.

Seventh House: While traversing the 7th house from Moon, Mercury produces uneasiness. The sociability of the person weakens. Strain develops with his wife. Chances of persecution again become imminent. The individual suffers from mental worry. He gets affected by fatigue and is unable to devote adequate energy to his professional activities.

Eighth House: When Mercury traverses the 8th house from Moon, it induces the individual to exercise his skills and intelligence in exploring the secrets of Nature. He tends to delve into the abstruse and inaccessible realms of thoughts and emotions and reveals his experiences and findings through literary activities. During this transit Mercury becomes sharp, active and expansive. It often results in a child -birth and in attainment of one's desired objectives. The individual during this period gains in status. He feels satisfied and happy. But there is also another side of the situation. Mercury in weak situations leads to mental instability, untruthful speech and loss of appetite.

Ninth House: The transit of Mercury in the 9th house from Moon leads to questioning of the devotional approach to life. It makes the individual skeptic and agnostic. He seeks explanations for every action whether religious or mundane. During this period, when Mercury is not very strong in the natal horoscope, the individual even gets afflicted in his mind. He experiences sorrow. He is opposed in his thought and actions. People become hostile to him and they create many impediments to his life and to his work. He takes untimely food and suffers physically too.

Tenth House: The 10th transit of Mercury is auspicious and effective. During this period, the individual receives unusual planetary support. He attains success in his endeavours and victory over enemies. His success sometimes antagonizes a few persons who speak against him and create much difficulties for him and his activities. But the individual sails through clearly and finally overcomes them. At the end he receives appreciation for his work, ideas and publications.

Eleventh House: The transit of Mercury through the 11th house from Moon is helpful in many ways. During this period, the individual expects accrual of money, success in commercial ventures, renown, good social relationships and special favour from his superiors. He hopefully expects happiness in his married relation, good news about his children and happiness from women companions, friendship with supportive individuals and ownership of good vehicles. The individual's ideas are well received during this period.

Twelfth House: When Mercury is ahead of Sun, the transit of Mercury through the 12th house from Moon produces happiness by providing the person the pleasures of the bed and literary and business trips. It also leads to insatiable desire for acquiring new commodities for one's personal use that may lead to debts. As a general rule, Mercury in the 12th house transit is not very welcome. It produces loss of wealth, indebtedness, decreased happiness and inner discontent. All endeavours of the person seem futile. He is disgraced in his society. Physically he suffers from weakness and he may even be afflicted with low blood pressure. Psychologically, he is indifferent to his wife and generally is not averse to extra -marital relationships. He is unable to relish even good food and he experiences all round impediments and difficulties.

Moon

General: Moon is a quick moving planet staying in one house for only about 2 and 1/2 days. It takes only about month to complete its round through the entire zodiac. There is also a unique relationship between the 2 and 1/2 years transit of Saturn in a sign and that of Moon in 2 and 1/2 days in it. Both these transits are profoundly connected with activating and stabilising the life-sustaining energy. The methods of their operation are however different. When Moon is weak, it functions like a malefic but during its position of strength it shows its affinity with Jupiter which is also in an enduring manner connected with life-sustaining energy. Moon works through emotion arousing sensitivity, a function of Venus, and is linked with higher mind, *Buddhi,* an aspect of Mercury. Moon receives its marching order from Sun whose rays it reflects. Thus the role of Moon is poly-dimensional. It is indeed sustentive for the life of the individual. Its effects are, however, so quick, and so fleeting that the transit results of this planet are often overlooked though its tremendous significance is assigned to its natal position. Moon gives auspicious results in the 1st, 3rd, 6th, 7th, 10th and the 11th houses from itself provided it does not suffer from *Vedha* points correspondingly in the 5th, 9th, 12th, 2nd, 4th, and 8th signs from itself. There is no *Vedha* between Moon and the Mercury.

First House: During the transit of Moon over natal Moon, the individual is full of emotion, contented and positive towards life. Physically, he feels fit, emotionally he is happy and socially he is very courteous. He is interested in enjoying the pleasures of life. The individual however is liable to suffer from afflictions of eyes. He encounters difficulties in his job. His mind gets worried and he suffers from some kind of unknown and unspecified fear.

Second House: The transit of Moon through the 2nd house from its natal position is not very agreeable. During this period the individual gets unpalatable food to eat. He suffers from affliction of the eyes. He encounters difficulties in his job. His mind is very worried. He suffers from fear.

Third House: During the course of its 3rd house transit from its natal position, Moon produces very agreeable conditions. It induces the individual to receive news of his victory over adversaries. Physically, he feels sound in health. Psychologically, he feels equable. He is in a fit frame of mind for taking up any assignment that needs patience and perseverance. He receives money and gifts.

Fourth House: When Moon transits the 4th house from its natal position, the emotional life of the person gets disturbed. He loses his sleep. His mind is worried and he suffers from uncertainties. He is abused and ill-spoken of. His own people ignore and dislike him. He is vulnerable to pressure on his heart, both pathologically and metaphorically.

Fifth House: While transiting the 5th house from its own natal position, Moon does not produce agreeable results. It leads to mental disturbances, sorrowful disposition and unpleasant environment. Humiliation takes place during this period. One is attracted to objects impossible to achieve. The individual suffers from arthralgia. During these few days, he feels unhappy, frustrated and confused. He does not make any headway in his undertakings.

Sixth House: Moon gives very favourable results during its 6th house transit from its natal position. These few days are ordinarily very happy for the individual. He feels a sense of pride, pleasure in vanquishing an important adversary of his own and in achieving something extraordinary. A feeling of superiority dawns on the individual. He receives gifts, good company and comfortable life.

Seventh House: During the Moon's 7th house transit through its own natal position, the individual goes on a short pleasure trip. He comfortably moves from place to place. He passes his time pleasantly. His wife becomes very cooperative towards him. He receives some good news. Gain of money, appreciation at work, good food and happiness in one's disposition are some of the other results of this transit.

Eighth House: When Moon traverses the 8th house from itself, the individual gets dreadful dreams and becomes afraid of unknown fear. Psychologically, he gets disturbed. He is caught unaware in some situation from which it is difficult to extricate himself. His mind runs on unusual channels. He gets into difficulties with the people around him. He experiences pain in his ankle.

Ninth House: When Moon transits through the 9th house from its natal position, the individual gets much shaken. He suffers from stomach ailment. His father becomes unhappy with him. Even his superiors reprimand him. Friends, relations, children and every one who comes in contact with him find him unpleasant and shun his company. Setback occurs even in his undertakings. He fails to observe his religious duties and austerities.

Tenth House: Moon transiting through the 10th house from itself makes the individual optimistic and holds his head high. He receives influx of higher powers and succeeds in his worldly ventures too. He becomes interested in his immediate surroundings and acts effectively therein. Others appreciate him. The rapport between the individual and his environment improves. The people around him hold him in high esteem.

Eleventh House: The beneficial impact of Moon's transit through the 10th house from its natal position continues even for the following few days when Moon transits through the 11th house from its natal position. During these days the individual is likely to receive guests who bring precious gifts and good news for him. He becomes much in demand and is likely to get invited to amiable social parties and get-togethers. He receives good news, precious stones like pearl and sea food or fish. There is every possibility of his receiving valuable gain in speculative transactions. Generally these are happy days in every individual's life.

Twelfth House: The transit of Moon in the 12th house from its own natal position makes an individual suffer from excessive expenditure, pressure from creditors and fruitless travels. He gets forced to go on short journeys. He becomes indisposed, receives disturbing news and there are problems with regard to his professional activities. His relatives get annoyed with him. During the period of these few days, the individual is caught in a web of unnecessary mental anguish and depression.

CHAPTER#3

Annual or Progressed Horoscope

Annual or progressed horoscopes are cast on the assumption that the natal position of the Sun depicts an abiding significance. Whenever the Sun traverses this point, it energizes this point and stimulates the original impulse. Hindu Astrology believes the Sun to be the custodian of human destiny. It takes special care of every individual and guides him on his special path of evolution. Every year when the Sun transits over its natal position for the individual, it reverberates the original impulse and prepares him to absorb more and more planetary influences so as to proceed further in tune with his destined path. The planetary configuration at the moment of the solar ingress to this original point reveals the twists and turns programmed for the individual during the year. Annual horoscopes recapitulate the task ahead of the individual assigned to him by his destiny.

The status of an Annual horoscope hinges around this highly sensitive point occupied by the Sun at the time of the individual's birth. Every time the Sun or any other planet traverses this point, the magnetic field around it gets stirred. The cosmic energy latent within it begins to flow out. It engulfs within it all the planets and saturates them with its influence so as to assist and support the individual in his eternal journey. The planetary configuration at this time becomes important to direct this energy-channel to the individual. It affects the welfare of the individual in a significant manner till the solar return next year alters the astro-magnetic field of cosmic energy flow again. The planetary configuration at his anniversary represents the latent energy released for its actualisation during the year. The natal planetary configuration and the configuration at the time of the solar ingress at its natal point are both connected with the same system of stellar operation centered on the natal solar position. It is through the significance of this pivotal point that Hindu Astrology is linked with Vedic metaphysics. An exploration in this aspect of astrology leads us to various postulates relating man with Sun or the Cosmic

Unity. It should however be recognized that the determination of the natal position of the time of birth is very difficult and highly problematic.

When sidereal longitude of the Sun becomes equal to the longitude occupied by it at birth, that moment is reckoned as the moment of solar return. It is this point that gets energized, revivified and sensitized as a result of the solar ingress. The cosmic energy is poured into the life of the individual through this point. The precise delineation of the longitude of the Sun at birth and for the moment of its return to this point is done in many ways. We may not go into the details of these theoretical postulations. Here we wish to stress the point that the annual chart can be cast in the same manner as one does for erecting the natal horoscope. The chart for the year is cast on the same principles as for natal horoscopes. The usual method for casting the natal horoscope is adopted for determining the details of longitudes of different planets and for precise calculation of the ascendant as well as the Medium Coeli (M.C.) and so on.

Annual horoscope is merely an instrument for assessing the general effects of the planets for the year under study. The planetary impulses are studied in relation with the natal chart. The analysis of the results of annual horoscope depends upon certain special rules. These rules are significantly different from those applied for in the interpretation of natal horoscopes. The interpretation of annual or progressed horoscopes for example, takes into account the *Dvādaśavargīya Bala* of the planets in an important manner. Under this method, 12-fold strength of a planet is taken into account. Some factors in the calculation of planetary strength are common in astrological interpretation of both natal charts and progressed horoscopes. The progressed charts however lay much greater and very special importance on these calculations. The 12-fold strength calculation for a planet takes into consideration the planetary rulers of the different parts of a sign as well as their presiding deities. Another aspect of progressed horoscope is the calculation of five-fold strength or *Pañcavargīya Bala* of planets. These calculations are important in relation with annual horoscope for the determination of the Lord of the Year which is not done in the case of natal horoscopes. While determining the rulership for the year, one comes across the concept of *Munthā*. It is a concept that deserves special attention. The Western astrologers familiar with the technique of planetary progression may find this concept very fascinating. *Munthā* depends upon the yearly progression of ascendant by a sign. It is an imaginary point but it emphasizes a cyclic repetition of astro-cosmic influence on different aspects of one's life. The annual charts also lay emphasis on *Sahamas* which emphasizes togetherness of certain sensitive points in a chart. These sensitive points are based on detailed calculation of longitudes of certain planets alongwith the precise ascendant point. Sometimes even cusps of certain house-divisions are considered under this concept. The classical texts described 119 such sensitive points in which each one produces special results. *Sahamas* are not very popular in connection with natal horoscopes but their importance in annual horoscopes is considerable. Even if they are not directly related with the determination of the Lord of the Year, it is helpful to be familiar with them. Some of the *Sahamas* lead to very accurate results if they can be properly worked out.

Planetary Strength

The planetary results are worked out on the basis of the precise location of planets in different signs of the zodiac. Each sign is divided into sub-sections of varying extensions. There are 12 such divisions, each of which is related with different planetary rulerships. These rulerships are different from the rulership over the signs as a whole. Under these sub-divisions, each sign is divided into various segments and each segment is assigned to a planet, which need not be the same as the ruler of the sign. The same zodiacal sign itself in its broad spectrum may therefore be put to one planet (for example, Capricorn under Saturn). But its sub-sections are made depending upon the number of the division of the whole sign. There may be different planets ruling over its different segments. The strength of the planet occupying the sign is indexed on the basis of its location in the segment in which it is present. The *Dvādaśavargīya* strength as well as *Pañcavargīya* strength of planets in the annual horoscope are based on such considerations.

Dvādaśavargīya Bala

The 12-fold strength depends upon the following twelve divisions of a sign. (i) When the sign is considered as a whole, it is known as a *Rāśi* and it extends over 30° of the sign, (ii) *Horā* represents two-fold division of a sign. Each division under *Horā* segment comprises 15° of the zodiac, (iii) Drekkan likewise refers to three-fold division of the sign. Every segment of it comprises 10° of the sign, (iv) *Caturthāṁśa* refers the four-fold division of the sign, (v) *Pañcasmāṁśa* is five-fold division, (vi) *Ṣaṣṭhāṁśa* or the six-fold division, (vii) *Saptamāṁśa,* the seven-fold division, (viii) *Aṣṭamaṁśa* or the eight-fold division, (ix) *Navamāṁśa* or the nine-fold division of a sign, (x) *Daśamāṁśa* or the ten-fold division, (xi) *Ekādaśamāṁśa* or the eleven-fold division, and (xii) *Dvādaśamāṁśa,* or the twelve-fold division of a sign. The planetary ownership of different segments of these divisions is given below :

Rāśi: The planetary ownership of the zodiacal sign is the same as given in all astrological textbooks. Planets ruling the different zodiacal signs are as follows: Aries (Mars), Taurus (Venus), Gemini (Mercury), Cancer (Moon), Leo (Sun), Virgo (Mercury), Libra (Venus), Scorpio (Mars), Sagittarius (Jupiter), Capricorn (Saturn), Aquarius (Saturn), and Pisces (Jupiter).

Horā: The first half of *Horā* division in odd signs such as Aries, Gemini, Leo and so on, is ruled by Sun while the next half is ruled by Moon. This sequence is altered in the case of even signs such as Taurus, Cancer, Virgo and so on. In these cases, the first half of the division is ruled by Moon and the second half by Sun.

Drekkan : The ruler of the sign itself rules over the first 10° of the division. The next 10° that is, 10° to 20° is ruled by the ruler of its 5th house. The ruler of the 9th house from the sign rules the last 10° of the sign. It implies that Mars rules the first Drekkan in Aries, the second by Leo and the third by Jupiter. As far as Taurus is concerned, it's first *Drekkan* is ruled by Venus, the second by Mercury, and the third by Saturn.

Caturthāṁśa: The four divisions of a sign made under it comprises 7° 30' each. The first segment of it is owned by the planet ruling over the sign. Mars rules the first segment under Aries in this division. The ruler of its second quadrant rules the second segment. In the case of Aries, the second quadrant belongs to Cancer. So the ruler of the second division under *Caturthāṁśa* is Moon. The third segment under this division belongs to the ruler of its third quadrant. So the ruler of the third division is Venus. The fourth division of it belongs to the ruler of the fourth quadrant of it that makes Saturn its ruler.

Pañcamāṁśa: Each portion of *Pañcamāṁśa* consists of 6°. In odd signs such as Aries, Gemini, Leo etc. these five-fold divisions are ruled by Mars, Saturn, Jupiter, Mercury and Venus respectively. The sequence for the even signs such as Taurus, Cancer, Virgo etc. is reversed so that the first division is ruled by Venus, the second by Mercury, third by Jupiter and so on.

Ṣaṣṭhāṁśa : The ownership of different segments under *Ṣaṣṭhāṁśa* is based differently. One may for this division consider the 360° of the zodiac divided into 72 equal division of 6° each segment. Thr first six divisions that comprise the whole of Aries will have the control of the lords of the first signs of the zodiac. It implies that the six divisions under Aries will have the ownership of Mars, Venus, Mercury, Moon, Sun and Mercury respectively. The next six divisions that comprise the whole of Taurus will be under the control of the rulers of the next six signs. It implies that the six segments of Taurus will be ruled by Venus, Mars, Jupiter, Saturn, Saturn and Jupiter. The next six segments that comprise the six segments under Gemini will be ruled by the lords of the following six signs. The sequence under Gemini will synchronize with that of Aries. The 12 zodiacal signs consisting of 72 divisions of five degrees each will in this way have six rounds of lordships assigned to the lords of each sign.

Saptamāṁśa: Under this division a sign is divided into seven segments. Each of these is equal to (30° ÷ 7 = 4.2/7 degrees) or 4°17' 8" approximately. In this division, the ownership over different segments begins with the ruler of the first zodiacal sign namely Aries and follows the sequence as in the preceding division till Libra. Thus the planet of the first division becomes Mars and Venus becomes the ruler of the seventh division. The sequence of rulership continues and the seven-fold divisions in the second zodiacal namely Taurus begins with Mars which is the ruler of the eighth zodiacal sign namely Scorpio. The second division of this sign becomes Jupiter which is the owner of the following sign Sagittarius. The sequence continues and the fifth division in Taurus comes under the ownership of the ruler of Pisces, which happens to be Jupiter. The sixth division will come under the rulership of Mars, which owns Aries, and Venus will control the seventh division as the ruler of Taurus. Beginning with Gemini, the first segment of it will be ruled by the lord of the sign Taurus which ended the previous zodiacal sign's *Saptamāṁśa*. The first division of Gemini is ruled by Mercury and ends with Jupiter, the lords of Gemini and Sagittarius respectively. The first segment of Cancer begins with the lordship of Saturn, which owns Capricorn and its last division is owned by Moon, the ruler of Cancer. In this way the entire zodiac will be covered in its *Saptamāṁśa* divisions by the rulers of consecutive sign-lords. There would in this way be seven rounds of rulers of every sign of the zodiac under *Saptamāṁśa* division.

Aṣṭamāṁśa: This division divides the sign in eight equal segments each of which is equal to 3° 45'. The sequence of ownership of these segments is a little different from the previous one. Beginning with the first segment in Aries, the rulership of the first *Saptamāṁśa* in this sign is assigned to Mars, the planet owning the first zodiacal sign. The second segment of it is assigned to the ruler of the second sign, third to the ruler of the third sign, and so on. This rule is applicable in all the movable signs namely Aries, Cancer, Libra and Capricorn. All of these begin their first segment of Aṣṭamāṁśa with Mars, the ruler of the first zodiacal sign. The second segment in each of these signs will be ruled by Venus the ruler of the second sign and so on. In all the fixed signs namely Taurus, Leo, Scorpio and Aquarius, the first division in their *Aṣṭamāṁśa* is ruled by Sun, the owner of Leo and the sequence begins thereafter. The sequence of ownership of subsequent segments follows seriatim. The rulers of their second divisions will be Mercury, the ruler of Virgo and of the third segments, Venus, the ruler of Libra, and so on.. The common signs namely, Gemini, Virgo, Sagittarius and Pisces begin the lordship of their first division with the ruler of Sagittarius and follow the sequence seriatim thereafter. Consequently, Jupiter followed by Saturn, the lord of the following sign Capricorn and so on, rules the first segment in Gemini, Virgo, etc. The chain of these lordships requires eight rounds of repetition to cover all the signs in a zodiac.

Navamāṁśa: Under this division each sign of the zodiac is divided into nine segments. Each segment comprises 3° 20'. *Navamāṁśa* is an important division of a sign both for the interpretation of natal as well as annual horoscopes. Under this division, the first segment in Aries is ruled by Mars, the ruler of Aries, the next segment is ruled by Venus, the ruler of Taurus and the sequence of ownership continues seriatim. The ninth segment under Aries is owned by Jupiter, the ruler of Sagittarius, the ninth zodiacal sign. The first *Navamāṁśa* under Taurus is ruled by Saturn, the lord of the following sign named Capricorn. Thereafter the rulership of Navamāṁśas continues seriatim as before till we arrive at Virgo owned by Mercury which rules over the last segment of the ninefold division under Taurus. The first *Navamāṁśa* under Gemini begins with the rulership of Venus, the owner of Libra. The sequence follows once again as before. In this way, the lordship of the first *Navamāṁśa* in Aries, Leo and Sagittarius goes to Mars, the owner of Aries. The ownership of the first *Navamāṁśa* in Taurus, Virgo and Capricorn begins with Saturn, the owner of

Capricorn. In the case of Gemini, Libra and Aquarius, the first Navamāṁśa is owned by Venus, the ruler of Libra that is followed by Mars, the ruler of Scorpio and so on. Cancer, Scorpio and Pisces begin their first Navamāṁśa with the ruler of Cancer namely Moon.

Daśamāṁśa: Each segment of *Daśamāṁśa* consists of 30°. In odd signs, such as Aries, Gemini, Leo etc, the first lordship under this division is the same as that of the sign. It implies that the first *Daśamāṁsa* in Aries will be ruled by Mars followed by the ruler of Taurus namely Venus, and so on while the first segment in Gemini will be ruled by Mercury and so on. In Gemini, it will be Mercury, and in Leo it will be Sun that will rule over the initial division in the tenfold division. In even signs such as Taurus, Cancer, Virgo etc, the lord of the ninth sign from that under consideration becomes the lord of the first division of *Daśamāṁśa*. Thus, the initial rulership in Taurus under this division goes to Saturn, the ruler of Capricorn, the ninth house from it (Venus). In the case of Cancer it will be Jupiter, the ruler of Pisces that happens to be the ninth sign from Cancer Other rulerships follow the same sequence.

Ekādaśamāṁśa: Each segment of this elevenfold division is equal to (30°÷11=2.8/11) or 2°43'38". The rulership of different portions of this division begins with the lord of the 12th sign counted from the sign whose *Ekādaśamāṁśa* is under consideration. In the case of Aries, its first segment is ruled by the 12th sign namely Pisces ruled by Jupiter. The next segment for this division is ruled by Mars the ruler of Aries, the sign that follows the previous one. Its third portion is under the control of Venus that rules over Taurus, the sign that follows Aries. The sequence of lordship under this division continues in this order.

Dvādaśamāṁśa: Each sign under this division is divided into 12 equal parts each of which covers 2°30" of the zodiac. The lord of the sign itself rules the first segment of the division. The lord of the second sign rules the second segment and the sequence continues in this order.

The various divisions indicated above are taken into account for assessing the strength of various planets as well as for determining the planetary periodicity taking sway over the individual during different periods of the year. These twelve divisions of different magnitude are needed also for deciding the benefic or the malefic nature of the plane in the annual horoscope. The relative strength of the planets depends upon the nature of the sign they occupy and their relationship with the lords of different segments of the signs. The traditional relationships between different planets namely friendship, neutrality etc. between the planets and the lords of the sign they occupy to a great extent modify their *temporary* relationships. For this purpose the planets occupying 2nd, 3rd, 4th, 10th, 11th and 12th houses from any other planet are friendly to one another. Those that are occupying the 1st, 5th, 6th, 7th, 8th and 9th houses in their relationships are inimical. Based on these features the interplanetary relationships between them located in different portions of the sign are tabulated under friendly, neutral and inimical relationships. Different values are assigned for the various relationships. Total value based on such considerations is very important for the assessment of annual horoscopes. In case favourable relationships exceed the adverse ones, the planet will produce favourable results during the year. It will be so even if the planet is malefic one or is adversely placed in the natal chart. Larger number of inimical relationships will lead to adverse results of the planet even if it is a benefic one in the natal chart. The balance between the two sides will neutralize the results of the planet making it ineffective either to produce good or adverse results.

The following table illustrates the exercise. Assuming that the planetary positions in the Annual Chart are as follows:

Sun	296°15'
Moon	311°25'
Mercury	272°33'
Venus	281°39'
Mars	17°32'
Jupiter	32°59'
Saturn	256°7'
Rāhu	311°11' and
Ascendant	191°56'

The relationships between the planets under the twelve kinds of planetary strength are indicated in *Table 1*. This table helps in assessing the benefic and adverse disposition of different Planets in annual horoscopes. This table shows the number of friendly and rulership positions among the various *Dvādaśavargīya* divisions. It also shows the number of inimical and neutrality positions in these divisions. By counting the number of such occurrences in these categories one can find out the number of favourable, adverse and neutral positions. For example, in *Table 1* there are 6 auspicious occurrences comprising 2 Rulership positions and 4 Friendly positions. Similarly there are 4 Inimical Positions and 2 Neutrality positions. As 6 is more than 4, so Sun will be auspicious for the individual during the year. *Table 2* is prepared on the basis of such calculations. It shows the favourable and adverse disposition of planets for the year.

Table 1

Interplanetary Relationships Based on Their 12 - Fold Strength. (F=Friendly Relation; N=Neutrality; I=Instrengthimical Relation; and R=rulership of the Planet)

Planets	*Sign*	*Hora*	*3-fold*	*4-fold*	*5-fold*	*6-fold*	*7-fold*	*8-fold*	*9-fold*	*10-fold*	*11-fold*	*12-fold*
Sun	I	R	N	I	F	F	I	F	R	I	N	F
Moon	N	F	F	N	N	F	N	N	N	N	N	F
Mercury	N	I	N	N	F	F	I	N	N	R	N	N
Venus	F	I	R	N	F	N	F	I	I	N	N	R
Mars	R	F	F	N	F	F	F	F	I	I	I	R
Jupiter	I	F	I	I	I	I	I	F	N	N	I	I
Saturn	N	I	I	F	N	I	N	I	I	F	I	F

Table 2

Assessment of Beneficence of the Planets

Planets	*Auspicious Placements*	*Neutral Position*	*Adverse Placements*	*Overall Effect*
Sun	6	2	4	Favourable
Moon	4	8	Nil	Favourable
Mercury	3	7	2	Favourable
Venus	5	4	3	Favourable
Mars	8	1	3	Favourable
Jupiter	3	2	7	Adverse
Saturn	3	3	6	Adverse

The benefic of a planet depends upon its strength under *Dvādaśavargīya Bala* or the 12-fold classification as in the above illustration. Jupiter and Saturn are adverse in the illustrative example. As such they will lead to unpleasant results such as physical ailments, psychological disturbances and impediments to the enterprise of the individual. Sun, Moon, Mercury, Venus and Mars are favourable. They are expected to produce happiness, wealth, psychological cheers and professional preferment. The number of favourable points attained by a planet indicates the intensity of its impact. Mars has 8 favourable points and only 3 adverse ones. It is indicative of the situation wherein the intensity of Martian auspicious results will predominate. It will be much higher than the few adverse events that may however occur during the year. The neutral points in this classification refer to absence of any kind of support, either good or bad, of a planet. Moon has 8 neutral points and only 4 auspicious ones. Moon does not have any adverse point. Moon will not produce any impediment in the life of the person during the year and it will mostly remain indifferent to him or her. It will only be occasionally that Moon can lead to some pleasant happy events but that again will be very much restricted. The difference between the auspicious and the adverse points shows the spread of a particular kind of impact. If the favourable points exceed the adverse points by a substantial margin, there will be a large number of pleasant events. If the gap between the two is narrow, the excess of favourable points can not lead to an overall beneficial results in any marked way. In such cases there can be numerous pinpricks with several favourable opportunities and any successful outcome from these cannot be assured.

Lord of the Year

The concept of the *Lord of the Year* is special in relation with progressed horoscope. No such term exists for the interpretation of natal charts. Under this concept, the planet that will take special chart of the individual is determined. This concept is different from that of Planetary Periodicity. The *Lord of the Year* is decided on the basis of relative evaluation of the strength of five claimants for this office. The following are the five claimants for this Lordship:

1. The Lord of the Ascendant in the Natal chart.
2. The Lord of the Ascendant in the Progressed or the Annual Chart.
3. The Lord of *Munthā*.
4. The Lord of *Trirāśi*.
5. The Lord of the Sign occupied by Sun if the birth anniversary falls during day time, or the Lord of the Moon -Sign if the anniversary falls during night.

The ascendant lord, in the natal and in the Progressed Charts is easy to identify. The planets ruling over the signs occupying the ascendant in these charts become the Lords. The concepts of *Munthā* and *Trirāśi* are however special requiring special methods for determination. *Munthā* stakes its claim for the lordship of the year alongwith four others, but even otherwise this is very important in influencing the events during the year. *Munthā* plays an important role in annual prognostication. It expresses certain special features of the ascendant itself. *Munthā* is an imaginary point and its position is arrived at by progressing the ascendant every year by 30°. An individual born at 16°25' in Aries has *Munthā* coincident with the ascendant. At the conclusion of one year, when the individual begins his second year, *Munthā* will be at 16°25' in Taurus. At his third birth anniversary, *Munthā* will have moved to the same longitude in Gemini. This course continues for ever. Every month, this imaginary point moves by 2½ degrees. *Munthā* is never retrograde. It completes the zodiacal cycle in 12 year period. Thereafter it is at its original position in the ascendant. So in order to find the location of *Munthā* at any age, one has to divide the number of years elapsed and divide the figure thus obtained by 12 and add one to it. The final figure, that is the remainder plus one will indicate the house in which *Munthā* will be located during the year under consideration.

Trirāśi is related with the sign of the ascendant at the time of the solar ingress. It also takes into account the birth anniversary falling in day or night time. The various signs of the zodiac are classified in three categories for the determination of *Trirāśi*. Each of these consists of four signs of the zodiac. Every sign in the first category consisting of Aries, Taurus, Gemini and Cancer is assigned to Sun, Venus, Saturn and Venus respectively in case the birth anniversary is in daytime. Their rulership is assigned to Jupiter, Moon, Mercury and Mars respectively if the birth anniversary occurred during night time. Signs in the second category namely Leo, Virgo, Libra and Scorpio are ruled by Jupiter, Moon, Mercury and Mars respectively if the birth anniversary is in day time and by Sun, Venus, Saturn and Venus respectively if the birth anniversary occurs in the night time. In the third group of zodiacal signs namely Sagittarius, Capricorn, Aquarius and Pisces the ownership is based on a different principle. In the two groups of the signs, the planets, which rule over the first four signs for the daytime anniversaries rule in the same order over the second set of the four signs for the night-time birth anniversaries while those planets that rule the first set of the signs for the night time birth anniversaries rule the next four signs in the same order for day-time birth anniversaries. The third set of the four signs namely, Sagittarius,

Capricorn, Aquarius and Pisces are ruled by Saturn, Mars, Jupiter and Moon respectively without any distinction for the day or night-time birth anniversaries. The following table shows the relationship between the signs of the zodiac and their planetary ownership for day and night-time birth anniversaries.

Table 3
Rulership of Zodiacal Signs Under Trirāśi Classification

Zodiacal Signs	*Daytime Anniversaries*	*Night Time Anniversaries*
Aries	Sun	Jupiter
Taurus	Venus	Moon
Gemini	Saturn	Mercury
Cancer	Venus	Mars
Leo	Jupiter	Sun
Virgo	Moon	Venus
Libra	Mercury	Saturn
Scorpio	Mars	Venus
Sagittarius	Saturn	Saturn
Capricorn	Mars	Mars
Aquarius	Jupiter	Jupiter
Pisces	Moon	Moon

As mentioned earlier, the *Lord of the Year* is finalized by assessing the relative strength of the lords of the ascendant in a natal chart and in progressed horoscope according to the solar ingress birth anniversary, *Munthā, Trirāśi* and the lord of the sign occupied by Sun or Moon based on the event of birth anniversary falling in daytime or during night time. Their relative strength is assessed according the their *Pañcavargīya Bala* or the five-fold strength. These five-fold classifications are different from the *Dvādaśavargīya Bala.* Some of the criteria are however common to both of these which we shall presently examine. In case there is a tie up, some further conditions are imposed. The most important criterion is that the Lord of the Year must be related with the ascendant either by association or by aspect and the latter is a preferred condition. If the tie still persists another elaborate method is used to resolve the bind which we shall discuss later on. Prior to that it is necessary to understand the features of *Pañcavargīya Bala.*

Pañcavargīya Bala

The five-fold strength of planets is based on five factors namely *Kṣetra Bala, Ucca Bala, Hadda, Drekkan* and *Navamāṁśa.* We have already discussed *Drekkan* and *Navāmaṁśa. Kṣetra Bala* denotes the residential strength or the strength derived on the basis of a planet's location in a sign. It is decided according to the relationship existing between the planet and the ruler of the sign in which it is placed. There are four kinds of relationships under such a connection. These relationships are based on ownership of the sign, its friendship, neutrality, and enmity with the rulers of the sign in which it is placed. The strength of these relationships is measured on a scale of total 30 points. The highest strength is assigned to ownership of a sign enjoying 30 points on the basis of its location.

Those planets, which occupy their friendly signs that is the signs belonging to their friendly planets, qualify for 75% of the total (30 points). They receive 22.5 points. Neutrality of the relationship earns only half the total that is only 15 points. Those planets, which occupy their enemy's sign, get only 25% of the total that is they receive only 7.5 points.

Uccabala: The strength of planet is highest during its exaltation and the lowest when it is debilitated. *Uccabala* measures the strength of the planet according to its distance from these two points. It is worked out by dividing the difference in degrees between the distance of the planet either from its exaltation or debilitation point and dividing the same by nine. If the distance is measured from the exaltation point, the value is subtracted from 20, but if it is measured from its debilitation point no such reduction is needed.

Hadda ordinarily means the 'limit'. In the present context it has acquired a special connotation. *Drekkan* represents the three-fold division of a sign each of which is associated with a planetary rulership. *Navamāṁśa* represents the nine-fold division of a sign each of which like the previous one, is also assigned to a planetary rulership. Drekkan and Navamāṁśa have already been described earlier. On the basis of these five-fold indices of strength the relative claim for the lordship of the year is determined. Each of these indices is worked out on certain age-old assumptions.

Kṣetra Bala: As mentioned above, Kṣetra Bala denotes the residential or locational strength of a planet. The strength is assessed on the basis of the relationship existing between the planet and the ruler of the sign in which the planet is placed. There are four kinds of relationships mentioned in this regard. These are the relationships of (a) rulership, (b) friendship, (c) neutrality, and (d) enemity between the two planets. These indicators are measures on a scale of total 30 points. The highest strength is assigned to ownership criterion of the relationship which enjoys 30 points. Those planets which occupy their friendly signs get 75% of the total that is, 22.5 points. Neutrality of the relationship carries only half of the strength that is only 15 points while those planets which are in their enemy's sign receive only 25% or only 7.5 points.

Table 4
Kṣetra Bala of Planets in the Illustrative Horoscope

Planets	*Locational Sign*	*Ruler of the Sign*	*Relationship*	*Kṣetra Bala*
Sun	Capricorn	Saturn	Inimical	7.5
Moon	Aquarius	Saturn	Neutrality	15.0
Mercury	Capricorn	Saturn	Neutrality	15.0
Venus	Capricorn	Saturn	Friendly	22.5
Mars	Aries	Mars	Rulership	30.0
Jupiter	Taurus	Venus	Inimical	7.5
Saturn	Sagittarius	Jupiter	Neutrality	15.0

Ucca Bala or the Exaltation Index: Uccabala is worked out according to proximity or distance of a planet from its exaltation point. The exaltation point for Sun in Aries is 10° and its debilitation point at Libra is 10° which is 180° away from its exaltation point. The exaltation point of other planets are as follows : Moon - ♉3°, Mercury - ♍15° Venus - ♓ 27°, Mars - ♑28°, Jupiter - ♋5° and Saturn - ♎ 20°. The debilitation points of the planets are as follows : Sun ♎10°, Moon ♏3°, Mercury - ♓15°, Venus - ♍27°, Mars ♋28°, Jupiter - ♑5° and Saturn ♈20°. Each planet earns 20 points on exaltation whereas no point is assigned to it at its debilitation. The planets lose their Uccabala gradually when they move towards their debilitation and gradually regain their strength on their way towards their exaltation. Half-way removed from the either end i.e. when they are 90° away from their exaltation (which also means when they are 90° away from their debilitation point) the planets have only 10 points of their strength. Based on the exact location of a planet, its exaltation index is accordingly worked out. A short-cut method of working out the Uccabala is as follows:

Table 5
Exaltation index for Planets in the Illustrative Chart

Planets	*Exaltation*	*Debilitation Point*	*Actual Longitude*	*Distance*	*Exaltation Index*
Sun	♈10°=10°	♎10°=190°	296°15' =296.25°	296.25–190 =106.25	106.25÷9 =11.81
Moon	♉3°=33°	♏3°=213°	311°25' =311.42	311.42–213 =98.42	98.42÷9 =10.94
Mercury	♍15°=165°	♓15°=345°	272°33' =272.55	272.55–165 =107.55	107.55÷9 =11.95
Venus	♓27°=357°	♍27°=177°	281°39' =281.65	281.65–177 =104.65	104.65÷9 =11.63
Mars	♑28°=298°	♋28°=118°	17°32' =17.53,or 360+17.53 =377.53	377.53–298 =79.53	79.53÷9 =8.84; 20.0–8.84 =11.16
Jupiter	♋5°=95°	♑5°=275°	32°59' =32.98, or 360+32.98 =392.98	392.98-95 =297.98	297.98÷9 33.11–20 =33.11; =13.11
Saturn	♎20°=200°	♈20°=20°	256°7'= 256.12	256.12–200 =56.12	56.12÷9 =6.24; 20.0–6.24 =13.76

Hadda Index assumes certain limits within which different planets are more effective than at other places. The first six degrees of Aries are very sensitive to Jupiter, next six degrees are so to Venus, the middle eight degrees to Mercury, followed by Mars and Saturn having five degrees each. The following table *(Table 6)* gives the limits within which the planets have special affinity with specified sections of the zodiacal signs. The relationship between the Hadda lords and the planets of the progressed horoscope are assigned certain values, the highest of which is 15 points. The synchronicity of the planet under consideration with the Hadda lord fetches the highest value of 15 points. If the two are friendly, the planet gets 75 per cent of the total that is 11.2 points and under neutral relationship, the planet qualifies only for half, that is, 7.5 points. If the Hadda lord and the planet are inimical, it gets 25 per cent of the total, i.e. merely 3.75 points. *Table No. 7* shows the Hadda points of the planets in the above illustrative horoscope.

Table 6

Lords of Hadda and the Extension of their zone of Influence

Zodiacal Signs	*Extension of First Hadda*	*Extension of Second Hadda*	*Extension of Third Hadda*	*Extension of Fourth Hadda*	*Extension of Fifth Hadda*
Aries	0°-6°	6°-12°	12°-20°	20°-25°	25°-30°
	Jupiter	Venus	Mercury	Mars	Saturn
Taurus	30°-38°	38°-44°	44°-52°	52°-57°	57°-60°
	Venus	Mercury	Jupiter	Saturn	Mars
Gemini	60°-66°	66°-72°	72°-77°	77°-84°	84°-90°
	Mercury	Venus	Jupiter	Mars	Saturn
Cancer	90°-97°	97°-103°	103°-109°	109°-116°	116°-120°
	Mars	Venus	Mercury	Jupiter	Saturn
Leo	120°-126°	126°-131°	131°-138°	138°-144°	144°-150°
	Jupiter	Venus	Saturn	Mercury	Mars
Virgo	150°-157°	157°-167°	167°-171°	171°-178°	178°-180°
	Mercury	Venus	Jupiter	Mars	Saturn
Libra	180°-186°	186°-194°	194°-201°	201°-208°	208°-210°
	Saturn	Mercury	Jupiter	Venus	Mars
Scorpio	210°-217°	217°-221°	221°-229°	229°-234°	234°-240°
	Mars	Venus	Mercury	Jupiter	Saturn
Sagittarius	240°-252°	252°-257°	257°-261°	261°-266°	266°-270°
	Jupiter	Venus	Mercury	Mars	Saturn
Capricorn	270°-277°	277°-284°	284°-292°	292°-296°	296°-300°
	Mercury	Jupiter	Venus	Saturn	Mars
Aquarius	300°-307°	307°-313°	313°-320°	320°-325°	325°-330°
	Mercury	Venus	Jupiter	Mars	Saturn
Pisces	330°-342°	342°-346°	346°-349°	349°-358°	358°-360°
	Venus	Jupiter	Mercury	Mars	Saturn

Table 7

Points Attained Under Hadda indexing by Planets in the Illustrative Chart

Planets	*Location (Longitude)*	*Hadda Lord*	*Relationship with the Planet*	*Points Attained*
Sun	296°15'	Mars	Friendly	11.25
Moon	311°25'	Mercury	Friendly	11.25
Mercury	272°33'	Venus	Friendly	11.25
Venus	281°39'	Venus	Rulership	15.00
Mars	17°32'	Mercury	Friendly	11.25
Jupiter	32°59'	Venus	Inimical	3.75
Saturn	256°07'	Venus	Friendly	11.25

Drekkan Index: The relationship between the planetary lord of the *Drekkan* in which the planet is located and the planet itself is measured by Index. As indicated earlier, Drekkan is a three-fold division of each sign each comprising 10° of the zodiac, and every zodiac is ruled by a planet. The lordship over the first portion is assigned to the lord of the sign itself, the second portion is assigned to the lord of the Fifth sign from it, and the third one is ruled by the lord of the Ninth house from the sign under consideration. The highest value earmarked under Drekkan Index is 10 points. A planet occupying its own Drekkan attains the full value of 10 points. Those placed in friendly Drekkan attain three-fourths of the total i.e. 7.25 points. Planets located in neutral Drekkan qualify for 50 percent of 5-points while the planets which occupy the Drekkan ruled by inimical planets are assigned only a quarter of the total or 2.25 points. The Drekkan indices of the planets in the illustrative horoscopes given earlier are indicated in the following table.

Table 8
Drekkan Indices of planets in the Illustrative Chart

Planets	*Location in Longitude*	*Drekkan Lord*	*Relationship*	*Drekkan Index*
Sun	296°15'	Venus	Inimical	2.50
Moon	311°25'	Mercury	Friendly	7.50
Mercury	272°33'	Saturn	Neutrality	5.00
Venus	281°39'	Venus	Own Drekkan	10.00
Mars	17°32'	Sun	Friendly	7.50
Jupiter	32°59'	Venus	Inimical	2.50
Saturn	256°07'	Mars	Inimical	2.50

Navamāṁśa Index: The relationship between the Navamāṁśa lord and a planet is measured under Navamāṁśa index. Mention has already been made of Navamāṁśa and its various lords. The relationship between Navamāṁśa lord and the planet is measured on a scale of 1.25 to 5 points. The highest point is attained by those planets which occupy their own Navamāṁśa, while that pertaining to a friendly planet qualifies the planet for 3.75 points. A planet occupying neutral Navamāṁśa gets 2.50 points. A planet which occupies the Navamāṁśa of an inimical planet is entitled to only 1.25 points.

Table 9
Navamāṁśa Indices of Planets in the Illustrative Chart

Planets	*Location*	*Navamāṁśa Lord*	*Relationship*	*Index*
Sun	290°15'	Sun	Ownership	5. 00
Moon	311°25'	Saturn	Neutrality	2. 50
Mercury	272°33'	Saturn	Neutrality	2.50
Venus	281°39'	Mars	Neutrality	2.50
Mars	17°32'	Mercury	Inimical	1.25
Jupiter	32°59'	Saturn	Neutrality	2.50
Saturn	256°07'	Sun	Inimical	1.25

Pañcavargīya Bala: The five-fold strength of a planet is assessed on the basis of the above mentioned five indices. It is calculated by totalling the Kṣetra Bala, Ucca Bala, Hadda, Drekkan and Navaṃāṁśa indices and dividing the same by 4 to indicate the relative strength of the planets in the progressed horoscope. The highest point that can be attained is 20 and the lowest is 3.75. A planet scoring 15-20 points is considered powerful, while those with 10-15 points are above the average. Ordinary planets secure 5-10 points and they are unable to make any significant impact. These planets securing less than 5 points are insignificant. The relative strength of different planets in the illustrative horoscope is given in *Table 10.* In this example, Mars and Venus are very powerful while Moon, Saturn and Mercury are of average strength. Other planets are not likely to make any significant impact during the year.

Table 10
Five-fold Strength of the Planets in the Illustrative Horoscope

Planets	*Kṣetra Bala*	*Ucca Bala*	*Hadda Index*	*Drekkan Index*	*Navamāṁśa Index*	*Total Points*
Sun	7.50	11.81	11.25	2.50	5.00	38÷4=09.52
Moon	15.00	10.94	11.25	7.50	2.50	47.19÷4=11.80
Mercury	15.00	8.07	11.25	5.00	2.50	41.82÷4=10.46
Venus	22.50	11.63	15.00	10.00	2.50	61.63÷4=15.41
Mars	30.00	13.11	11.25	7.50	1.25	63.11÷4=15.78
Jupiter	7.50	13.11	3.75	2.50	2.50	29.36÷4=07.34
Saturn	15.00	13.76	11.25	2.50	1.25	43.76÷4=10.94

The Pañcavargīya Bala of different planets is important for deciding their role during the year. In order to qualify for the rulership over the year, a planet should not merely score the highest total of the five-fold strength, it should also aspect the ascendant. Unless it does so, it is disqualified for this position. In case several planets with equal strength aspect the ascendant, it is the index of the aspect which resolves the tie. The rules for determining the relative aspect strength of a planet is different for progressed horoscope from those for the natal chart. These rules stipulate four kinds of aspects. These are known as clearly friendly, hidden friendly, hidden inimical and clearly inimical. The 1st and the 7th aspects are clearly inimical in progressed charts. They create impediments, destroy happiness and lead to strife and disputes. These aspects are the most powerful and are assigned 100 points. The 5th and 9th aspects are considered clearly friendly. They possess three-fourths power with 75 points assigned to them. These aspects strengthened the friendliness between the two planets. The planets in progressed charts also aspct their 3rd and 11th houses. They are concealed or hidden friendly aspects. They lead to success and fulfilment of one's objectives. They score half of the total or 50 points. Hidden inimical aspects pertain to the 4th and 10th aspects, which produce differences between the planets. These aspects weaken the aspected planets. They qualify for 25 points or one-fourth of the total strength. Some authorities concede even 2nd and 12th aspects, which are auspicious but they secure only 15 points. The planets are said to cast even 6th and 8th aspects but these are ineffective in producing any significant impact.

The planets in progressed horoscope have their aspects restricted to a specific range. They do not extend beyond that extent. They do not spread to the whole of the house as assumed in natal charts. The different magnitude of aspects for various planets are as follows:

Sun: $\pm$ 15°; Moon: $\pm$ 8°; Mercury: $\pm$7°; Venus: $\pm$7°; Mars: $\pm$12°; Jupiter: $\pm$9°; Saturn: $\pm$ 9°.

The planetary aspects for deciding the rulership of planets over the year are based on their exact longitude and the extension of their aspects. In case of a tie-up between the planets on the basis of their strength and aspect on the ascendant, which also includes the cases of more than one planet qualifying on these criteria, the lordship over the year is decided with reference to *Munthā*. Whichever of these planets has stronger relationship with *Munthā* for the year is the acclaimed lord of the year. If this does not resolve the issue, one has to resort to another condition. If the birth anniversary falls during the day time, the lord of the Sun sign, otherwise the lord of the Moon sign in the event of the anniversary falling during the night time, is assigned the role of the lord of the year. Some opinions suggest that the tie between equally eligible planets can be resolved by assigning the rulership over the year to the planet which is associated with or forms combination with Moon. In case no such association or combination is present, Moon itself can be considered so. According to another view, if no planet on the basis of *Pañcavargīya Bala* qualifies for the role, the planet aspecting the ascendant in spite of its lack of requisite strength can be assigned the role.

Periodicity of Planets

The timing of events during the course of the year is decided in three ways. These methods differ from one another. The selection of any specific method depends upon the personal predilection and experience of the astrologer. Each of these methods has its advantages as well as shortcomings which cannot be objectively decided. These methods are calculated on the basis of (i) *Kṛsāṁsas* and *Pātyaṁśas,* (ii) *Muddā* system, and (iii) the Viṁśottarī system of periodicity as modified for the progressed horoscopes.

Kṛsāṁsas and *Pātyāṁśas: Kṛsāṁśas* are worked out by arranging in an ascending order the distances of the planets traversed from the beginning of the zodiacal sign in which they are placed. For example, a planet occupying 11°39' in Capricorn will have precedence over the planet occupying 17°12' in Aries. These distances tabulated in an ascending order are known as *Kṛsāṁśas.* In this exercise, even ascendant is included. Retaining the lowest or the first number, the distances are written in such a way that the second number is written as the difference from the preceding one. The initial longitude, irrespective of the sign, remains the base. The next higher longitude is mentioned merely as its distance from the previous one. Totalling all the digits including the first or the lowest one can test the correctness of the tabulation. The total thus arrived should be equal to the highest longitude in the series. It would be the last number in the series. The series thus worked out is known as *Pātyāṁśas.*

The next step involves converting *Pātyāṁśas* into periodicity of the planets. This is done by dividing the duration of the year, i.e. 365 days 6 hours or 365.25 days by the total of *Pātyāṁśas.* The total would be equal to the *Kṛsāṁśas* of the planet in the series. The quotient should be multiplied by the *Pātyāṁśa* of the planets. The first *Daśā* under this system pertains to the initial planet in the series. The subsequent periods follow the sequence as they exist in the *Kṛsāṁśa* table. The various steps involved in this calculation aim at converting the planetary sequence over different portions of the year under consideration and assigning certain values that can show the duration of the rulership of the planet.

Table 11
Different Stages in the Calculation of Kṛśaṁśa Daśā

Planets	*Longitude*	*Kṛśāṁśas*	*Pātyāṁśa*	*Planetary Duration*
	s ° '	° '	° '	(13.9143)×(Pātyāṁśa)
Mercury	9 2 33	2 33	2 33	35.48 days
Jupiter	1 2 59	2 59	(2°59' - 2°33') = 0 26	5.98 days
Moon	10 11 25	11 25	(11°25'- 2°59') = 8 26	117.44 days
Venus	9 11 39	11 39	(11°39'-11°25')= 0 14	3.20 days
Ascendant	6 11 59	11 59	(11°59'-11°39')= 0 20	4. 59 days
Saturn	8 16 07	16 07	(16°07'-11°59')= 4 08	57.47 days
Mars	0 17 32	17 32	(17°32'-16°07')= 1 25	19.76 days
Sun	9 26 15	26 15	(26°15'-17°32')= 8 43	121.33 days
			$\sum$=26°15'=26.25 degrees	$\sum$365.25 days

Duration of the rulership of each planet in the illustrative chart
=[(365.25 days of the year)÷(26.25)] × (Pātyāṁśa of the Planet)
=(13. 9143) × (Pātyāṁśa of the Planet)
Planetary Duration for Jupiter, for example=(13.9143) × (0.26) days
=5.98 days.

The first *Daśā* in the above example is of Mercury. The duration of its periodicity is 35.48 days, or 35 days 11 hours and 31 minutes. This period will be followed by Jupiter lasting for 5.98 days, Moon for 117.44 days and so on. The last period is that of Sun that lasts for 121.33 days. At the expiry of this period, the year itself must have ended.

The sub-period during the main planetary period is obtained by multiplying the two periods as given above and dividing the resultant by 365.25 days. The first sub-period during the main period of a planet is that of the planet itself while the planetary sequence is the same as given in *Pātyāṁśa* table.

Muddā System: The planetary periodicity under this system is somewhat similar to *Viṁśottarī* system. It begins by noting the serial number of the asterism in which Moon is located and progressing that number by one for every year of the age. The total number thus obtained is divided by 9. The quotient is rejected and the remainder is taken to represent the planet that will have the first rulership. Number 1 as remainder signifies that the Sun will have control first during the year. The significators of other planets are as follows: 2 - Moon, 3 - Mars, 4 - Rāhu, 5 - Jupiter, 6 - Saturn, 7 - Mercury, 8 - Ketu and 9 - Venus. The order of the planetary rulership in this system follows the same sequence as under *Viṁśottarī* system. It means that the sequence will be as follows: Sun, Moon, Mars, Rāhu, Jupiter, Saturn, Mercury, Ketu and Venus. Under Muddā system Rāhu and Ketu are also taken into consideration though under *Kṛsāṁśa* they are left out.

The duration of planetary rulership under this system is worked on the assumption that the total duration of rulership of these planets corresponds to 365.25 days. This duration is proportionately distributed over various planets relative to the duration assigned to them under the *Viṁśottarī* system.

If a planet enjoys its rulership, say, for one year under *Viṁśottarī* system, that planet under *Muddā* system will have the rulership of (365.25)÷(120) days. This gives a multiplier of 3.04375 or, 3.044. Sun has the rulership of 6 years under *Viṁśottarī* system but under *Muddā* system it rules only for (6) × (3.044) or 18.26 days. The different planets under this system have their rulership period as follows : Sun (18.26 or 18 days and 6 hours), Moon (30.44 or 1 month 11 hours), Mars (21.31 days or 21 days and 8 hours), Rāhu (54.79 or 1 month 24 days and 19 hours), Jupiter (48.70 or 1 month 18 days and 17 hours), Saturn (57.83 or 1 month 27 days and 20 hours), Mercury (51.74 or 1 month 21 days 18 hours and 53 minutes), Ketu (21.30 or 21 days and 8 hours) and Venus (60.88 or 2 months and one day). They should total 365. 25 days of the year.

The sub-planetary rulership under *Muddā* system is worked out by multiplying the two periods assigned to the two planets and dividing the resultant by 365.25 which gives the sub-planetary rulership in days. In this system the first sub-period is that of the main planet and the cyclic order follows the same sequence as in Viṁśottarī system. The commencement of the first rulership period does not begin at the very beginning of the periodicity. The distance traversed by *Muddā* in the *Nakṣatra* should be reckoned as the periodicity of the planet already elapsed. This is analogous to the *Viṁśottari* system of rulership.

The *Viṁśottarī* system as applied to progressed horoscope implies that the Moon's position in the asterism at the commencement of the birth-anniversary is noted and the planetary periodicity accordingly worked out. The determination of the initial rulership and the sequence is analogous to *Viṁśottarī* system under the natal chart but the duration of planetary rulership as under the *Muddā* system will be applicable in the present case.

Lord of the Year

The annual horoscope provides supportive tool for the working out of the timing of events. The three methods described above do not have the same degree of acceptance. The solar ingress charts are very popular among the seasoned practitioners who often take help of *Viṁśottarī* system but *Muddā* system of planetary rulership is generally at discount. The interpretation of results is done on the basis of the Lord of the Year for detailed prognostication.

The lord of the year oversees the various events occurring during the year. The happiness of the individual is assured if the lord of the year in strength is located in a house other than 6th, 8th and 12th houses. Under this condition he will have good health during the year. He will have psychological satisfaction, elevation in social and official status and the fulfilment of his objectives. If the lord of the year is also the ascendant lord either in the natal chart or in the progressed one, the individual will experience enduring achievement and fulfilment of his long-term objectives. The other planets will exert their influences during the different parts of the year according to their periodicity but these results will be within the overall conditions laid down by the lord of the year.

When the lord of the year combines with a planet, either by association or by aspect, the combined effect of the planets becomes significant. When the lord of the year approaches a benefic or a malefic, the latter becomes sensitive to the advancing planet and precipitate good results as far as possible according to its nature. Even if the approached planet is a malefic, it becomes favourably inclined towards the person for the time being and produces uplifting influence on him and accelerates his inner unfoldment. If the lord of the year is ahead of a benefic, the latter supports the year-lord in all auspicious results but if such a planet is a malefic, the whole year can be full of impediments, loss, destruction and completely demoralizing events.

The lord of the year has important role even in the natal horoscope. It affects the different planets during the course of their planetary periodicity in fructifying their results. If the ascendant lord of the progressed chart or the lord of the year is ahead of such a planet in the natal chart, the fructification of the result is cancelled. The efforts made by the individual are thwarted. He receives setback in his activities. The planetary possibilities of the natal chart are available to the person only when this kind of relationship is not present during the year. If the ascendant lord or the progressed and the lord of the year either together or alone approaches a fructifying planet during the course of the year, the likely results of the natal planets can be effective and favourable. The absence of such relationships will allow the natal planets to produce their results according to their own natal disposition. It is a general rule in astrology that a planet in a natal chart is effective in fructifying the natural results of a *bhāva* if it owns that house. This result is denied if the lord of the year forms a separating relationship with the lord of the house even if both of these are placed together. [Separating relationship is formed if the distance between the two planets increases].

The results of the lord of the year follow according to the natural disposition of the different planets which occupy this position. The results follow the general guidelines indicated below:

Sun: During the course of the year when the Sun occupies the status of the lord of the year, there is enormous downpour of Divine life-force. It makes the individual extremely dynamic, powerful, effective and successful. His health improves. He may even receive some honour and reward. He can be entrusted with greater responsibilities. His reputation increases far and wide. There is a chance of his begetting a child, producing some enduring work, and supporting important philanthropic activities. During this period, the creative energy of the individual endears him to the people around him, makes him effectively helpful and inculcates in him a sense of psychological fulfilment. Weakness in the strength of the Sun distorts the expression of this power. In that case the individual becomes egotistic. His relationship with his relations and close associates deteriorates. He gets involved in legal disputes and faces humiliation.

Moon: When Moon assumes the lordship of the year, it produces effective results if it approaches an auspicious planet or receives such aspects from a favourable planet. Left alone, Moon makes the individual material minded living in his own fantasy. Personal acquisitions and pleasures of the world such as house, landed property, wife and children, social prestige and good health will mark the year. The individual will like others to acknowledge and appreciate his achievements, praise him for his activities, and offer him precious gifts. Weak Moon leads to physical and mental sufferings, misunderstanding with friends and family relations, change of residence, unprofitable travels and excessive expenditure. Under favourable Moon associated with Ṣun, the individual can expect support from important individuals in power. This combination makes the mind of the person very creative. The association of Mars with Moon produces danger from accidents, injury from lethal weapons and much restlessness. Mercury's association with Moon, depending upon strength of both the planets, leads the individual to publish quality literary works, forge important social relationships, make fruitful journeys and secure substantial gain in business enterprises and trading associations. Venus in such a relationship intensifies sensual enjoyment, produces festivities like marriage and other anniversaries in the family. It leads to professional preferment. The association of Moon with Saturn leads to mental depression, impediment to activities and loss of honour. Rāhu and Moon, when Moon attains rulership of the year, externalize certain karmic results which create difficulties in the life and activities of the individual or enables him to acquire much deeper insight and understanding into the mysteries of life. Ketu in such a situation leads to strange visions, suddenness of events and unexpected movements. The strength of Moon gets greatly increased in association with Jupiter. It leads to general welfare, construction of a new house and festivities like marriage and joyous celebrations.

Mercury: As lord of the year, Mercury activates the mind principle. Strong Mercury with favourable influence on it sharpens the intellect of the person. He becomes quick-witted, capable of producing treatises, giving learned discourses and adept in refined social manners. He acquires special skill in mathematics, logic and occult sciences. He also acquires much wealth. His efficiency in trade negotiations and diplomatic exchanges becomes exceptional. Mercury in average strength produces business discernment and enables the individual to secure much profit from trade and commerce. He becomes helpful to his family members, relatives and friends. Unfavourably disposed, Mercury as the lord of the year makes the individual lose his mental composure, speak ill of others, become quarrelsome and experience difficulties in professional activities.

Mercury is another planet, besides Moon, which is much influenced by its association with other planets. Associated with Sun, Mercury sharpens the intellect, enables the individual to acquire renown and honour and bestows upon him unexpected respectability and wealth.

In association with Moon, Mercury leads to much travel and fanciful imagination. This combination can be highly productive when combined with some concretizing planet. Otherwise, the time will pass in making schemes only without their implementation. Mercury in association with Mars is very troublesome and strenuous but under their impact the individual even receives much warmth in his social relationship. Mercury and Venus together intensify the results of each other. Mercury and Jupiter generally make life comfortable, and time passes with celebrations and socialization but nothing concrete or substantial emerges during the year. Saturn's association demoralizes the individual, induces him to indulge in socially unapproved sexual relations. Rāhu's impact on Mercury is productive of good results whereas Ketu is very disruptive and distressing.

Venus: As the lord of the year, Venus leads to a year of luxurious life, sensual pleasures and cultivation of dance, drama and music. Much of its results depend upon the strength as well as other connections of the planet. Venus makes the individual highly vulnerable to the influence of others. In the company of righteous persons, the immorality and lack of control over his senses will not manifest and he will be supportive of artistic and philanthropic activities. But in association of lowly type persons, no sin is beyond the reach of the person. Generally a strong and well disposed Venus makes the individual contented with material attainments around him. He derives pleasures from his wife and his social status. He is true to his friends and relations. He is engaged in helpful social interactions. But with weak and badly disposed Venus, the individual runs into difficulties of various kinds, encounters, scandals, suffers from ignominy and gets afflicted with venereal diseases.

Mars: As lord of the year, Mars produces abundant vitality and the individual gets enthusiastically engaged in different programming. His efforts get directed towards physical activities. The Martian impact is significant throughout the year in implementation of difficult programming, carrying out of constructional activities, agricultural operations, military strategy and mechanical instrumentation. Powerful Mars leads the individual to success in his enterprises, increase of wealth and property, destruction of enemies and obstacles, favourable decisions in respect of any dispute or court cases in which he may be involved. He is expected to receive special honour and precious gifts. Ordinary or weak Mars is not much opportune. With average strength it does produce valour but the direction of energy gets perverted leading to loss of prestige and displeasure of the superiors. Self-centeredness of the individual increases, pride takes sway over the person and he suffers from physical illness and accidents. Weak Mars arouses troubles due to impulsive reactions of the individual which often become serious. He loses wealth, gets afflicted with diseases and physical infirmities. He is disgraced and meets defeat. He is likely to leave his mother country and dwell far away from his place of birth in a very pitiable situation.

Jupiter: When Jupiter attains the position of the lord of the year, the year is full of joyous events. There is much honour and prestige for the individual. He gets surrounded by good and religious people. His time is spent in religious and spiritual pursuits. Jupiter produces comfortable life. It enables the individual to secure wealth and success. There is an aura of holiness around him. The divine grace flows to him uplifting him and those around him. His family is held in high esteem. There is much festivity in the family. Contentment, righteous living, interest in higher values in life and philanthropic activities are some of the features of Jupiter which take place during the year. If Jupiter is not strong, it produces illness and heavy expenditure. It induces the individual towards materiality and material sciences. It brings about changes in one's place of residence as well as in service conditions. Whatever happens during this period is primarily concerned with the psychology of the person and his general attitude to life. Jupiter is efficient primarily in protecting and nurturing the good qualities of the individual. It does not lead much to material riches rather produces a kind of noble attitude to life and psychological contentment with whatever happening to the person.

Saturn: One must not dread Saturn as the lord of the year. In fact, it is Saturn that produces much that ordinary individual desires. The lordship of the year to Saturn enables the individual to acquire additional property, new houses, furniture and new gadgets of comfortable living. The individual secures money and wealth from overseas during this period and spends a substantial portion of it on construction of buildings, gardens and in securing new instruments of daily use. During this period the social status of the individual may rise. These are some of the results that accrue if Saturn is strong. During the same period, however, the ethical standard of the individual gets perverted. He begins to take interest in extra-marital relationship. He is inclined to consort with courtesans. A weak Saturn during its rulership of the year arouses much hostile forces around the individual and isolates him even from his own close relations.

Munthā

Munthā as indicated earlier is ascendant progressed by a sign (30°) for every year of the age. It is given a motion of 2½ degrees per month. During the course of its progression, this highly sensitive point in a natal chart preserves much of its inherent nature and produces every year, in fact, in every month of the year, its impact according to its changing relationship by way of conjunctions and aspects with other planets. *Munthā* produces intense results. It is as important as the lord of the year is. Its occupancy is important both in the natal chart as well as in the progressed horoscope. When *Munthā* enters a sign, it vitalizes the lord of the sign and the *bhāva* ruled by the planet. *Munthā's* association with a planet also draws from that planet much influence to its own advantage. In this way, it secures special capabilities. This situation is strengthened during the course of its combining or separating relationships that may occur either due to association or aspects. When in a progressed horoscope *Munthā* is placed in a sign and is aspected by the lord of that sign and by other benefic planets, it enables the effects of the house occupied by the sign in the natal chart to blossom luxuriously. If *munthā* is aspected by malefic, its result is opposite. If the lord of the year is sufficiently strong, the affliction caused by *Munthā* gets cancelled.

Munthā is very favourable in ascendant, 9th, 10th and 11th houses, especially in a progressed chart. In a natal chart, *munthā* produces destruction of adversaries and complete elimination of every impediment bestowing dignity and social status on the individual. It leads to the birth of children and acquisition of property, expansion of glory, honour from the state, gifts from friends and attainment of physical welfare. In the 9th house, it induces the inner-man towards righteous living and engagement in welfare work for the people at large. When such a situation arises, the individual becomes the head of an organization and acquires much wealth during the year. He directs the wealth towards religious festivities, welfare and happiness of his wife and children and spiritual regeneration. His activities earn him popularity and renown in the society and meritorious deeds in the world hereafter. If *munthā* in the progressed chart occupies the 11th house from the natal ascendant, it produces for the person such favourable conditions that he earns the goodwill of the authorities and gets opportunities to help others and be helped by them in return. He attains success in his undertakings. He earns much glory through devotion to elders and performance of righteous deeds. In the 9th house, *munthā* provides the individual pleasures of sex, contentment from his attainments and a psychological feeling of upliftment. He attains much satisfaction from his friendly associations, from the success of his *family* members and his own personal fulfilment of desires.

Munthā in the 2nd house in the progressed horoscope produces enormous amount of money and wealth. It enables the individual to attain higher status in his office and the society, receive support from the state and respect from brothers and friends. Even in the 3rd house, the effects of *Munthā* are heartening. The individual earns wealth, glory and comfortable living with his own efforts. He spends his time religiously and devotes himself to the service of elders. When *munthā* is placed in a sign and is aspected by the lord of that sign and by other benefic planets in a progressed horoscope, it enables the effects of the house occupied by the sign in the natal chart to blossom luxuriously. If *munthā* is aspected by malefic, instead of benefic, its result is opposite. If the lord of the year is sufficiently strong, the affliction caused by *Munthā* gets cancelled.

The adverse results of *munthā* occur when, during the course of the year, it is placed in the 4th, 6th, 7th, 8th, and 12th houses from the natal chart. In the 4th house, *munthā* causes much mental anguish, physical ill health, and differences with brothers and friends, enmity with adversaries and humiliation in the society. In the 6th house, the whole year is full of difficulties of different sorts. There is setback in health, increase in opposition from enemies, fear of theft and loss of property and wealth. The individual loses in litigation and earns displeasure of the authorities. He himself becomes depraved and serious difficulties arise in his professional career. The occupancy of *munthā* in the 7th house from the natal ascendant upsets the individual so much that he fails to take right decisions. Misfortune becomes so intense that he becomes perplexed completely, his relationship with his own relations as well as with others becomes erratic causing much friction in life. Initiative in work becomes absent virtually, enthusiasm in life is almost gone and there is much loss of wealth and neglect of righteous deeds. In the 8th house, *munthā* produces physical and psychological difficulties. The mind of the individual becomes unbalanced and he suffers from many complicated diseases. He gets involved in nefarious activities. He associates himself with many illegal undertakings. In the 12th house

Munthā enables the individual to earn money with his own efforts but his expenditure exceeds much more than his income. He gets associated with undesirable characters, indulges in sex orgies, becomes physically diseased and loses much money. He incurs the displeasure of a large number of persons.

Munthā associated with or aspected by different planets produces special effects. Its location in different signs of the zodiac supports the impulse generated by the rulers of those signs. The association of *munthā* with a sign or a planet produces powerful combinations. When it occupies Leo or is associated or aspected by Sun, the individual receives special assignment from the state. He works closer to the central seat of power. He develops special expertise and invitations from overseas seeking his assistance and expertise are expected. When *munthā* is posited in Cancer or related with Moon, the individual develops interest in religious thoughts and activities. He becomes renowned, improves his health and attains the psychological feeling of immense satisfaction. Unless *Munthā* is adversely affected by a malefic, it contributes substantially to the lunar influx. When *munthā* is associated with Mercury or Venus in any way, it contributes to much pleasurable experience unless it is afflicted by any adverse malefic. *Munthā*'s association with these planets sharpens the individual's intellect, makes him travel extensively both on business and for holidaying. Under this situation, the individual enjoys the company of beautiful girls. His married life becomes a bed of roses. He gets much happiness, good social relations and widespread renown and power. The association of *munthā* with Mars emphasizes its malefic nature. Occupying Aries or Scorpio while it is associated with Mars either by combination or aspect, *munthā* makes the individual vulnerable to accidents, diseases connected with blood, surgical operations and industrial injuries. In association with Jupiter or with the signs ruled by Jupiter, *munthā* makes the person very content. His children prosper and his wife feels respectfully affectionate towards him. He receives property, ornaments, precious gifts besides honour from the state. The impact of Saturn on *munthā* is unpleasant. Under its influence, the individual receives impediments of all kinds. There is setback in his enterprises, his health deteriorates, his social status decreases, he loses money and property, his married life runs to rocks and he feels extremely depressed.

Munthā forms special relationship with the nodes of the Moon. It is specially so because the nodes have certain distinguishing features much different from other planets. Rāhu for example, moves backward. So it traverses from the end of a sign towards its beginning. *Munthā* on the other hand has a forward motion. So has the other planets. They move from the beginning of a sign towards its end. As a result of this feature, *munthā* and the usual planets do not meet face to face as it does in relation with Rāhu. When *munthā* occupies an area yet to be traversed by Rāhu, that is, the front of Rāhu, the individual secures much happiness and gifts of happiness. During this phase of confrontation between Rāhu and *munthā,* the individual becomes wealthy, attains renown and glory, enjoys comfortable living and secures deeper understanding of life and the process of its unfolding. When *munthā* in association with Jupiter and Venus confronts Rāhu, the individual receives precious gifts, gems and jewellery, good clothes and even a new house or a new vehicle. When *munthā* occupies the 7th house from Rāhu, implying thereby that it forms association with Ketu, the adversaries of the individual become powerful and create terror for him. The individual during this period suffers from unidentified fear and from other unhappy events in his life. Any affliction of *munthā* by a malefic is adverse which destroys the peace of the individual's mind and he gets confronted with numerous difficulties.

The affliction of the lord of the sign in which *munthā* is placed also seriously affects the wellbeing of the individual. When the lord of the sign occupied by munthā is located in the 6th, 8th, 12th or 4th from it, and it is retrograde, associated or aspected by a malefic planet, or when the lord of the sign occupies the 4th or the 7th house from the malefic, under such conditions *munthā* is not auspicious. In fact, it even nullifies the good results likely to occur otherwise. The individual under this condition suffers physically and incurs much loss of wealth.

The auspicious nature of *munthā* is greatly vitiated by its relationship with the lord of the 8th sign. When the lord of the sign occupied by *munthā* is associated in the progressed horoscope with the lord of the 8th house, the person may even die during that year. The result becomes acute when *munthā* is associated with any other planet. The same is the result when the lord of the sign in which *munthā* is located casts an evil or malefic aspect on the lord of the 8th house from ascendant lord in the progressed chart.

When *munthā's* position in the natal chart during the course of any year is such that *munthā* or the lord of the sign occupied by it receives either aspects of benefic planets or is associated with them, the individual receives the consequential auspicious results during the first half of the year. The same combination in progressed horoscope produces the relevant results during the second half of the year.

Sahamas, the Sensitive Points

Sahamas are the sensitive points formed by special relationships between certain planets and some highly significant positions in the chart. These sensitive points arise as a result of interplanetary relationships considered alongwith the ascendant. The house division in which the *Sahamas* lie during the year that *bhāva* gains special significance in that period. *Sahamas* are not identical with house-divisions, they are merely sensitive points. The rationale of these points is not well-known but their efficacy has been evident. About 120 of them are specified in various astrological texts but all of them are not of the same importance. A few of these are described below.

Puṇya Sahamas: It is an important sensitive point. It is calculated by adding together the longitude of Sun, Moon and the ascendant. If the solar ingress at the birth-anniversary occurs during day time, the longitude of Sun is deducted from that of Moon to which the degree of the ascendant is added. In the event of the birth anniversary taking place during night, the position is reversed. In this case the longitude of Moon is subtracted from that of the Sun. The resultant figure is added to the ascendant. According to some texts, this formula for *Puṇya Sahama* is applicable when the ascendant lies between that which is subtracted from that. Otherwise, another 30° is added to the result obtained after the subtraction. The latter view is more popular.

Puṇya Sahama represents a pipeline for the downpour of divine benediction which brings to the individual such auspicious results as performance of meritorious deeds, accrual of wealth, enjoyment of joyous events,and great inner satisfaction. If this *Sahama* lies in the 6th, 8th or the 12th house from ascendant, the result is opposite. There is destruction of meritorious deeds, loss of status and the experience of ignominy. If this sensitive point while occupying any of these adverse houses is aspected by a benefic or by the lord of these houses, the individual encounters adverse results at the beginning of the year, but the end is more favourable. The affliction of this point by a malefic planet if aspected by a benefic leads to auspicious results only during the latter part of the year. When this *sahama* is associated with benefics but is aspected by malefics, the sequence of good and adverse events is reversed. It will produce favourable results during the first half of the year and the adverse ones during the latter half. If the point is in conjunction as well as in aspect of benefics, the entire year is favourable. It will bestow much affluence, wealth and honour to the individual. Malefics in such a situation of affliction and aspecting the *sahama* will make the entire year a miserable one.

Māhātmya Sahama is relevant for ascertaining the possibility of achieving greatness in any specific area during the year. Greatness in the present context refers to attainment of some enduring virtues such as perseverance, stability, seriousness and intelligence born out of struggles in life. This kind of greatness is different from the social status of a person resulting from power and wealth. It is also different from glory and renown. *Māhātmya Sahama* is worked out by subtracting the longitude of Mars from *Puṇya Sahama* and adding to it the degree of the ascendant. If the birth anniversary is in day time, the longitude of Mars is subtracted from *Puṇya Sahama* and added to the result of the longitude of the ascendant. But for the night time birth anniversary, *Puṇya Sahama* is subtracted from the longitude of Mars and the longitude of the ascendant is added to the result thus obtained. The auspicious and adverse result of this *sahama* is decided on the same lines as in the case of *Puṇya Sahama.*

Samartha Sahama is important for finding out the possibility for acquiring strength and physical power as well as the capacity to overcome one's adversaries. It also differs from the solar ingress taking place during the day time or night time. In case, this anniversary commences during day time, the degrees of ascendant lord is subtracted from that of Mars and in the case of birth anniversary occurring in night time, the longitude of Mars is subtracted from that of the ascendant lord. In both the cases the resultant is added to the degree of the ascendant and progressed by a sign. In case, of Mars being the ascendant lord itself, in both the cases the longitude of Mars is subtracted from that of Jupiter with which the ascendant and 30° is added to arrive at *Samartha Sahama.*

Gaurava Sahama indicates the sensitive point highly propitious for providing to the individual glory, renown, honour, good clothes, vehicles and professional preferment. In the case of day time solar ingress, the longitude of Moon is subtracted from that of Jupiter and that of Sun is added to the resultant. In the event of night time birth anniversary, the longitude of Sun is subtracted from that of Jupiter and that of Moon is added to the resultant. In the case of day time birth anniversary, if Sun is not placed in between the minuend (a number from which another is subtracted) and the subtrahend (a number that is subtracted from another) and Moon is not placed likewise for the night solar ingress, 30° requires to be added to the formula. When this sensitive point is associated or aspected by its own sign lord and other benefic planets, the entire year is favourable for the flow of wealth, honour, prestige and happiness. If it is associated with or aspected by malefic planets, the individual may be thrown out of job and may have to face unemployment. If the *Sahama* is aspected or approached by malefic planets, the first half of the year can be troublesome while the approach of benefics indicates the attainment of happiness, vehicles and many different kinds of machinery and gadgets.

Karma Sahama: This sensitive point is worked out by the subtraction of the longitude of Mercury from that of Mars for day time birth anniversaries and vice versa for those who have solar ingress during the night time. The result thus obtained is added to the longitude of the ascendant and it is progressed by 30°.

This sensitive point produces strong impulse for intense activities which lead to accrual of precious metals, landed property, fixed assets and much riches. Favourable position of *Karma Sahama* and its lord alongwith favourable disposition of the 10th house and its lord lead to a joyous year. During this period the individual receives plenty of wealth and gifts. In case the lord of the 10th house and the lord of *Karma Sahama* both are retrograde, there will be much toil and little gain. The association of Saturn or its aspect with these two lords creates impediments thwarting all chances of success.

Roga Sahama: This sensitive point is worked out by subtracting the longitude of Moon from the ascendant with the resultant added to the degree of the ascendant and the total being progressed by a sign of the zodiac. It is related with the possibility of any disease afflicting the person. It is determined by finding out the nature of the lord of the *sahama*. When the lord of this sahama itself is a malefic and is associated and aspected by another malefic, the individual suffers from illness and long drawn diseases for the whole year. When the lord of *Roga Sahama* approaches the lord of the 8th house, there is danger of death. When the lord is weak in this relationship, the death is painful. If the *sahama* is associated or aspected by its own lord as well as by other benefics, or when the lord of the *Sahama* is placed in a house other than the 6th, 8th or the 12th, the individual does not suffer from any illness.

Manmatha Sahama : It is worked out by subtracting the longitude of the ascendant lord from that of the Moon if the birth anniversary commences in day time while the sequence is reversed for the night time birth anniversary. The result obtained is added to the degree of the ascendant and 30° is added to the same. If the ascendant lord is also the Moon, the longitude of the Moon should be subtracted from Asun for the night as well as day anniversaries, and the resultant is added to the degree of the ascendant and progressed by a sign of the zodiac. The point is sensitive for the arousal of lust.

Para Dārā Sahama: This sensitive point refers to the possibility of adultery and extramarital liaisons during the year. It is obtained by subtracting the longitude of Sun from that of Venus. The result is added to the longitude of the ascendant alongwith an addition of 30° to it.

Vivāha Sahama : It is obtained by subtracting the longitude of Saturn from that of Venus and the ascendant and the result is progressed by another 30'. It refers to chances of actualization of any marriage proposal during the year.

Deśāntara Sahama : This sensitive point is connected with the possibility of foreign travel during the year. It is obtained by subtracting the longitude of the lord of the 9th house from the cusp of the 9th house and adding the result to the degree of the ascendant and the final total progressed by a sign.

Yogas, or the Stellar Combinations

The mystic significance of stellar impulses is deciphered through their configuration. The astrological texts have indicated many such combinations, usually known as Yogas. They reveal the special planetary disposition in a natal chart. Similar combinations exist also in progressed horoscopes. These planetary interrelationships have special features of their own. They also require special rules for their interpretation. The planetary combinations in a natal chart and the progressed horoscopes are different and they require very careful consideration.

One such combination which is similar to many Yogas in a natal chart is defined as Ikkavāla Yoga. All the planets except Rāhu form it and Ketu spread over the quadrants i.e. 1st, 4th, 7th and 10th houses and Paṇaphara houses viz. 2nd, 5th, 8th and 11th houses. This sort of planetary configuration enables the individual to enjoy royal status. The combination induces the individual to lead a very dynamic life full of activities. He establishes good social relations, and receives honour from the state. There is accrual of wealth as well as psychological buoyancy and optimism. When this combination takes place, the individual achieves some spectacular result and he considers the year as very remarkable for him.

On the other hand, there is an equally unhappy combination formed by all the above planets concentrated only in four houses viz. 3rd, 6th, 9th and the 12th houses. It is known as *Induvara Yoga.* When this combination takes place, the individual meets many impediments. During this period, his efforts fail and the expected results are denied. Ill health and serious allegations become imminent. He receives setback in his enterprises. He may have to leave his home and go to some unknown, inhospitable distant land.

There are several combinations in respect of progressed horoscopes, which nullify the adverse planetary results or accentuate the favourable ones. Many of these combinations are connected with "applying" and "separating" combinations. These are the combinations, which are special in progressed horoscopes. Such specific combinations applicable specially to progressed horoscopes (and in horary astrology) are not generally examined in relation with natal charts. There are two special distinguishing features of these yogas. The first relates to the method of determining strength of a planet involved in these combinations, and the second is connected with their aspects. The first feature has already been discussed earlier. As far as planetary aspects are concerned, it may be indicated here that in the interpretation of natal charts, they are broadly considered from house to house or from sign to sign (as in the case of Jaimini system). In progressed horoscopes, one does not assume that the planetary aspects pertain to house to house or from sign to sign, but they are primarily angular distances between two planets. Moreover one also assumes that the aspects are concentrated at the central point of the focus. Every planet has an area around this focal point at which its aspect is very concentrated. This area of concentration is known as *Dīptāṁśa* meaning the degree of radiance. The limits of these restricted aspects are as follows for different planets: Sun - 15°, Moon - 12°, Mercury - 7°, Venus - 7°, Mars - 8°, Jupiter - 9° and Saturn - 9°. Beyond these points, the planetary aspects are ineffective. While considering the planetary combinations in progressed horoscopes, even the average speed of the planets during the course of their movement plays an important role. During the course of applying and separating relationship, the relative speed of different planets is a determining condition of much significance. Many of the combinations in progressed horoscopes depend mainly on such relative speeds. Moon is the fastest planet, which takes only 2½ days in a sign. Mercury takes about two weeks, Venus 3-4 weeks and Sun takes a month in traversing a sign. Mars takes about 6 weeks, Jupiter takes a year and Saturn 2½ years. The relative motion of these planets decides the primacy of a planet in producing any specific result.

Among the various applying and separating combinations, *Muthaśila* also known as *Itthaśāla,* and Mūsarifa also known as *Īśarābha* are the two basic ones. The former is formed by fast moving planet at the time when it establishes a relationship with another planet either by occupation in a sign or by its aspect. Even occupation of the same sign is considered having an aspect but of a malefic nature. In some cases, if a planet is at the last degree of a sign while another planet occupies the next sign but within its "orb" or the zone of its radiance, they establish relationship between them. This combination is considered auspicious. The fast moving planet in such cases lends its support to the slow moving planet ahead of it. It enables the slow moving planet to fructify its results. It assumes that the fast moving planet is a benefic and it is going to help the slow moving planet, which has the power to produce certain good results. The support lends by the fast moving planet enables the slow moving planet to quicken the actualization of the auspicious results.

A fast moving planet occupying a forward position keeping a slow moving planet behind it even by a degree or less than that forms Mūsarifa yoga. It assumes that the distance between them is on the increasing side. The two planets separate from each other. As a result of this combination, the fast moving one reduces the auspicious potentials of the slow moving planet. The combination is considered inauspicious. The harmful results of this combination fructify under its impact. It happens primarily when a malefic is involved in the combination. If a fast moving planet is a benefic, the adverse effects may not take place when this combination is formed. The natural results of the planets under this relationship are neither augmented nor annulled if both the planets involved in the combination are benefic planets.

Muthaśila, the former combination is of three kinds, immediate, complete and forthcoming. The first one, namely the immediate Muthaśila arises when the slow moving planet is ahead of a fast moving planet even slightly say, by half a degree or so. In such cases, the fast moving planet is not yet occupying the same longitude as the slow moving planet but is going to do so very soon. In the second case, the fast moving planet occupies the last degree of a sign while the slow moving planet occupies the next sign but within the orb of the next planet. In such cases, the fast moving planet lends its effective support to the slow moving planet in fructifying the results inherent in it. A third possibility arises when a fast and a slow moving planet are located in such a way that the orb or the zone of radiance of the former does not touch that of the latter but is likely to do so in near future. This kind of *Muthaśila yoga* indicates the related results of the concerned planets will soon be available to the individual.

An interesting variety of *Muthaśila* arises when two planets are situated in such a way that they are similar to this relationship in some ways. This is known as *Naktha Yoga.* A fast moving planet intervening between two planets, especially between the ascendant lord and another planet forms it. The second planet can be a *kāraka* planet, which causes the fructification of certain *bhāva.* The latter needs support from the former but by itself it does not establish the Muthaśila relationship. With the presence of a fast moving planet, a connection is established between the ascendant and the other planet by its own orb of radiance which becomes an important link in this relationship. This combination can be illustrated in the following manner. In case, Mercury as the ascendant lord is situated at Leo 10° while Jupiter is at Pisces 12°. The two planets do not aspect each other because there is no aspect between the 6th and the 8th houses. Thus there is not Muthaśila relationship between Mercury and Jupiter. If a planet such as Moon, which moves faster than either of them, occupies Taurus 11°, the Moon occupies 3rd place from Jupiter and 10th from Mercury. There is a 3rd and 10th aspect, which exists between these three planets. So a kind of Muthaśila relationship of formed between them because the two planets are also located within the lunar orb of aspects. Under this combination the result fructifies with the help of a person who is not directly connected with the event.

Yamaya yoga: Yamaya yoga is also another variant of the above combination. In this yoga, the two planets under consideration are not related. Another slow moving planet establishes special connection with them. The intervening planet establishes association according to its angular relation with the Kāraka planet as well as with the ascendant lord. By establishing a link between these two planets it absorbs the energy from the ascendant lord and transmits the same to the Kāraka in order to enable it to actualize the result. In this combination, the slow moving planet receives energy from the related fast moving planet and passes that to the relatively slower one among them. In such cases the results are obtained through a third person. An example of this combination is given as follows. Assuming that Libra is the ascendant with its lord placed in Aries at 25° while Moon is placed at Taurus 14°55', which happens to be the 8th house. There is no relationship between Moon and Venus as the *dīptāṁśa* of the latter ends at Taurus 2°5' and that of the former begins from 2°55'. But the presence of Jupiter at 6° in Taurus establishes a relationship between them. The *dīptāṁśa* of Jupiter links the two planets. So *Muthaśila yoga* is established by its presence as a result of which success can be possible through the intervention of possibly an elderly and pious third person.

Manau Yoga : It is an inauspicious formation. The association of malefic planets like Mars and Saturn establishes this combination. When either of the two is within the orb of a fast moving planet whether ahead or behind it, while the other two are not forming the Muthaśila, in that case, Mars or Saturn takes the strength of the faster planet and afflicts the slower one. This relationship destroys any likely auspicious influence of the former planet. For example, in case two planets namely Venus and Moon, the two fast moving planets are within the orbit of Muthaśila formation but another malefic viz. Saturn or Mars intervenes between them and occupies a place within the orb, say, of Moon. The position of the malefic between the two planets vitiates their good effect likely to result under the Muthaśila. There could be several variations of this yoga. It turns the auspicious Muthaśila into an unhappy combination. These unhappy combinations lead to unhappy experiences, rise of enemies, involvement in debts, quarrels and loss of wealth. Retrogression or combination of a planet producing such variants of Muthaśila cancels the yoga. Moon combining with any of the two planets forming Muthaśila combination intensifies their auspicious nature.

If the lord of the ascendant and the lord of the house under consideration as well as the friends of the lord of the ascendant and the friends of the lord of the sign under consideration are aspected by the lords of the signs in which they are located, the result of the combination is similar to that of Muthaśila yoga in producing auspicious results.

Many other combinations based on factors other than the applying and separating aspects of planets also exist for the interpretation of progressed horoscopes. The weakness of the lord of 9th and 2nd houses while a malefic planet in the progressed chart occupies the ascendant destroys the long-earned money. The debilitation of Moon and combustion of Mercury, Venus and Jupiter make the year full of troubles. The individual suffers from physical ill health, mental worry, financial loss and separation from loved ones. If a planet in the natal chart occupies the 8th house while in the progressed chart it occupies the ascendant this planet makes the individual suffer intense mental agony during the year. Even death may occur if his Moon and the ascendant lord in the progressed horoscope are weak. It so happens even if the lords of the sign occupied by Moon and the ascendant lord are weak.

On the other hand, if during any year the ascendant lord in the progressed chart is strong and placed in the 5th or the 9th house or a quadrant house and is aspected by or associated with a benefic planet, the individual in that year transcends all difficulties and earns much wealth and attains happiness. Jupiter occupying a quadrant or a trine house in the progressed chart and unaspected by any malefic while aspected by benefics eliminates several difficulties created by the weaknesses of the ascendant, Moon and Muntha. It even bestows much wealth and happiness on the individual. If the 4th house in a progressed chart is occupied by its own lord or is aspected by benefic, the individual receives happiness, renown and much wealth. If Jupiter occupies either the ascendant or the 3rd house and the ascendant lord is in the 4th house, much wealth and happiness flow to the individual.

If, during the year, the lord of the 7th house is placed in the ascendant alongwith Jupiter without any malefic aspect while benefic planets aspect it, the combination produces much happiness. The individual receives royal favour. It elevates his social status. He acquires much money and wealth, and it leads to much happiness. Similarly strong lords of the 9th and 2nd houses placed in the ascendant unaspected by malefics will lead to tremendous wealth during the year. The occupancy of malefic planets in any of the 3rd, 6th and 11th houses while the quadrants and the trine houses are occupied by benefic planets leads to the attainment of much precious gifts, wealth, renown and happiness.

The progressed horoscope is a sort of status report which displays the actualization prospects of the latent potential indicated by the natal chart. The periodicity of planetary rulerships, transits of planets and the progressed horoscopes always operate within the general parameter of the natal horoscope and they indicate the important milestones towards the fulfilment of individual's ultimate destiny.

Glossary

AFFLICTION	Malefic influence of a planet on another planet or on any specific Division in any natal chart.
ANTAR	Inter-period during main planetary periodicity.
APACAYA	1st, 2nd, 4th and 7th house -divisions in a natal chart.
ASPECT	Look or seeing by a planet any other planet or a house-division in a chart.
AṢṬAKAVARGA	Eight -fold strength of a planet depending upon its occupancy in relation with Moon and other planets but also including ascendant.
ATICĀRA	Accelerated motion of a planet.
AYANA	Direction.
AYANĀṀŚA	The term has a special significance in astrology. The vernal equinoctial Point of Aries is taken as the starting point for measuring of celestial longitudes. The celestial longitude of a heavenly body measured from this Initial point is known as the tropical longitude in sayana longitude. Due to precession of the equinoxes as the Vernal Equinoctial point is receding back over the ecliptic at the rate of about 50.3" per year as a result of which the longitude of fixed stars are increasing every year at the rate in order to stabilize the zodiac, a point has been taken as the origin which is permanently fixed on the ecliptic and this point is different from the vernal equinoctial point, or in other words the tropical longitude of the initial point is called the Ayanāṁśa.

BHAUMA	Son of Earth; Mars.
BHĀVA	One of the 12 divisions of a natal chart.
BHUKTI	A directional measure; sub-period of a planetary periodicity.
BĪJASPHUṬA	Index of male procreative power.
BRAHMA	The Supreme creative energy; one of the earlier manifestation of the primordial creative power (viz. Lord Mahạdeva. Śiva). The initial expanding and projecting aspect of the Godhead which results in full manifestation: the principle which links the physical and spiritual aspects of the human personality.
BUDDHI	Intelligence or the principle which links the physical and spiritual aspects.
BUDDHIC PLANE	The realm of pure intelligence where highly spiritual entities are said to dwell and pure intelligence of the human being operate.
CARA RĀŚI	Motional strength of a planet.
CEṢṬĀ BAḶA	Motional strength of a planet.
DHARMA	Righteousness; Harmonious evolutionary impulses to live correctly and in accordance with the law of nature; that which upholds and maintains existence.
DĪKṢĀ	Initiation; special relationship between an aspirant and his (personal) teacher; certain special teachings or *mantras* for developing special occult powers; a stage in the inner development of the ego which takes place in secrecy and at specially prepared secret and secluded places.
DREKKAN	One -third division of a sign or the house-division.
DVĀDAŚAVARGĪYA BALA	The 12-fold strength of a planet depending upon 12-fold division of a sign e.g. Horā, Drekkan, Navamāṁśa etc.
EKĀDHIPATYA ŚODHA	Reduction of aṣṭakavarga index due to a planetary ownership of two signs (or houses) in a chart.
FOHAT	A term used to represent the active (male)

	potency of female reproductive power in nature. The essence of cosmic electricity.
GOCARA	Planetary transit; a system if astrological prediction based on planetary Transits in different houses and in different zodiacal signs.
GRAHA	A planet.
GRAHA YUDDHA	Planetary warfare.
HADDA INDEX	Certain limits within which certain planets are more effective in producing their results than at other places.
HOROSCOPE	Natal chart representing planetary position of the planets in the sky at the time of the birth.
HOROSCOPE PROGRESSED	A predicative calculation under which the relationship between the planetary position at the moment of solar ingress at its natal longitude to show the likely events during the ensuing year.
INDRIYA	There are ten external agents; the five senses that are used for perception are known as Jñāna-indriyas and there are five used for action, which are known as Karma -Indriyas.
JANMA RĀŚI	The sign occupied by Moon at the time of birth, sometimes the sign occupied by the Sun is called Janma Rāśi.
KĀLA	Time; the God of Death.
KĀLA PURUṢA	Time represented in a human form.
KARMA	Physically, action; metaphysically, the Law of Retribution, the Law of causation.
KENDRA	Angles, the quadrant or cardinal houses in a natal chart.
KṚṢṆA PAKṢA	Dark half of the lunar month.
KṢETRASPHUṬA	Index to ascertain the fertility for conception in a woman.
KUṆḌALINĪ	Serpent Fire. The coiled potential resting in Nature and in the body of men. When it awakens in Nature, Life-forms emerge from the planet; when it awakens in men, several qualities begin to unfold, intellectual

	capacities are unveiled, intuition awakens, and creativity is expressed.
LAGNA	Ascendant, the first house in a natal chart.
LAGNA-AṢṬAKAVARGA	Benefic points in aṣṭakavarga preparation contributed by the ascendant.
MANDA	Dull, Saturn.
MŪLA TRIKOṆA	Trine position of a planet enjoying strength in between its exaltation and ownership positions.
MUNTHĀ	The yearly progression of Ascendant by a sign for every year since birth-year.
NIRAYANA	Fixed zodiac.
PAÑCAVARGĪYA BALA	The five -fold strength of a planet depending upon its position in a sign, which are Kṣetra Bala (locational strength), Uccabala (strength due to its exaltation position or due to its proximity to this position) Hadda, Drekkan and Navamāṁśa positions.
PĀTYĀṀŚA	A stage in the working out of progressed horoscope.
PRĀṆA	Life-energy. The life-force which pervades Nature and gives life to an individual.
RĀJA YOGA	Planetary combination for material or political affluence. The term also refers to a system of spiritual austerity in which the aspirant controls his actions, feelings, thoughts and other actions without subjecting the body to any serious austerities.
REKHĀ	A line. In connection with Aṣṭakavarga preparation, it refers to malefic (or benefic) strength as assumed.
SAHAMAS	Sensitive points formed by special relationships between certain planets and some highly significant positions in a chart.
SARVĀṢṬAKAVARGA	An overall picture of all aṣṭakavargas in a natal chart.
SARVĀṢṬAKAVARGA	An overall consideration (total) of aṣṭakavargas for all Planets in a natal chart.
SAUMYA	Balanced and graceful visage; Mercury.
SŪRYA	The planet Sun.

TRIKOṆA	Trine houses; 1st, 5th, and 9th houses in a natal chart.
TRIKOṆA ŚODHA	Reduction on account of triangular signs in aṣṭakavarga calculations.
UCCA BALA	Strength of a planet at its exaltation position.
UPACAYA HOUSES	3rd, 6th, 10th, and 11th houses in natal chart.
VARGOTTAMA	A planet occupying the same sign in natal and in Navamāṁśa chart.
VEDAS	The sacred books of the Hindus, four in number.

Index

Horoscope, Annual 1
Progressed xviii, xix, xx, 1, 139-146, 164, 168
Houses, Apacay 98
Cardinal 5
Trine 5
Upacaya 98

I

ignorance, veil of 38
innovation, agricultural 48
investigation, scientific 73

J

Jung, Carl. G. xiii

K

Karma, Law of vii, 32, 34
Lords of 32
Sancita 32
Karmic agents 69
forces 1, 6
omissions 76
reservoir 68
results 68
retribution 39

L

Light, Inner 38
luxurious life 90

M

Mansions, Lunar xvi
martyrdomn 61
material attractions 77
measures, remedial xiv
meditation 26
metaphysics, Vedic 137
Muddā system 151, 157
mundane predictions 61
Munthā 138, 164-168
Mysteries, Hidden 44
mythic relationships 104
Mythology, Hindu 41
Myths and symbols xvi

N

Nakṣatras 3, 105
Navamāṁśa 142

O

Occult attainments
knowledge 45
perception 36
preparation 126
Occultism 119

P

Pañcavargīya Bala 149-156
Parāśara 2
Permissive relationship 46
Phlegmatic disorders 65
Photosynthesis 45
Planets, Bādhaka 103
malefic 6
tertiary 21
shadowy 33
of disillusionment 43
irritability
wish fulfilment 46
Periodicity of 156-159
(also see Planetary periodicity)
Planetary configuration xvii, 97
control 2
deities 2
hierarchy xi
periodicity 6, 23, 47, 130, 152